P9-DOF-228

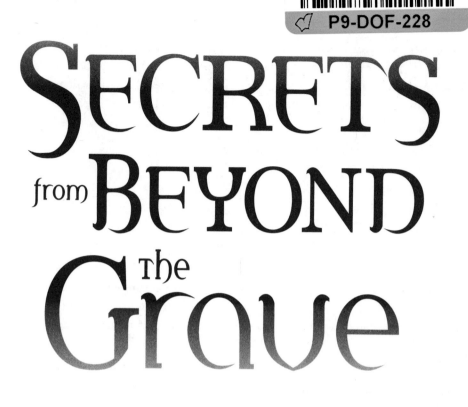

# SECRETS from BEYOND the Grave

## PERRY STONE

Charisma
HOUSE
A STRANG COMPANY

Most STRANG COMMUNICATIONS BOOK GROUP products are available at special quantity discounts for bulk purchase for sales promotions, premiums, fund-raising, and educational needs. For details, write Strang Communications Book Group, 600 Rinehart Road, Lake Mary, Florida 32746, or telephone (407) 333-0600.

SECRETS FROM BEYOND THE GRAVE by Perry Stone
Published by Charisma House
A Strang Company
600 Rinehart Road
Lake Mary, Florida 32746
www.strangbookgroup.com

This book or parts thereof may not be reproduced in any form, stored in a retrieval system, or transmitted in any form by any means—electronic, mechanical, photocopy, recording, or otherwise—without prior written permission of the publisher, except as provided by United States of America copyright law.

Unless otherwise noted, all Scripture quotations are from the New King James Version of the Bible. Copyright © 1979, 1980, 1982 by Thomas Nelson, Inc., publishers. Used by permission.

Scripture quotations marked AMP are from the Amplified Bible. Old Testament copyright © 1965, 1987 by the Zondervan Corporation. The Amplified New Testament copyright © 1954, 1958, 1987 by the Lockman Foundation. Used by permission.

Scripture quotations marked KJV are from the King James Version of the Bible.

Scripture quotations marked RSV are from the Revised Standard Version of the Bible. Copyright © 1946, 1952, 1971 by the Division of Christian Education of the National Council of the Churches of Christ in the USA. Used by permission.

Quotations from the Quran are from *The Quran Translation*, 7th edition, translated by Abdullah Yusef Ali (Elmhurst, NY: Tahrike Tarsile Quran, Inc., 2001).

Cover design by Justin Evans
Design Director: Bill Johnson

Copyright © 2010 by Perry Stone
All rights reserved

Library of Congress Cataloging-in-Publication Data

Stone, Perry F.
  Secrets from beyond the grave / Perry Stone.
      p. cm.
  Includes bibliographical references.
  ISBN 978-1-61638-157-8
  1.  Future life--Christianity. 2.  Conversion--Christianity.  I. Title.

  BT903.S76 2010
  236--dc22

                                        2010018030

First Edition

10 11 12 13 14 — 9 8 7 6 5 4 3 2 1
Printed in the United States of America

# CONTENTS

## Chapter 12

## Chapter 13

## Conclusion

# The DEAD ARE PRAYING for YOU NOT to GO WHERE THEY ARE!

Today no one knows his name. We do know that he was a very wealthy individual who dressed lavishly in purple linen and enjoyed banquets in his private dining hall, feasting daily. The historical record lists that he had five brothers in his family. (See Luke 16:19–31.) Without warning, he was suddenly found dead in his house. Yet in reality, he was actually alive and living in another world—a strange dimension, a rather mysterious realm identified as *Sheol* or *Hades*. Although his body was buried, his soul and spirit operated with all five senses, recalling his past life well, remembering his prosperity, and remembering that a beggar at the gate of his house died of starvation while he, being rich, had willfully ignored the poor fellow's plight.

This rich man was now an eternal prisoner in a land of departed souls. The hollowed-out chambers in that place are identified in the inspired Scriptures as being situated under the crust of the earth, which I will show in this book. Although this former aristocrat had no time for God and no compassion for poor people while living in his mansion and gorging himself with the finest foods, he now had forever to imagine what could have been, in a land where time ceases to exist.

In this world of departed souls, he learned how to pray. Oddly, he never asked if he could get out of this underground prison of heat and flames, as he knew there was no escape. His prayer was for the living. A *dead man* was praying for the *living*. His request was to send the poor beggar back from the dead to the house of this former rich man to warn his brothers not to come to this place. His prayer was never answered. His brothers had "Moses and the prophets" (Luke 16:29), or they had knowledge of the Scriptures. The rich man was told: "If they do not hear Moses and the prophets, neither will they be persuaded though one rise from the dead" (v. 31).

In this book, however, I am partially answering the thousands-of-years-old prayer of this rich man. I am going to take you through a journey into the underworld to show you what you will experience and what you can expect if you depart this life without a redemptive covenant. The prayer of this former millionaire is: "Please don't come where I am."

Then there was the beggar—a man whose name was Lazarus. He is not the Lazarus Christ raised from the dead, but another man with the same name. His earthly life was one of continual misery. Not only was he a beggar whose boney, trembling hands were held out asking for mere crumbs from the rich man's table, but also his entire body was covered with painful, bleeding sores. The only friends this feeble and penniless piece of humanity had were the dogs that came and licked his sores. This poor man was begging at the rich man's estate, but neither the unnamed rich man nor his five brothers paid attention to his needs.

It appears that the rich man and beggar died at about the same time. The rich man closed his eyes in death and woke up in a world of heat, flames, and torment. The old beggar received a personal escort of angels to a place of comfort where he personally met the patriarch of the Hebrew faith, Abraham, and was comforted in the afterlife.

This story, spoken by Jesus, is only recorded by one of the four Gospel writers—Luke, who was a physician (Col. 4:14). As a medical physician, Luke was often detailed in presenting information that would have intrigued him from a rational, medical perspective. Doctors deal with birth, suffering, and death. Luke gives great detail to the virgin birth of Christ and the miraculous events surrounding the birth of John the

Baptist (Luke chapters 1 and 2), to the sufferings of Christ as His "sweat became like great drops of blood" (Luke 22:44), and to the story of two men and their life-after-death experiences (Luke 16:19–31).

I have debated with individuals who do not believe in the afterlife and who especially doubt the existence of a place called *hell*. They claim the story Luke recorded was simply a parable told by Christ to illustrate a spiritual point. However, the identifying marks found in the parables of Christ are all missing in this story.

In Christ's day there were two main religious groups that often opposed His teaching: the Pharisees and the Sadducees. The Pharisees believed in the body, soul, and spirit, and that the spirit departed the physical body at death. The Sadducees, however, did not believe in the eternal spirit within a man or in the departure of the human spirit from the body at death. Thus, this account in Luke 16, spoken by Christ and recorded by Doctor Luke, was a direct blow to the unbelieving Sadducees.

A parable is a story that holds another *hidden* meaning within the story. Christ's parables were stories with other interpretations within the stories. For example, the wheat and tares are the children of the kingdom and the children of Satan (Matt. 13). The parable of the sower reveals the four ways men respond to the gospel message (Mark 4).

In parables, Christ never gave specific names, yet in this account He names Lazarus, Abraham, and Moses. Before Christ's crucifixion, both the righteous and unrighteous went into lower chambers under the mountains, and there was a great chasm between the upper level where the righteous dwelt (Abraham's bosom) and the lower chambers called hell (Luke 16:22–31).

If for some reason you have never read the account of the death of these two men and their lives beyond the grave, then this book will explain the afterlife in great detail. If you have read or heard that this story is not literal but only a parable, I will give you ample information to prove that the afterlife does indeed exist. If you do believe in two worlds beyond this one world, and if you desire more insight into what you will encounter seconds after departing this life, then this book will answer your questions.

We who are presently living will eventually pass from this life, "as it is appointed for men to die once, but after this the judgment" (Heb. 9:27). When we depart from this shell of clay, there are only two locations where our eternal spirit and soul will remain until the resurrection and Judgment Day. It is this unseen world of departed souls that I want to explore with you. In one location, the dead are praying you will never come there. In the other location, there is a High Priest making intercession for you that you will finish your journey and wake up in the paradise of God. You will choose your destiny.

# Chapter 1

# JOURNEY BEYOND
# the GRAVE

There are three worlds, one seen and two unseen. Yet the unseen realm is as real and tangible as the seen. These three dimensions are written about in the following passage:

> That at the name of Jesus every knee should bow, of things in heaven, and things in earth, and things under the earth.
> —PHILIPPIANS 2:10, KJV

"Things in earth" are living human beings. "Things in heaven" include God, Christ, and the angels. "Things under the earth" include chambers where fallen angels are bound in chains of darkness while waiting for the day of their judgment (2 Pet. 2:4). According to the New Testament, there are also the souls and spirits of departed men and women, some being reserved in a special region in heaven and others in chambers located under the earth.

The location of those now residing in heaven is identified by the apostle Paul as a heavenly paradise, alluded to in 2 Corinthians 12:1–4. The opposite *holding chambers*, known as the land of the departed unrighteous souls, are located under the earth and include a series of large caverns and chambers, deep under the crust of the mountains, where the unrighteous souls and spirits are taken immediately following their physical death on Earth. (See Numbers 16:30–33; Luke 16:23–31.)

## The Creation of the Underworld

Moses recorded that, "In the beginning God created the heavens and the earth" (Gen 1:1). Prior to when God formed Adam in the Garden of Eden, angels preexisted with God and were watching the activities of Creation as the Almighty spoke it into existence (Job 38:4–7). Some scholars point out that in Genesis 1:1, the Hebrew word for "created," which is *bara'* (baw-raw'), indicated the heavens and Earth were formed in a perfected condition.[1]

However, in Genesis 1:2 we read that the "earth was without form, and void; and darkness was on the face of the deep." Darkness is on the "deep." The Hebrew word for "deep" is *tehom* and alludes to the subterranean chambers under the earth where the waters are stored.[2] This apparent chaos seen in verse 2 has been identified among some biblical students as the time of the fall of Satan and his angels from heaven (Isa. 14:12–15; Luke 10:18; Rev. 12:7–10), thus causing a chaotic event to occur on the earth.

Thus, between the mysterious and unknown "ages past" of Genesis 1:1 and the fall of Satan in Genesis 1:2, the expulsion of Satan from heaven to Earth struck the planet like lightning (Luke 10:18), and, as some suggest, this was the time when God created a place called *hell* in the heart of the earth. It is clear that hell was never created for man but originally was intended only for Satan and his rebellious angels. We read in Matthew 25:41:

> Then He will also say to those on the left hand, "Depart from Me, you cursed, into the everlasting fire prepared for the devil and his angels."

While the details of the expulsion of Satan from heaven and the creation of hell remain somewhat of a mystery, the waters covering the earth in Genesis 1:2 are believed by some to be the waters cooling the planet down after chamber after chamber of hell had been formed in the center of the earth. Oddly, there are scientists who believe the earth was at one time a ball of fire that eventually cooled (with water) and formed the planet we now dwell on. The difference between what I am sharing and the scientific "slow-evolving planet theory" of the earth is the time element. Scientists believe the formation process took billions of years. However, although in ages past the original Creation of Genesis 1 may have occurred millions of years ago, the time frame recorded from Genesis 3:3 onward—of God creating the light, plants, and man—was slightly more than six thousand years ago according to traditional theology. Whether hell was prepared *before* the fall of Satan (Gen 1:1) or *afterward* (Gen 1:2), Scripture and science agree on these facts: there are different levels under the earth, and the center of the earth is fire.

## The Underground Chambers

Throughout the Bible there are five different words used to identify the area I call the underworld: These words are:

- *Sheol*—an Old Testament Hebrew word
- *Hades*—a New Testament Greek word
- *Gehenna*—a New Testament Greek word
- *Tartaroo*—a New Testament Greek word
- *Abyss*—a New Testament Greek word

The word *Sheol* is used sixty-five times in the Old Testament. It is translated as "hell" thirty-one times in the Bible, thirty-one times as "grave," and three times as "pit." The word *Hades* is translated as "hell" ten times in the New Testament. It is also found in 1 Corinthians 15:55, where the English word is *grave*. The only exception is Revelation 6:8. In that passage the pale horse rider is Death, and hell (Hades) follows him.

By definition the word *Hades* is "the region of departed spirits of the lost (but including the blessed dead in periods preceding the ascension of Christ)."[3]

The early church fathers commented on Hades. One Ante-Nicene father commented:

> This is the torment compartment of Sheol-Hades where wicked souls have always gone and will always go until the end of the Millennium....Hades is a place in the created system, rude, a locality beneath the earth, in which the light of the world does not shine; and as the sun does not shine in this locality, there must necessarily be perpetual darkness there.[4]

The third word, *tartaroo*, is a Greek word translated as "hell" and found in only one place:

> For if God did not spare the angels who sinned, but cast them down to hell and delivered them into chains of darkness, to be reserved for judgment...
>
> —2 PETER 2:4

Tartarus was considered both a spirit or a deity in Greek mythology and the place of a chamber lower than Hades in which the most wicked spirits were confined. It was believed to be the first place created in the regions of the underworld, as angels fell into sin ages before Adam was created and sinned. Peter reveals that this is the chamber of the fallen angels.

Just as Satan will be cast into the abyss in the future and have a seal placed over the pit preventing his escape for one thousand years (Rev. 20:3), so those angels who were in revolt against God during the fall of Lucifer and those who corrupted themselves in the days of Noah by producing the offspring of giants (Gen. 6:4) are now chained in pits of darkness in the lowest parts of the earth. There is no indication that human souls are in this region, but only fallen angels. Jude wrote:

And the angels who did not keep their proper domain, but left their own abode, He has reserved in everlasting chains under darkness for the judgment of the great day.

—Jude 6

The next word revealing another chamber under the earth is the Greek word *abussos*, which is translated in English as the word *abyss*. This word is found nine times in the New Testament and is translated in the Book of Revelation as "bottomless pit" (Rev. 9:1–2, 11; 11:7; 17:8; 20:1, 3). This word alludes to an unspecified area under the earth that is a huge void, an empty cavity that cannot be measured. This place was known to the evil spirit Christ encountered during His ministry. On one occasion, Christ expelled a large host of demons from a man, and the chief evil spirit requested not to be confined in the "deep" (Luke 8:31, KJV). The King James Version says "deep," but the Greek word is *abussos*, or the abyss. Thus, as far back as almost two thousand years ago, the world of fallen and evil spirits under Satan's authority was fully aware of their final doom—the abyss.

The spirit world knows the Scriptures, as evidenced during Christ's temptation when Satan quoted from Psalm 91. (Compare Psalm 91:11–12 with Matthew 4:6.) The prophet Isaiah predicted that Lucifer would one day "be brought down to hell, to the sides of the pit" (Isa. 14:15, KJV). In Christ's time, the evil spirits He encountered knew that their final doom would be confinement in a "pit." Perhaps after seeing Christ, they believed the time of their destruction had arrived!

In the Hebrew text, when alluding to the underground chambers the word *deep* (*tehom*) is considered the "primeval sea." In the Septuagint (the Old Testament translated from Hebrew to Greek), the word *abyss* is used in the place of *tehom*. Thus, the word *tehom* is linked to the sea in Job 28:14 and to the depths of the earth in Psalm 71:20. In the Apocalypse, John reveals that the evil entity that will one day become the Antichrist of Bible prophecy (identified by John as the "beast") will be possessed and controlled by a spirit that will arise out of the abyss:

The beast that you saw [once] was, but [now] is no more, and he is going to come up out of the Abyss (the bottomless pit) and proceed to go to perdition.

—REVELATION 17:8, AMP

## The Area of Ge-Hinnom

The final word found in the New Testament that is translated as "hell" is the Greek word *geenna*, transliterated in English as "Gehenna." The Greek word *geenna* is found twelve times in the Greek New Testament and is translated eleven times in the four Gospels (Matthew, Mark, Luke, and John) as "hell." The word itself, however, has a more detailed historical and broader meaning than "just a Greek word for 'hell.'"

First, there is an area of Jerusalem that historically and biblically is named Ge-Hinnom. There is today a very deep ravine and valley outside of the southwestern walls of the old city of Jerusalem, known in the Old Testament as the Valley of the Sons of Hinnom, called in the early times Tophet.

For Tophet is ordained of old; yea, for the king it is prepared; he hath made it deep and large: the pile thereof is fire and much wood; the breath of the LORD, like a stream of brimstone, doth kindle it.

—ISAIAH 30:33, KJV

In early Israel the valley served as a border between the tribes of Judah and Benjamin (Josh. 15:8; 18:16). In the days of the Canaanites the area later was called Ge-Hinnom, or the Valley of the sons of Hinnom. The early inhabitants worshiped an idol called Molech. This man-made god was originally an Ammonite god that sat on a brass pedestal and appeared as a man from the waist down and a calf from the waist up. Those who worshiped Molech would pass their children through the fires (2 Chron. 33:6).

Jeremiah spoke of this dreadful act in Jeremiah 7:31:

> And they have built the high places of Tophet, which is in the Valley
> of the Son of Hinnom, to burn their sons and their daughters in the
> fire, which I did not command, nor did it come into My heart.

Rashi, a famous twelfth-century rabbi, penned a commentary on Jeremiah 7:31:

> Tophet is Molech, which was made of brass, and they heated him
> from his lower parts; and his hands being stretched out, and made
> hot, they put the child between his hands, and it was burnt, when it
> vehemently cried out, the priests beat a drum, that the father might
> not hear the voice of his son, and his heart might not be moved.[5]

Thus, from the earliest times, the Valley of Hinnom became linked with idol worship, fire, and the passing of the children through the fires of Molech.

In the New Testament, the area of Hinnom was located outside of one of Jerusalem's main gates, the Dung Gate. Having been to Jerusalem more than thirty times and having stood in the Valley of Hinnom, I am aware of a piece of fascinating history linked to the area. In the time of Christ, the valley was actually the garbage dump of the city. It was also a place where the carcasses of dead animals were burned. The area was a very deep gorge and had slick, high rock walls on either side of the valley that went from the deep gorge up to the top of the hills. A fire continually burned in the valley, accompanied by the normal odors that follow burning trash.

When Christ alluded to hell in the New Testament, He used the Greek word *geenna* and was able to present a visual imagery to His listeners, who were very familiar with the garbage at Gehenna.

> There are two palm-trees in the valley of Ben-Hinnom, between
> which a smoke arises: and this is that we learn, "The palms of the
> mountain are fit for iron." And, "This is the door of Gehenna."[6]

Christ often used visible objects to illustrate spiritual truths. He spoke of sheep and goats, using these two animals as an analogy for the righteous and the unrighteous. The same is true with the wheat and tares. These natural grains, which were common in Israel, are used as imagery to describe the children of the world (the tares) and the children of the kingdom (the wheat). (See Matthew 13:24–38.)

Skeptics teach that because Christ used the word *geenna* for hell and because this place was located in Jerusalem, hell does not exist and was only a valley in Jerusalem. This *theory* is like saying that Christ spoke of Jerusalem, and because Jerusalem was an actual city in His time, then the New Jerusalem mentioned in Revelation 21 and 22 is an allegory and does not really exist in heaven. When speaking of hell, Christ used this word to paint a clear image in the minds of His listeners, who were familiar with the deep pits, the continual fires burning, and the smoke that rose from the area—comparing it to the actual underworld of departed souls.

## Ge-Hinnom and the Death of Judas

One of Christ's original twelve apostles was Judas Iscariot (Matt. 26:14). Judas identified Jesus by a kiss (v. 49) and betrayed Christ for thirty pieces of silver (Matt. 27:3). Judas later regretted his actions, but he repented to himself and not to God (v. 3). After throwing the silver money on the temple floor, Judas went out and hung himself on a tree (v. 5). Later, when the apostles were replacing Judas, Peter stated: "Now this man purchased a field with the wages of iniquity; and falling headlong, he burst open in the middle and all his entrails gushed out" (Acts 1:18). Critical scholars say this is a contradiction: one statement says Judas hung himself, and the other says he fell headlong. As always, there is a simple explanation to these *complex* theological debates.

I have stood in the area numerous times and even visited a monastery that sits on the top of the hill overlooking the Valley of Hinnom. On top of the hill there are numerous trees whose branches reach out over the cliffs to the valley below. It becomes apparent that Judas took a rope and hung himself by jumping off the cliff, with his body dangling from the tree branch. At some point, the branch snapped, and the body of Judas plummeted below, dashing upon the jagged rocks that protrude along the cliff walls and landing on rocks at the bottom of the valley. Thus there is no contradiction. He hung himself first, and after the branch broke, his body fell. The impact caused the results mentioned in Acts 1:18. Concerning Judas, Peter wrote:

> To take part in this ministry and apostleship from which Judas by transgression fell, that he might go to his own place.
> —ACTS 1:25

Judas was a part of the apostolic ministry and fell into sin when "Satan entered him" (John 13:27). After his death, Peter said he went "to his own place." The word *place* in Greek is *topos* and alludes to a certain location. It can allude to a place (room) that a person occupies (Luke 14:9–10). Some scholars suggest that this phrase "his own place" alludes to a special room in hell where Judas was taken for betraying Christ. Christ had said that for the person betraying him, "It would have been good for that man if he had never been born" (Mark 14:21).

In summarizing the life and death of Judas:

- He was chosen as one of the twelve apostles (Matt. 10:1–4).
- He is called a "bishop" based on a prophecy in Psalms (Ps. 109:4–8; Acts 1:20).
- He was given spiritual authority over demons and disease (Matt. 10:1).
- He was appointed the treasurer of the ministry (John 12:6).
- He was called a thief before he ever betrayed Christ (John 12:6).
- He eventually sold out his ministry for money (Matt. 26:15).
- He was called a "devil" by Christ (John 6:70).

- He allowed Satan to enter his heart at the final supper (John 13:27).
- He betrayed Christ with a kiss and gave Him over to the soldiers (Matt. 26:48).
- He realized his sins but repented to himself and not to God (Matt. 27:3).
- He went out and took his life (Acts 1:18).
- His soul and spirit were taken to their own location under the earth (Acts 1:25).

## Blood Money for a Graveyard

Since the thirty pieces of silver was money used to betray an innocent man and shed innocent blood, a curse was placed upon anyone who shed innocent blood. Since Christ's blood was shed as a result of Judas's action, the money could not be returned to the coffers in the temple. It was used to purchase a field in which to bury strangers who died in Jerusalem. The field, called *Aceldama*, meaning the "field of blood," was purchased in the valley where the lifeless corpse of Judas was found. While standing in the area of Aceldama in Jerusalem, I realized that this field is located on the edge of what was known as the Valley of Hinnom, or Ge-Hinnom. Judas literally took his life on the edge of what was labeled as hell in his time!

Christ used the word *Gehenna* to describe hell. There are various historical and Jewish commentaries that give their insights and opinions on the subject of hell. Among the Jews there are seven names of seven different divisions of Gehenna and a belief that the entrances to this underworld are both in the sea and also on the dry land. According to Josephus, the Essenes described Gehenna as a cold and dark cave.[7]

This area throughout history was a place to bury the dead, as indicated by Jeremiah:

> They will bury in Tophet until there is no room.
>
> —JEREMIAH 7:32

These words—*Hades, Sheol, Tartarus, Gehenna,* and the *abyss*—are the five main words used to identify the underground world of fallen angels, certain evil spirits, and the souls of the unrighteous.

## The Location of the Underground Chambers

After spending hundreds of hours in researching the possible locations and entrances to this rather mysterious underground world, there are three important facts that emerge.

First, these chambers and caverns are all located underneath the earth's surface. In the Scriptures heaven is always identified as being *up*, and hell is always referred to as being *down* or beneath (Num. 16:30; Job 11:8). Never is hell spoken of as being up, and never is heaven's location given as down. Second, these underground holding places for the unrighteous and fallen angels are under the mountains, as revealed in the story of Jonah (Jon. 2:6). Finally, a lesser-known and -taught aspect of the underworld is that many of the entrances are located under the seas (Job 26:5).

Hell is definitely located down and under the earth:

- "Go down quick into hell" (Ps. 55:15, KJV).
- "Shalt be brought down to hell" (Isa. 14:15, KJV).
- "Cast him down to hell" (Ezek. 31:16, KJV).
- "They also went down into hell" (Ezek. 31:17, KJV).
- "God spared not the angels that sinned, but cast them down to hell" (2 Pet. 2:4, KJV).

One example of hell being under the crust of the earth is in the case of the rebellion of Korah against Moses. Korah was jealous of Moses's and Aaron's authority over the people and sought to led a coup against these men of God. The Almighty brought a sudden judgment on Korah and his rebels:

> And the earth opened its mouth and swallowed them up, with their households and all the men with Korah, with all their goods. So they and all those with them went down alive into the pit; the earth closed over them, and they perished from among the congregation.
> —NUMBERS 16:32–33

This word *pit* is not the word for a small opening in the ground, like a crack caused by an earthquake. The Hebrew word is *Sheol*—the world of departed spirits. This was a supernatural event, for following their descent into the underworld, the earth closed up and sealed the opening to prevent others from falling into the chasm. The rebels went *down* into the pit.

A second point is that a person must descend below the mountains in order to reach the caverns and pits of the underworld. There is interesting insight into the story of the *death* of Jonah, reported in the Book of Jonah. Children are taught that Jonah was thrown off a ship, and a whale swallowed him, allowing Jonah to live for three days in belly of the fish. However, when a person carefully examines the words and statements made by Jonah himself, the rebellious prophet actually drowned, and the fish preserved his body from being eaten by other sea creatures. After three days of being preserved, God raised Jonah from the dead and brought him out of the belly of the fish. Here is what Jonah wrote:

> Then Jonah prayed unto the LORD his God out of the fish's belly, and said, I cried by reason of mine affliction unto the LORD, and he heard me; out of the belly of hell cried I, and thou heardest my voice. For thou hadst cast me into the deep, in the midst of the seas; and the floods compassed me about: all thy billows and thy waves passed over me. Then I said, I am cast out of thy sight; yet I will look again toward thy holy temple. The waters compassed me about, even to the soul: the depth closed me round about, the weeds were wrapped about my head. I went down to the bottoms of the mountains; the earth with her bars was about me for ever: yet hast thou brought up my life from corruption, O LORD my God. When

my soul fainted within me I remembered the LORD: and my prayer
came in unto thee, into thine holy temple.

—JONAH 2:1–7, KJV

Jonah recalled that after he was thrown off the ship, the waves of the sea passed over him, and his head became entangled in seaweed. He described his soul fainting within him, which would be a reference to his soul preparing to depart from his body through death. He describes going to the "bottoms of the mountains," and the "bars" were about him forever. Yet God brought him up from "corruption," which is an allusion to physical decay after death. Notice Jonah did not pray *in* the belly as some modern translations indicate but *out of* the fish's belly. Jonah described crying out of the "belly of hell." The Hebrew word here is *Sheol*, the common word for the subterranean world of the departed dead.

Jonah literally drowned, and after his death he went into the belly of the subterranean world for three days. As Jonah cried unto the Lord, God brought Jonah's spirit back into his body. This is the reason Christ compared His three days and nights in the heart of the earth to Jonah's three days and nights in the belly of the fish (Matt. 12:39–40). Just as Lazarus was dead for four days, and Christ raised him back from the dead, Jonah was dead for three days; the Almighty brought the prophet's spirit and soul from Sheol back into a body that had been preserved in the belly of a large fish. Matthew's Gospel translates the Greek word *ketos* as a "whale" (Matt. 12:40, KJV), but the word means "a large fish" or a "sea monster" (used in the Septuagint in Job 7:12; 9:8; 26:13). Men have assumed the great fish was a whale, since this would have been the largest sea creature with the capacity to swallow a human body.

Jonah spoke of the bars under the mountains that closed on him. When Job and his friends were speaking about death, we read:

Have the gates of death been revealed to you?
Or have you seen the doors of the shadow of death?

—JOB 38:17

While most scholars believe these "doors" are simple metaphors, there must be portals or entrances to both heaven and to the underworld. This brings us to the third point: the openings of the underworld that are located under the waters. Notice the references to these openings in the following scriptures:

> They shall go down to the bars of the pit, when our rest together is in the dust.
>
> —JOB 17:16, KJV

> The dead tremble,
> Those under the waters and those inhabiting them.
> Sheol is naked before Him,
> And Destruction has no covering.
>
> —JOB 26:5–6

> Or who shut in the sea with doors...
> Have you entered the springs of the sea?
> Or have you walked in search of the depths?
> Have the gates of death been revealed to you?
> Or have you seen the doors of the shadow of death?
>
> —JOB 38:8, 16–17

> Let not the floodwater overflow me,
> Nor let the deep swallow me up;
> And let not the pit shut its mouth on me.
>
> —PSALM 69:15

In the context of these scriptures, these passages all allude to either death or hell, and some mention gates and bars that are entrances to the pit, or to hell. I would suggest that just as the New Jerusalem in heaven has twelve entrances into the Holy City, there are also entrances scattered around the world that lead to the subterranean world of Sheol.

While it may be impossible to prove with visible evidence, there are some rather mysterious places where bizarre magnetic activity occurs in and around certain seas. One such noted location is the Bermuda

Triangle, with its borders touching Puerto Rico, Bermuda, and Florida. The exact size of the Bermuda Triangle depends on the source describing it, but it is in the range of two hundred thousand square miles off the Atlantic Coast. It is reported to have claimed more than a thousand lives in fifty years. Since 1945, more than a hundred ships, boats, and planes have reportedly vanished.

The Bermuda Triangle is one of two places on the earth where a magnetic compass does point toward true north. Normally it points toward magnetic north. The difference between the two is known as compass variation. The amount of variation changes by as much as twenty degrees as one circumnavigates the earth. If this compass variation or error is not compensated for, a navigator could find himself far off course and in deep trouble.[8] Strange, glowing white water and green fog have been spotted there from satellites. The Bermuda Triangle has a deep trench near San Juan measuring twenty-seven thousand feet deep.

Another area where the same strange phenomena occur is the Devil's Sea. The sea is located on the other side of the world, opposite the Bermuda Triangle. The area is located east of Japan between Iwo Jima and Marcus Island. The Japanese government labeled this area as a danger zone. Near Guam is the world's largest underwater trench, measuring thirty-six thousand feet deep.[9] It is unknown why these areas have such strange magnetic fields, and this book will not detail research related to these incidents. However, there are numerous places in the world where there is odd magnetic activity that occurs on a consistent basis, including areas where the compass actually goes in the opposite direction.

A man named Ivan Sanderson, a professional biologist who founded the Society for the Investigation of the Unexplained in Columbia, New Jersey, claims to have discovered twelve electromagnetic vibrations around the world, called by some the "Ten Vile [Strong] Vortices." In 1972, Sanderson wrote an article in *Saga Magazine* calling his discovery "The Twelve Devil's Graveyards Around the World." Sanderson had researched the areas around the world where ships and planes had allegedly disappeared and discovered ten regions of the world, spaced equally apart, that experienced these strange phenomena.[10]

These areas of strange magnetic and space–time phenomena are situated with five above the equator and five below at equal distances from the equator. Adding the North and South Poles, there are twelve areas. Sanderson claims the ten main areas are located at seventy-two-degree intervals, which include the Bermuda Triangle and the Devil's Sea. Sanderson has laid the areas that produce the electromagnetic energy in a grid and believes these may be portals or vortices. East of the Bermuda Triangle is the Sargasso Sea, an area where the compass of Columbus acted strangely during his journey. The ten areas are:

1. Bermuda Triangle
2. Algerian Megalithic Ruins (south of Timbuktu)
3. Karachi (Pakistan)
4. Devil's Sea Triangle (near Iwo Jima, Japan)
5. Hamakulia, southeast Hawaii (focal point is in the ocean southeast of Hawaii)
6. Megalithic structures at Sarawak (Borneo)
7. Nan Madol (Pohnpei Island, Micronesia)
8. The seat of the Incan culture in South America
9. Easter Island
10. Gabon (West Africa)[11]

One of the explanations for difficulties with ships and planes in these areas is the frequent crosswinds of hot and cold air that form in the atmosphere over the sea. However, it does not explain why there are so many large stone monuments, called megaliths and dolmens (stone tables), erected in the areas where the magnetic activity is the most intense.

I personally visited one such area in the Golan Heights in Israel. The place is a paleomagnetic park known as the *Magnetic Stones*. If you place a compass near the stones in this area, the compass points in the opposite direction of true north. This abnormality has various explanations. However, this area also has more than three thousand large stones called dolmens, which are also found scattered in other places around the world, including Easter Island, thousands of miles away from the Golan area. Biblically, this area was once the home of the biblical giants, a race of very large men who lived before and after the flood of Noah (Gen. 6:1–4). Secular historians question how a normal man could have moved such large stones, which require a special mechanical lift just to erect them in an upright position. The simplest explanation is that the biblical giants were a part of these areas and assisted in the building of these megalith monuments. It is, however, a mystery as to why these monuments are found in the same areas where strange magnetic activity is occurring.

## Spirits Under the Euphrates

A region of the world that is alluded to in biblical prophecy is the Euphrates River. In the Apocalypse, this famous ancient waterway will dry up, and four mysterious angels will be released from their confinement (Rev. 9:14). The Euphrates River originates in the Taurus Mountains and flows through Syria and Iraq, eventually joining the Tigris in the Shatt al-Arab and emptying into the Persian Gulf. The apocalyptic prophecy that mentions the loosing of the four angels also reveals that a dangerous angel named Apollyon, or Abaddon (Rev. 9:11), will be released from the abyss near the same time these other four angelic beings are released from their captivity, where they are confined in caverns under the waters of the Euphrates.

Much of the future prophetic activity mentioned in the Old Testament and in the Apocalypse will unfold in and around the Middle East. Since this future activity is identified as occurring near the Euphrates River, and one of the evil agents released on the earth is called Abaddon, could this evil angel that is now in the abyss be released somewhere in the Persian Gulf area, because the Euphrates and Tigris eventually empty into the Gulf? It is interesting to note that the Euphrates and Tigris join and empty into the Persian Gulf in a place where there is a famous island. This island, called Abadan, is forty-two miles long and twelve miles wide and is presently a main oil refinery island for Iran. It was the centerpiece of the war between Iraq and Iran in the 1980s. The location of the island is just below where the Euphrates and Tigris come together at a place in southern Iraq called Bosera, joining as one river and flowing into the Persian Gulf.

The Hebrew name of this demonic being that will be released from the bottomless pit at some point during a time of tribulation on Earth is Abaddon. The Hebrew has no vowels, and the name of the oil-rich island has some of the same Hebrew letters of the Hebrew name Abaddon, indicating that there may be a linguist link, however weak, to this island and to the release of the spirit called Abaddon from a black-smoke-filled pit. Since the location is near the Euphrates, which is mentioned by name in the prophecy, the spirit called Abaddon could be bound under the earth in this region of the world. Strong prince spirits often take on the same name of the region they control, such as the prince of Persia and the prince of Grecia (Dan. 10:13, 20).

When this "pit" (Rev. 9:1) is opened, black smoke fills the air, darkening the entire area. Because the Abadan Island is used to refine oil, any form of explosion could literally cause black smoke to billow into the atmosphere, thus fulfilling the visual description given by John in Revelation 9:2. During the Gulf War in 1991, hundreds of oil wells were set on fire, causing the air in Kuwait and the surrounding area to be filled with a black smoke that covered the sun, and, at times, the chemicals that remained in the atmosphere caused the moon to have a reddish appearance.

These fallen angels are bound both "under the waters" and "in the pit" (abyss). The inspired writers of Scripture speak of the gates under the sea:

> Or who shut in the sea with doors,
> When it burst forth and issued from the womb?
>
> —JOB 38:8

> Have you entered the springs of the sea?
> Or have you walked in search of the depths?
> Have the gates of death been revealed to you?
> Or have you seen the doors of the shadow of death?
>
> —JOB 38:16–17

## Spirits Are Under the Waters

When studying the Scriptures, many times it becomes important to examine the original meaning of words to ensure that the English translation has correctly presented the true interpretation. Below is one example:

> Dead things are formed from under the waters, and the inhabitants thereof. Hell is naked before him, and destruction hath no covering.
> —JOB 26:5–6, KJV

In this passage Job mentions hell (Sheol) but also mentions destruction, which is the Hebrew word *abaddon,* the same name of the evil angel mentioned in Revelation 9:11! Another word to examine is the word *dead,* which in this passage is the Hebrew word *rapha´* or *rephaim.* What makes this word unique is that the word *rephaim* is used in the English translation of the Bible as one of the common names for a race of giants that once roamed the earth. The name is found in 2 Samuel as a valley in Jerusalem once ruled by the giants (2 Sam. 5:18, 22; 23:13). The word *giants* is found throughout the English translation of the Old Testament and is the word *rapha´,* the root word for *rephaim.*

Job 26:5 says: "Dead things [*rapha´*] are formed from under the waters." The word *form* in Job 26:5 in Hebrew is *chuwl,* and it can mean "to writhe in pain." Since fallen angels are now bound in *tartaroo* (2 Pet. 2:4), then these fallen angels are now confined under the waters, under the mountains in the lowest subterranean chambers, experiencing eternal pain.

> And the angels who did not keep their proper domain, but left their own abode, He has reserved in everlasting chains under darkness for the judgment of the great day.
> —JUDE 6

These will be part of the angels that at the Great White Throne Judgment will be brought out of hell, and the saints will judge them

(1 Cor. 6:3; Rev. 20:11–15). They are reserved (the word *reserved* means "to be kept under watch and guard") until the day of their judgment!

## On the Edge of the Triangle

I have ministered many times at a great church in Huntington, West Virginia. Years ago I was informed of an amazing story concerning a former pastor, Reverend Roland Garner. In 1977–1978, Pastor Garner went on a two-week diving expedition in the areas of the Bahamas and Bermuda, serving as a chaplain for the diving crew. The researchers and divers on the expedition were researching activity near the Bermuda Triangle and why the mysterious magnetic activity occurred.

On the boat a man named Wingate and a close associate of Jacques Cousteau were leading the scuba expedition. During one dive the men found under the water what appeared to them to be the black basalt stones of an ancient temple, including a perfect marble column. During another dive, after twenty minutes the diver came up and told the others that he was not "going back down there." When Pastor Garner asked him why, the fellow replied, "I could hear something groaning under the floor of the sea. It sounded like it was dragging chains." Pastor Garner did tell the diver that there were fallen angels somewhere under the earth, and perhaps that is what he heard. They never returned to this area. It was noticed that at times a yellow smoke could be seen.

Pastor Garner returned and told the entire story to his congregation and gave details about the strange expedition. He believed, and taught, that it was possible the area was once a pre-Adamic region of the world where Lucifer once ruled prior to his fall. He also believed that these places where the electromagnetic field does bizarre things may be entrances to these biblical chambers.

## Gates to Heaven and Hell

Many times when a biblical researcher or scholar does not fully believe in or accept a literal interpretation of a word of verse, he or she will immediately write off the word or passage as a metaphor, an allegory, or a myth. Such is often the case when the subject of hell comes up. Often someone will comment, "I believe there is a heaven, but not a hell. God would never permit anyone to spend eternity in such a place of torment." Others interpret hell to be the difficulties one encounters on Earth; thus the only hell we ever experience is on Earth. Still others suggest that the warnings about hell were exaggerations to emphasize the importance of how to treat others in this life. Some believe that ancient Egyptians initiated the belief in the afterlife and all other religions picked up on the doctrine and simply modified their ideas to fit their own religion.

I have always said that when the plain passage of Scripture makes sense, don't seek another sense or you will lose the common sense. The Bible was not written by Harvard and Yale professors but by forty different authors whose backgrounds were as shepherds, farmers, fishermen, a tax collector, a doctor, and a well-educated Pharisee (Paul). They wrote very simply and literally. Angels are literal, demons are literal, and heaven and hell are literal. The streets of gold are not a picture of the *foundations of divine authority* (since gold represents deity in the Bible), but they are literal streets with literal transparent gold! The twelve gates of pearl (Rev. 21:21) are not a representation of the apostolic ministry of the twelve apostles (since in the parable of the kingdom a pearl is the gospel [Matt. 13:46], and the apostles spread the gospel), but there are twelve literal gates to the heavenly city.

Any attempt to make hell a nonliteral place is futile, humanistic unbelief. Any effort to teach that the fire is spiritual and not literal also has no place in the true interpretation of the complete revelation of hell in both Testaments.

The apostle John was the only biblical writer to detail the size and appearance of the heavenly city, New Jerusalem. He alludes to twelve entrances or gates, guarded by twelve angels. These twelve gates are positioned with three on the north, three to the south, three to the east, and three to the west (Rev. 21:12–13). On the earth, we identify four points of the compass—the north, south, east, and west—and all people dwell in nations in one of those four directions. People from the north have a north gate, from the west a western gate, from the east an eastern gate, and those from the south could enter through a southern gate.

When a sinner departs from any part of the world, there may not be just one entrance to the underworld; but just as there are twelve gates in the New Jerusalem, there may be ten to twelve magnetic gates that actually lead to the underworld. Those from Australia enter the chambers in their regions, while the Africans, the Americans, and Asians use different entrances. All entrances lead to one main area under the mountains.

In the Garden of Eden, the tree of life was in the midst (center) of the garden (Gen. 2:9). Throughout the Apocalypse, the menorah is in the midst of the temple, and the Lamb is in the midst of the throne (Rev. 7:17). It may be possible that the very center or heart of the underground chambers on Earth is centered in Israel in a place known as the Dead Sea. As you will discover, the Dead Sea is not only filled with amazing history, but it is also a place of past spiritual conflicts and has numerous future prophecies linked to it.

# Chapter 2

# The DEAD SEA— the AREA of the FUTURE LAKE of FIRE

The first time I ever saw the Dead Sea was in May of 1986. It was my first tour of Israel. I was mesmerized with the rugged, rose-colored rocks rising like skyscrapers on the edge of the Judean wilderness and with the barren yet mystical appeal of the land surrounding the city of Jericho. I remember standing on a hill near the famous Qumran caves, overlooking the Dead Sea, and experiencing the most unusual desert silence and solitude imaginable. There was a strange, rather mystical and magnetic appearance to this bluish-green body of water. Little did I realize at that time—but after years of research I now do—that this sea might be the most unusual place on Earth.

The Dead Sea is 1,369 feet below sea level—the lowest spot on Earth. At the deepest part of the sea, the level is 2,300 feet below sea level. It lies in a 3,700-mile rift that stretches from Turkey into Africa. The sea is actually a lake that is gradually drying up. The entire area was formed by earthquakes and a boiling outburst of fire and hot water impregnated with sulfur and brimstone.

## Volcanic Activity

From the area of Northern Israel called the Bashan to the bottom of the Dead Sea, the entire area has been active with earthquakes and volcanoes from its earliest history. In the Bashan (the Golan Heights), located north of the Sea of Galilee, visitors can see huge black basalt boulders that are a silent reminder of earlier volcanic activity in the area. *Nature* magazine stated:

> Volcanoes may be more like hell than anyone realized. Eruptions disgorge streams of molten sulfur, the brimstone of evangelical preachers, which burns up before it can be preserved for posterity.[1]

The volcanic link to the Dead Sea is interesting. In the time of Abraham, there were five cities, called the "cities of the plain" (Gen. 13:12). These were Sodom, Gomorrah, Admah, Zeboiim, and Zoar (Gen. 14:2). Because of the iniquity of Sodom, four of the five cities were destroyed by fire and brimstone. "Then the LORD rained brimstone and fire on Sodom and Gomorrah, from the LORD out of the heavens" (Gen. 19:24). The evidence of this destruction can be seen in the layers of volcanic rock scattered across the ground in parts of Jordan, on the mountains of ancient Moab, on the eastern mountains above the Dead Sea, and in the small sulfur balls that lie in the ground not far from Masada on the western side of the sea. The shape of the salt mountains on the Israeli side of the Dead Sea also indicates a time in which there was a massive explosion in the region thousands of years ago.

Brimstone is a combustible sulfur substance that burns. I believe the destruction of the cities was a sudden eruption of an underground volcano that spewed hot rocks and lava into the air. Some scholars believe the cities were destroyed by an asteroid. However, this type of destruction by an asteroid would have devastated much more than the four cities. The only surviving city, the small city of Zoar, was built on a mountain. Lot and his two daughters were also delivered out of the destruction. A major asteroid would have wiped out everyone and everything, leaving no human or city in its path; thus the small town of Zoar and Lot with his two daughters would have become instantly evaporated.

## Asphalt and the Sea

There is strong geological evidence that there are subterranean fires under the Dead Sea. The waters of the Dead Sea contain about twenty-one minerals, twelve that are found in no other sea or ocean in the world. The salt content is high at 31 percent. Another odd feature is that in the past, the sea occasionally spit up black-looking asphalt, a tarlike substance, into small pebbles from deep crevices under the water. After earthquakes, chunks of asphalt as large as a house have appeared on the lake, giving it a nickname of Lake Asphaltites![2]

In the year 312 there were Greek mercenaries making money from the jellylike crude oil that surfaced from the waters in the center of the Dead Sea. Arabic tribesmen with reed rafts would be on shore waiting as these *bulls* of jellylike crude oil were collected. The Greeks carried them off like the plunder of war, and fights would break out over who obtained the substances. Once this black substance collected on shore, three men would chop it with axes and cover the sticky substance with sand, then placing in bags. Camels then carried the valuable crude oil to Alexandria, Egypt, where it was sold and used as a fuel for lighting fires.[3]

## The Dead Sea—the "Spiritual Link"

The *spiritual link* of biblical events occurring at or near the Dead Sea is more than just the location of the destruction of Sodom and Gomorrah. The wilderness of Judea, whose mountains run parallel to the Dead Sea on the Israeli side, is the site of the temptation of Christ.

> Then Jesus was led up by the Spirit into the wilderness to be tempted by the devil.
>
> —MATTHEW 4:1

The traditional location of this wilderness testing is the mountain directly behind the modern oasis of Jericho. From this mountain facing east, Christ would have seen the city of Jericho (Josh. 2); Gilgal, where Israel camped prior to the conquest of Jericho (Josh. 4:19); the plains of Moab, where Moses was buried (Deut. 34:6); the area where Elijah was translated alive into heaven (2 Kings 2:5–14); as well as the place at the Jordan River where Joshua crossed with the Israelites (Josh. 4:3–20).

It was in this region of Israel that Christ had a head-on confrontation with Satan during a forty-day fast. In the days of the temple, on the Day of Atonement the infamous scapegoat was led from the temple into the heart of the wilderness (Lev. 16:10), where it was pushed off a cliff to its death.

An interesting verse in the New Testament reveals that when an unclean spirit is expelled from a person, the demonic entity walks through dry places:

> When an unclean spirit goes out of a man, he goes through dry places, seeking rest, and finds none.
> —MATTHEW 12:43

Years ago during a Holy Land tour in Israel, I was reading this passage when I turned to my personal guide, Gideon Shore, and asked how his Hebrew Bible translated the phrase "dry places." After searching, he replied, "It would be the same meaning as the wilderness of Judea." At that moment I recalled another incident mentioning the wilderness, where a man possessed by evil spirits "was driven by the demon into the wilderness" (Luke 8:29). In the Old Testament of the English Bible the word *wilderness* is found 270 times.

From the earliest days, Jewish rabbis believed that certain strong demon entities had their dwellings in the deserts. There is no word for "demon" in the Hebrew; however, there is a word used to identify devils, *sa′iyr*, which is translated as "goat-demon." This word is a primitive Semitic word that was used to identify a spirit in the desert. This word, which means "hairy demons," is found in Leviticus 17:7 and 2 Chronicles 11:15. The word is also used in Isaiah 34:14 where the "goat-demons" greet one another in the ruins of Edom.

In the Old Testament, the goat was a creature often linked to deception. Jacob covered his arms in goatskin to deceive his father and take his brother Esau's blessing (Gen. 27:16–22). And later, Jacob himself was deceived into thinking his son Joseph had been eaten by a wild beast when Joseph's brothers presented his coat covered with blood (Gen. 37:31–34). Years later, on the Day of Atonement two identical goats were used, one marked for Azazel, and one marked for the Lord (Lev. 16:8). The goat for the Lord was slain on the altar, while the goat for Azazel had hands laid upon it and sin transferred from the people to the goat. This goat, called the *scapegoat*, would be led into the wilderness and eventually pushed off a cliff, meeting its death and thus releasing Israel from all their sins (Lev. 16:21–22).

Thus the wilderness became identified with Azazel, who, according to the Book of Enoch (and text found in manuscripts in the Qumran caves near the Dead Sea), was a fallen angel who came to Earth and revealed heavenly secrets that eventually caused mankind to sin.[4]

There is no direct biblical insight into why, but it appears that evil spirits dwell in the dry places. The children of Israel encountered "evil angels" during their wilderness wanderings (Ps. 78:49, KJV), and prior to Christ's public ministry, the Holy Spirit led Him "into the wilderness, being tempted...by the devil" (Luke 4:1–2). With the Dead Sea being the lowest spot on Earth, and with the biblical history of the area, including the Judean wilderness, this region of the world has certain features that mark it for spiritual judgment (Sodom and Gomorrah), temptation from Satan (Christ's temptation), and the fallen angels (Azazel).

## The Fire Under the Sea

If we go back hundreds or thousands of years and explore the historical references related to the Dead Sea, it becomes evident that there is a huge fire burning under the sea.

The first-century geographer Strabo said that it was "a land of fires," fueled by the substances from the area.[5]

About one hundred years before Christ, a Jewish writer wrote:

> Wisdom rescued a righteous man when the ungodly were perishing;
> he escaped the fire that descended on the Five Cities. Evidence of
> their wickedness still remains: a continually smoking wasteland.[6]
> —WISDOM OF SOLOMON 10:6–7, RSV

Diodorus, a first-century writer, said:

> The fire which burns beneath the ground and the stench renders the
> inhabitants of the neighboring country sickly and very short-lived.[7]

Philo was a writer and philosopher from the first century. When
speaking of Abraham, he wrote concerning the area of the Dead Sea:

> For the fire of the lightning is what is most difficult to extinguish,
> and creeps on pervading everything, and smouldering. And a most
> evident proof of this is to be found in what is seen to this day: for
> the smoke which is still emitted, and the sulphur which men dig up
> there, are a proof of the calamity which befell that country.[8]

Before 1787, there were biblical maps that showed smoke coming off of
the Dead Sea. It was reported:

> The south of Syria, that is, the hollow through which the Jordan flows,
> is a country of volcanoes [volcanic activity]: the bituminous and
> sulfurous sources of the Lake Asphaltis [the Dead Sea], the lava, the
> pumice stones thrown upon its banks, and the hot baths of Tiberius,
> demonstrate that this has been the seat of subterranean fire, which
> is not yet extinguished. Clouds of smoke are often observed to issue
> from the lake and new crevices to be formed upon its banks.[9]

During a scientific investigation in 1848, a traveler in the Holy Land
named William Francis Lynch wrote the following after spending time
in and around the Dead Sea:

The wind blew strongly...during the night, and brought with it a feted smell of sulphretted hydrogen....The great evaporation curtained it with a thin, transparent vapor its purple tinge contrasting strangely with the extraordinary color of the sea beneath, and...gave it the appearance of smoke from burning sulphur.[10]

Let us sum up the uniqueness of the Dead Sea:

- The Dead Sea is the lowest place on Earth.
- The southern part of the Dead Sea was the location of Sodom and Gomorrah.
- There is evidence of ancient volcanic activity in the region.
- The famed Judean wilderness's rose-colored jagged cliffs lie next to the Dead Sea.
- This wilderness is where Christ was tempted by the devil.
- The wilderness is where unclean spirits pass after being expelled from a person.
- There has been smoke, asphalt, and evidence of sulfur linked with the Dead Sea.
- There is a subterranean fire burning underneath the Dead Sea.

## Pits at the Dead Sea

One of the earliest references to the area of the Dead Sea is the battle between the four kings of Shinar and the five kings of the cities of the plain (Gen. 14:1–2). As the battle ensued, the kings of Sodom and Gomorrah met head-on in the "Valley of Siddim (that is, the Salt Sea)" (v. 3). The King James translation says: "And the vale of Siddim was full of slimepits; and the kings of Sodom and Gomorrah fled, and fell there" (v. 10).

Several years ago something strange began to occur around the edges of the Dead Sea in the places where the sea was receding and drying up. Because of lack of rain in Israel and the massive irrigation from the waters of the Jordan River (the only river that empties into the northern part of the sea), the Dead Sea is shrinking three feet each year. This has created sinkholes along the edges of the sea, some one hundred feet deep in this sponge-like terrain. The explanation given for these pits is: "The sinkholes happen because underground aquifers shrink and salt left by the receding Dead Sea waters erodes the earth."[11]

The reason for giving this unique information concerning the Dead Sea is the strange prophecies related to future events in this area, especially in relation to hell and the subterranean chambers where lost souls remain after death.

## The Sea Is Changing

In Ezekiel 47, the prophet Ezekiel predicted that the Dead Sea would eventually form two separate seas (vv. 1–11). One section would become fresh water, and the other half would be given completely to salt (v. 11). This *two seas* vision is impossible if the Dead Sea remains one large, forty-two-mile-long body of water. However, during recent years the Dead Sea has been drying up near the area of Masada, forming a peninsula and two separate bodies of water. The northern half is bluish green water where tourists swim and enjoy spas. The southern section is covered along the edges with multiple layers of salt and small salt pillars.

The peninsula that separates the northern and southern halves of the sea is visible to the natural eye, and the land links Israel and Jordan. There is a small channel dug from the northern half to the southern half to bring water from the northern section to the salty southern section.

## The Return of Christ—and the Dead Sea

In the Apocalypse, John saw Christ returning as the King of kings on a white stallion. He also wrote: "He [Christ] was clothed with a vesture dipped in blood" (Rev. 19:13, KJV). Why does Christ have a blood-soaked garment? The answer is found in Isaiah.

And all the host of heaven shall be dissolved, and the heavens shall be rolled together as a scroll: and all their host shall fall down, as the leaf falleth off from the vine, and as a falling fig from the fig tree. For my sword shall be bathed in heaven: behold, it shall come down upon Idumea, and upon the people of my curse, to judgment. The sword of the LORD is filled with blood, it is made fat with fatness, and with the blood of lambs and goats, with the fat of the kidneys of rams: for the LORD hath a sacrifice in Bozrah, and a great slaughter in the land of Idumea.

—ISAIAH 34:4–6, KJV

This prediction is fulfilled at the conclusion of the cosmic activity that occurs at the end of the Great Tribulation (Isa. 34:4; Matt. 24:29–30). The sword that will come down alludes to the same sword that is God's Word, which proceeds from the mouth of Christ when He returns (Rev. 19:15, 21). The blood on Christ's garment alludes to the battle that He alone will engage in at the areas of Bozrah and Idumea. Bozrah is a city located in northern Edom, which today is located in the nation of Jordan, situated on the east bank of the Dead Sea. The region of Idumea is situated on the Jordanian side of the Dead Sea, in the southern section. Years ago nothing but open fields, mountains, and a few ancient ruins were in these two areas. Today there are numerous farming communities and a growing population living on the east side of the sea.

Why would Christ fight a battle in this region? Many scholars believe that a remnant of Jews from Israel will flee out of Jerusalem and dwell in the wilderness during the midpoint of the seven-year Tribulation (Rev. 12:6). Satan (the dragon) will plot to destroy this remnant; however, he will fail. Christ Himself shall fight the battle to save this remnant when He returns to Earth.

The ancient biblical name for the modern nation of Jordan is Edom (and Moab), and the capital was (and is today) Amman. Hidden within the rugged, rose-colored mountains of Moab are the remains of a city, carved into the stone mountains, called Petra. Numerous scholars believe that this will be the hiding place in the wilderness where God will preserve this Jewish remnant for forty-two months, and this remnant will be delivered and spared from destruction at the return of Christ. Isaiah describes this battle:

> Who is this that cometh from Edom, with dyed garments from Bozrah? this that is glorious in his apparel, travelling in the greatness of his strength? I that speak in righteousness, mighty to save. Wherefore art thou red in thine apparel, and thy garments like him that treadeth in the winefat? I have trodden the winepress alone; and of the people there was none with me: for I will tread them in mine anger, and trample them in my fury; and their blood shall be sprinkled upon my garments, and I will stain all my raiment. For the day of vengeance is in mine heart, and the year of my redeemed is come.
>
> —ISAIAH 63:1–4, KJV

Isaiah foresaw the future Messiah (Christ) treading out His winepress (Rev. 14:19), and He was alone ("there was none with me"). The Messiah is declaring the day of God's vengeance in order to redeem His remnant on Earth (Isa. 61:4). Notice the region of the battle is Bozrah, and the imagery fits with the Apocalypse, where Christ has a blood-covered garment from fighting this battle alone for this remnant seed (Rev. 19:13).

When we compare John's vision of the return of Christ in Revelation 19 to the predictions of Isaiah 63 where the Messiah returns to Bozrah, we can see the parallel prophecies, indicating both prophets are seeing the same event, although their visions were hundreds of years apart:

- "Treads the winepress" (Rev. 19:15)—"trodden the winepress" (Isa. 63:3)
- "Robe dipped in blood" (Rev. 19:13)—"blood sprinkled upon My garments" (Isa. 63:3)
- "Makes war" (Rev. 19:11)—"I have trodden...and trampled them" (Isa. 63:3)

I believe the reason for Christ returning to this region is that Petra, the future hiding place of a Jewish remnant, is located about sixty miles from Bozrah in the mountains of Moab.

Isaiah further gives a prediction about the area of Bozrah and Idumea in Isaiah 34.

> Its streams shall be turned into pitch,
> And its dust into brimstone;
> Its land shall become burning pitch.
> It shall not be quenched night or day;
> Its smoke shall ascend forever.
> From generation to generation it shall lie waste;
> No one shall pass through it forever and ever.
> —Isaiah 34:9–10

This area, situated from the middle to the southern part of the Dead Sea, will be turned into pitch, brimstone, and burning pitch. In the Hebrew text these words are an important link to a future lake of fire that the Bible predicts will exist during the future millennial (one-thousand-year) reign of the Messiah! The word *pitch* is a liquid form of asphalt. The brimstone is a form of sulfur, and the burning pitch indicates that the area will become a fire pit that continually burns with the substances located in the area.

When the New Testament describes hell or the future lake of fire, it is a "lake of fire burning with brimstone" (Rev. 19:20) where the "smoke . . . ascends forever and ever" (Rev. 14:11). The fire "never shall be quenched" (Mark 9:43, KJV). In Abraham's and Lot's day when Sodom was burning, the Bible describes it as "the smoke of a furnace" (Gen. 19:28).

As previously stated, there are numerous chambers under the earth, including hell, tartarus, and the abyss. These caverns of the deep are located in specific regions of the underworld and are a part of the internal creation of the earth itself. Hell is presently the abode of the unrighteous dead. However, the Bible indicates that when the Messiah returns, there will be a certain cavern opened somewhere on Earth, and living men will be permitted to look into the depths of the underworld and will actually see the souls of men who have sinned against God. Human men will see the flames of hell.

## The Opening Into Hell

Without doubt, the Bible indicates there is fire in hell. This is interesting when considering the nature of the earth itself. The planet we live on consists of three *compositional* layers identified by scientists as the crust, the mantle, and the core. The outer crust is the outer layer consisting of trees, sand, and rock. The crust is between six to forty miles deep, depending on whether the measurement is being made from the top of a high mountain or from a low spot, such as the Dead Sea. The second layer is the mantle, and the center of the earth is the core.

The second layer, called the mantle, is a doughnut-shaped region that is twenty-nine hundred kilometers, or about eighteen hundred miles, thick.

> At the center of the Earth lies a two-part core. "The inner part is about the size of our moon," [Chris] Marone [Penn State professor of geosciences] says, "and has a density of essentially steel. The outer core surrounding it is an ocean of liquid metal 2,300 kilometers thick. The Earth's rotation makes this ocean flow and swirl, and the moving metal generates the planet's magnetic field."[12]

There have been numerous drilling projects since 1950. Project Mohole was an attempt in 1961 to drill into the earth's crust to discover the Mohorovicic Discontinuity, or Moho. Five holes were drilled off the coast of Guadalupe, Mexico, one at a depth of 601 feet beneath the seafloor.[13]

In 1970, the Russians bore a super-deep hole on the Kola Peninsula in Russia. Eventually, the hole reached a depth of 7.7 miles and was halted in 1994, as more research and further drilling techniques were needed. The following was reported:

> One of the obstacles scientists faced in drilling to such depths was the increasing temperature. Scientists attempted to counter this by

freezing drilling mud and pumping it down the hole. When the mud reached 7.5 miles (12 km), the drilling machine had reached the height of its heat tolerance. Scientists had estimated that rocks at that depth would be 100 degrees Celsius, but turned out to be 180 degrees Celsius....Scientists predicted that had they reached their 9.3-mile (15 km) goal, temperatures could have risen as high as 300 degrees Celsius.[14]

Some scientists and geologists suggest that the temperature at the very core of the earth may be as high as 11,000 degrees Fahrenheit, hotter than the surface of the sun.[15]

## Hell—Under the Earth?

It is interesting that all major world religions have a belief in some form of the afterlife, and even a belief in some form of hell. This belief goes all the way back to the ancient Egyptians and can be found in the Hindu, Buddhist, Islamic, Jewish, and Christian religions. Some skeptics believe that the older religions simply reinterpreted the hell idea to hold their followers in bondage to their religion and simply redefined the doctrine that someone a long time ago came up with to scare people into having faith.

The Book of Genesis gives the earliest accounts of world history from Adam to Nimrod, who constructed the Tower of Babel. According to Moses (the writer), after the Flood, all of mankind spoke one universal language (Gen. 11:1). Thus any beliefs in heaven, hell, angels, and demons were known and understood by all people. At the destruction of the tower, the languages were confused and the people separated among the nations. However, they would have carried with them their original beliefs, which would eventually become altered or changed over time.

I suggest that one reason so many world religions have a similar concept of hell and the afterlife may be because Adam and his descendants all knew of the existence of God, heaven, angels, the fall of Adam, the angels coming unto the daughters of men, evil angels, the Flood, and the existence of hell.

## The Worm Does Not Die

According to the Gospel of Mark, when Christ alluded to hell He emphasized eternal punishment. The phrase mentioned three times was: "Their worm does not die." Christ also warned five times: "And the fire is not quenched" (Mark 9:43–48). This warning did not originate with Christ's teaching, but it was penned six hundred years prior by Isaiah:

> And they shall go forth, and look upon the carcases of the men that have transgressed against me: for their worm shall not die, neither shall their fire be quenched; and they shall be an abhorring unto all flesh.
>
> —Isaiah 66:24, kjv

This phrase, "their worm shall not die," refers to the fact that after death, a human body encounters a natural decaying process and can actually produce worms that feed off the body itself. The Greek word for "worm" in Mark 9:48 is the word *skolex* (*sko´ lakes*) and means "a maggot" or "an earthworm." The implication is that the spirit of the person will never be destroyed but will endure forever. Some teach today that at some point in time God will destroy the spirits of those in hell and cause their memories to forever perish.

The main point that counters this theory is the phrase "eternal damnation" (Mark 3:29, kjv) or "everlasting fire" (Matt. 18:8). Both terms are used in connection to souls being in hell. In Matthew 25:46, Christ said: "And these will go away into everlasting punishment, but the righteous into eternal life." In the New Testament the Greek words *eternal* and *everlasting* mean "everlasting, perpetual, and never ending." Jesus spoke of everlasting life for the righteous and everlasting punishment for the wicked. Everlasting means everlasting—nothing more and nothing less. Why would we teach that the righteous continue to live forever (everlasting life) but that the same word used for the sinner (everlasting punishment) is a limited time and not perpetual? The scriptures dealing with future punishment all have the word *eternal* linked to the length of the punishment:

- "Everlasting punishment" (Matt. 25:46)
- "Everlasting chains" (Jude 6)
- "Eternal condemnation" (Mark 3:29)
- "Eternal judgment" (Heb. 6:2)
- "Eternal fire" (Jude 7)
- "Unquenchable fire" (Luke 3:17)
- "The blackness of darkness forever" (2 Pet. 2:17)
- "Darkness forever" (Jude 13)
- "Everlasting fire" (Matt. 18:8)

One reason that the afterlife is "everlasting" is that all humans consist of three parts—"spirit, soul, and body" (1 Thess. 5:23). The body returns to dust; however, the human spirit is eternal and cannot be destroyed or annihilated. God is a spirit (John 4:24), and angels are spirits (Ps. 104:4). Satan is an angelic being and thus a spirit. A spirit, whether an angel or a human spirit, can be separated from God, but it can never be annihilated. This would explain why God will never destroy Satan and the fallen angels but will confine them in the lake of fire "forever and ever" (Rev. 20:10). Since the body was made from the earth, it returns back to the earth (Gen. 3:19). At death, when the human spirit departs from the body, it returns to God, who gave it (Eccles. 12:7).

## The Dead Sea and Hell in the Millennium

When Christ returns to the earth, He will rule from Jerusalem for one thousand years (Rev. 20:2–7). Jerusalem is twenty-five hundred feet above sea level. The Dead Sea is about thirteen miles from Jerusalem and is thirteen hundred feet below sea level, which is the lowest place on earth. Because of the history of the region, from Sodom to the temptation of

Christ and the history of the brimstone, smoke, and fire in the region, the Dead Sea fits the best location for the following prophecy to be fulfilled:

> And it shall come to pass, that from one new moon to another, and from one sabbath to another, shall all flesh come to worship before me, saith the LORD. And they shall go forth, and look upon the carcases of the men that have transgressed against me: for their worm shall not die, neither shall their fire be quenched; and they shall be an abhorring unto all flesh.
>
> —ISAIAH 66:23–24, KJV

There are several translations of this passage:

> They shall go forth, and shall look upon the dead bodies of the sinners who have rebelled against my word; because their souls shall not die, and their fire shall not be extinguished; and the wicked shall be judged in Gehenna.[16]

> And they shall be to a satiety of sight to all flesh.[17]

> And they shall be as a vision to all flesh.[18]

> They shall be an astonishment to all flesh; So that they shall be a spectacle to all beings.[19]

The imagery from Isaiah is as follows. During the time of the future reign of the Messiah in Jerusalem, there will be an opening somewhere on the earth where living men can look into hell and see the departed souls of men whose "worm shall not die." This is not some metaphor or allegory, as Christ quoted this passage using the plain sense of the Scripture and a literal interpretation. Since the center of all global and spiritual activity will be in and around Jerusalem, and during the one-thousand-year reign all nations are required to attend the yearly Feast of Tabernacles (Zech. 14:19), then the logical *location* for this chamber to be opened for men to view would be in Israel.

At this present time there is a road that runs parallel with the western half of the Dead Sea, from the northern area of Qumran all the way past the southern salt sea. It continues south to the Gulf of Aqaba, a resort whose Red Sea waters are shared by four nations: Israel, Jordan, Egypt, and Arabia. This road will likely serve as the main road linking the horn of Africa (out of Egypt) with Israel during the reign of Christ. This road overlooks the Dead Sea, and you can actually see Jordan on the other side.

> In that day there will be a highway from Egypt to Assyria, and the Assyrian will come into Egypt and the Egyptian into Assyria, and the Egyptians will serve with the Assyrians. In that day Israel will be one of three with Egypt and Assyria—a blessing in the midst of the land.
>
> —ISAIAH 19:23–24

A logical question is this: *How can there be an opening in the earth if the Dead Sea is filled with water?* The explanation may possibly be that the Dead Sea has separated into two distinct and different bodies of water; one is a clear blue body of water, and the other a thick, salty body of mineral water. The area where the peninsula has been formed could very well be the region where an opening could emerge in the future.

I have personally met a leading Israeli geologist, Mr. Rothstein, whose department in Tel Aviv was responsible for researching and marking out the earthquake faults throughout Israel. Two major fault lines run parallel to the Dead Sea on both the eastern and western sides of the water. I believe at the return of Christ a major earthquake will strike Jerusalem on the Mount of Olives and send the famous mountain in two separate directions, the east and the west, creating a great rift running north and south. The gaping crevice will release huge amounts of fresh water, much of which will make its way though the winding mountains, eventually emptying into the northern half of the sea.

With the Dead Sea being close to Jerusalem, the fault lines will also release and cause a shifting in the geological positioning of the mountains. This could cause another opening along the western half of the

Dead Sea, chiefly in the area where the southern half of the sea is now dry. Once again, there is no better location on Earth to fit the astonishing Isaiah prophecy than inside of Israel near the Dead Sea, the area where the sinful cities of antiquity were destroyed by fire, which are "set forth as an example, suffering the vengeance of eternal fire" (Jude 7).

## The Tribulation Survivors

The next question is: *Who will be living on Earth at the time to go forth and look upon the carcasses of men?* During the seven-year Tribulation, there will be a major population reduction of perhaps billions of people—a result of war, plagues, and famines (Rev. 6:8; 9:15). However, there will be a remnant of men and women who survive the terrible Tribulation, and these individuals will eventually repopulate the earth during the millennial reign. Thus, the resurrected saints and those living on Earth will make up the millennial population.

The final question I have been asked is this: *Why would the Lord allow this?* The very idea of looking into a deep opening at souls who are separated from God seems to the rational mind to be cruel and very unusual. While the Scripture is silent as to the *purpose* of men seeing these departed souls, we do read that at the end of the thousand years, Satan will be loosed and will direct another rebellion against Christ, the saints, and Jerusalem with the assistance of Gog and Magog (Rev. 20:7–9). This new rebellion will not impact the saints, who will then enjoy a resurrected body, free from the presence and power of sin. It will, however, have an influence on the earthly inhabitants.

It is possible that the reason for this visual, "illustrated sermon" is to remind the inhabitants of the earth what happens when there is disobedience against God and the eternal consequences of rebellion. In a contemporary society, legislation is passed in the form of laws to help restrain crime and punish the criminal. Throughout the Old Testament, men would build altars, erect stone monuments, and mark spiritual visitations and historic events to remind future generations of that important moment in history. (See Genesis 35:3; Exodus 17:15; and Joshua 4:7.) The

Almighty instructed Israel that the observances of His yearly appointed feasts were to be passed from generation to generation (Lev. 23; 25).

When Satan is again loosed at the end of the thousand years, humans will again be subject to temptation. The opening to hell is to serve as a restraining influence against anyone who would reject the Messiah and join in the final rebellion with Satan.

Because the Dead Sea is the lowest spot on Earth, the underground chambers are actually closer to the surface of the earth's crust there than in any other place on Earth. Early historians wrote that fire would be seen creeping upon the ground in the very area where Sodom once existed. All geologists know that there are presently subterranean fires burning under the sea. The area of the Dead Sea is surrounded by high mountains on both sides—the mountains of Moab and the Judean wilderness. I have stood on the mountain overlooking the southern half of the Dead Sea many times. From the high points of the Judean wilderness, the entire sea, from west to east, can be seen.

## Sodom and Gomorrah Parallels

Because the destruction of Sodom and Gomorrah occurred in this region, these two cities are examples of future punishment.

> …and turning the cities of Sodom and Gomorrah into ashes, condemned them to destruction, making them an example to those who afterward would live ungodly.
>
> —2 Peter 2:6

> As Sodom and Gomorrah, and the cities around them in a similar manner to these, having given themselves over to sexual immorality and gone after strange flesh, are set forth as an example, suffering the vengeance of eternal fire.
>
> —Jude 7

The former location of these two wicked cities was in a well-watered area in the southern part of the Dead Sea, in the valley of Siddim. Their destruction serves as a warning to future generations who would follow the same sins of Sodom. These transgressions against God, recorded by Ezekiel, are:

> Look, this was the iniquity of your sister Sodom: She and her daughter had pride, fullness of food, and abundance of idleness; neither did she strengthen the hand of the poor and needy. And they were haughty and committed abomination before Me; therefore I took them away as I saw fit.
>
> —EZEKIEL 16:49–50

If our research proves correct, then the gaping hole in the earth seen by Isaiah would be within the same area where the two most famous cities of antiquity once stood. Thus the entire area is marked as a memorial and a remembrance of the eternal penalty of unrepentant sin—eternal death by fire.

## The Antichrist and the False Prophet

> Then the beast was captured, and with him the false prophet who worked signs in his presence, by which he deceived those who received the mark of the beast and those who worshiped his image. These two were cast alive into the lake of fire burning with brimstone.
>
> —REVELATION 19:20

The beast is identified as the Antichrist, the final world dictator, who will plunge the world into its most difficult time in history (Dan. 12:1–2). The false prophet of Revelation 13:11–16 will organize world religions around his counterfeit miracles, emphasizing worship of the Antichrist and this new system. Christ will fight the "battle of Bozrah" (Isa. 63:1–4), return to heaven with garments covered with blood, and organize a return to Earth with the armies of heaven (Rev. 19:14), appearing as the "lion of the tribe of Judah!" Christ will intervene in the battle of Armageddon (Rev. 16:16), head to Jerusalem, and touch down on the Mount of Olives (Zech. 14:4). Immediately Satan will be bound and cast into the abyss (Rev. 20:2–3).

This will be followed by the separating of men who have received the mark of the beast and worshiped his image, and the capture and removal of the Antichrist and false prophet from their global headquarters in Jerusalem to their confinement in a "lake of fire." This "lake" burns continually with fire and brimstone.

All of the predicted events related to Christ's return—Bozrah, Petra, Armageddon, and the Mount of Olives—center in and around Israel. Thus Satan's binding in the abyss and the casting of the beast into the lake of fire should be somewhere in the same region when the End Time events are unfolding.

## "Hell Cannot Be *Real*"

The thought of an eternal Creator condemning His creation into a confined cavern of fire, brimstone, and smoke is very unacceptable in our contemporary society. Thus, hell is considered an allegory or a metaphor, and many assert that the warnings of hellfire cannot be taken literally. Oddly, the same theologians who deny the existence of hell believe that heaven is an actual place and the dwelling place of God. Imagine this: God is real, but Satan is a metaphor. Heaven is real, but hell is an allegory. Streets of gold certainly exist, but the fire of hell is only symbolic of the fiery trials on Earth. Hell is mentioned twenty-three times in the New Testament, and not once is there ever an implication of hell being anything but a literal place with literal fire and the eternal abode of lost souls.

## "The Fire Cannot Be *Real*"

A second argument is that hell may be an actual place, but the fire mentioned in Scripture is not literal. In the New Testament, the word *fire* is found eighty-three times, and only six times is there a meaning other than *literal fire*. (For example, James said in James 3:6 that the tongue is a fire.) There is no biblical indication that the fire in hell is not literal fire.

There is a question, however, of how a spirit body reacts to literal fire. Consider the following. Elijah was carried into heaven in a "chariot of fire... with horses of fire" (2 Kings 2:11). Elisha and his servant saw the mountain where he lived surrounded by "horses and chariots of fire" (2 Kings 6:17), yet these fiery beings were not being consumed and burned up and were not uncomfortable with a spiritual body that consisted of fire.

The rich man in Luke 16 spoke of being "tormented in this flame" (v. 24). The word *flame* here is in the singular form, a single flame, and not *flames,* as many. The wealthy sinner also said he wanted Lazarus to "dip the tip of his finger in water and cool my tongue" (v. 24). If we were to touch a hot stove or get close to a fire, we would immediately jerk back our hands because the nerves in our bodies cannot handle the pain from the heat. However, a spirit body may actually react differently to fire than the physical body.

Consider this: The rich man refused to feed a poor man, and in hell the rich man's tongue (the inside of his mouth) was burning. The flame may have been the intense burning sensation in his mouth that was never relieved. He had refused to feed a poor man, and throughout eternity the rich, selfish man may burn in his mouth—the very thing (not feeding the poor) that sealed his destiny to this tormenting compartment. Compare this to the sins of mankind. If a person stole money without restitution or without repenting, then their hands (which took the money) would burn. If their mind plotted to do evil, and they acted it out without repenting for their evil ways, then their head will feel it is "on fire," burning without relief.

This concept of eternal suffering does not change the fact that there are literal flames and fire in the underworld. However, the spirits of men and women may be affected in a different manner than a physical body is when it contacts fire.

I have always contended that the worst things about hell would not be the smoke, fire, or outer darkness within the bowels of the earth. To me, the worst part would be the complete absence of the presence of God! The second most difficult fact would be separation from a loving family, especially children. There is no indication of innocent babies or children being in hell. (There will be more on this in the section "Who Will Be in Heaven?")

## The Greatest Warning

The greatest warning about hell was given by Christ Himself when He said:

> If your hand or foot causes you to sin, cut it off and cast it from you. It is better for you to enter into life lame or maimed, rather than having two hands or two feet, to be cast into the everlasting fire. And if your eye causes you to sin, pluck it out and cast it from you. It is better for you to enter into life with one eye, rather than having two eyes, to be cast into hell fire.
>
> —MATTHEW 18:8–9

In this bizarre warning, Christ mentioned two hands, two feet, and a person's eyes. This may be because these body parts are the *tools* used when a person commits sin. For example, guns do not kill people, but a gun in the wrong hands has taken innocent lives. Walking past a bar with a strip club is not a sin if you pass it by, but many men have walked into such a place never knowing their feet were carrying them on a road to destruction. It is not wrong to see a beautiful person, but if a man continually looks upon a woman, it can lead to sexual immorality. (Just ask King David!)

I know of no one who has ever requested a body part to be removed to prevent himself or herself from sinning. However, Christ is revealing that we must not be overly concerned about what occurs in the physical body, but we must fear spending eternity in hell.

> And do not fear those who kill the body but cannot kill the soul. But rather fear Him who is able to destroy both soul and body in hell.
>
> —MATTHEW 10:28

## Are There Levels of Punishment?

In heaven there will be some individuals who will not receive a reward, as their earthly works will be destroyed by fire at the judgment seat of Christ (1 Cor. 3:13–15). Christ warned, "Hold fast what you have, that no one may take your crown" (Rev. 3:11). Those who are "overcomers" are promised seven distinct blessings. (See Revelation 2–3.) Those who have been faithful to the covenant and who are workers in the Lord's harvest will be generously rewarded with crowns and assigned as rulers on the new earth (Luke 19:15–19).

Over the years I have been asked if I believe that those who were morally good but never received Christ will be punished in hell on the same level of those who were extremely wicked, such as the 9-11 hijackers, who willfully and joyfully took the lives of thousands of innocent people. A statement by Christ may indicate levels of punishment in hell.

> Woe unto you, scribes and Pharisees, hypocrites! for ye devour widows' houses, and for a pretence make long prayer: therefore ye shall receive the greater damnation.
>
> —MATTHEW 23:14, KJV

In the Old Testament there were two types of sins: those sins done with knowledge and those sins committed in ignorance (Lev. 4). There is a sin against knowledge, as it is written: "Therefore, to him who knows to do good and does not do it, to him it is sin" (James 4:17). To resist obeying the truth or to willfully sin against knowledge is a higher level of sin, as Christ stated: "No one, having put his hand to the plow, and looking back, is fit for the kingdom of God" (Luke 9:62). Those who knew the truth but did not walk in the light of the truth will be judged *more severely* than those who knew nothing of the truth. Those who sin in ignorance are judged less severely.

The word *damnation* in the Greek is *krima* and alludes to a judgment against a crime. The "greater damnation" alludes to a more severe punishment against a person. This warning from Christ in Matthew 23:14

was addressed to the Pharisees, who taught their followers one thing but themselves lived another. They fasted and prayed to be seen of men (Matt. 6:5). They enlarged the borders of their garments (perhaps their prayer shawls) and made their phylacteries (a small black box containing Scriptures attached with leather straps and pressed upon the forehead) larger as outward signs of their spirituality (Matt. 23:5). The hypocrisy of this religious group was so vile that Christ warned them: "Ye serpents, ye generation of vipers, how can ye escape the damnation of hell?" (v. 33, KJV).

There is a spiritual danger to having been spiritually illumined by the Scriptures and quickened by the Holy Spirit to experience the power of the world to come, then subsequently to turn back from a straight and narrow path. The writer to the Hebrews penned this warning:

> For it is impossible for those who were once enlightened, and have tasted the heavenly gift, and have become partakers of the Holy Spirit, and have tasted the good word of God and the powers of the age to come, if they fall away, to renew them again to repentance, since they crucify again for themselves the Son of God, and put Him to an open shame.
>
> —HEBREWS 6:4–6

In heaven, rewards for believers will be given based upon individual works, words, and special deeds performed while we were living on Earth. Just as there are various crowns, ruling positions for the future kingdom, and specific rewards for the faithful, I believe there are also levels of punishment and confinement based upon the sins and spiritual knowledge of each person, based upon if his or her actions were sins against knowledge or sins of ignorance. Christ taught that the people from His day would be judged more severely than those of the wicked cities of Sodom and Gomorrah. This is because the cities of Christ's day witnessed the miracles and yet refused to repent. However, if the wicked city of Sodom, in Lot's day (Gen. 19), had witnessed the miracles of Christ, they would have repented in sackcloth and ashes (Matt. 11:20–24).

The greatest eternal danger for any living person is to have known the true gospel, have been raised in a home with strong Christian faith, and to turn away from scriptural understanding, only to pass from this life having sinned against the truth. After all, there are only two worlds after this life, and it is important to know where your journey will end. And when you arrive, it will be a permanent stay.

Chapter 3

# I MET a MAN
# WHO SAW HELL

Throughout my lengthy traveling ministry I have personally met and spoken with individuals who encountered a brief afterlife experience. At times the experience was shortly after an accident or immediately after a major heart attack or some near-death experience. I will never forget a man I met in 1978 who was attending my grandfather John Bava's church. He related a very eye-opening and frightening experience, which changed his life. He experienced firsthand a journey into hell.

I had just begun my traveling ministry and was conducting a revival at my granddad's church, the Church of God in Gorman, Maryland. During my first revival, I met and interviewed a man name Bill Fishel, who related a dramatic event that totally transformed his spiritual life.

At the time of the incident, Bill was forty-one years of age and working as a coal miner. On the morning of November 7, 1974, he was suddenly stricken with chest pains and began having difficulty breathing. He was immediately released from work and was driven to Garrett County Memorial Hospital in Oakland, Maryland, where he was admitted. The nurses began IVs, including morphine, to control the pain. The medical papers indicate a lidocaine drip was begun. While lying on the table in the emergency room, Bill suddenly blacked out. The attending doctor,

Dr. Alverez, contacted a Dr. Van Ormer in Cumberland, Maryland, to advise on the situation. The last thing Bill remembered was everything fading before his eyes.

It was at this moment that Bill had what some would call an out-of-body experience. He heard voices in the hospital, which seemed to slowly fade into the distance. Suddenly Bill's soul and spirit were fully alert, and he was aware of moving rapidly into a dark tunnel, headfirst, going downward into the floor and under the crust of the earth. He described this tunnel as very "dreary and dark." His first questions to himself were: "If I have died, then why am I not going up to heaven? Why am I going down?" As he continued his descent, spiraling downward, he observed a faint light at the end of the long tunnel. Suddenly he was enveloped in this light and found himself standing in a very large field with no grass or trees. The light, he would later learn, was coming from a large cavern somewhere in the earth.

As he stood in this barren field, he described an intense heat that filled the atmosphere. The ground was desolate and hard. The air was very warm and uncomfortable to breathe. As he was wondering where he was, he noticed that people of various ages began to appear in the same field. Each bore an empty, blank expression on his or her face. No one was happy, and no one was speaking to the others. As these individuals began appearing in this unknown region on this barren field, a crowd began forming and filling up with many people. Bill would later realize these were the souls and spirits of men and women from around the world who had just passed away on Earth and were all drawn to this area prior to their final confinement.

## A Visual Look at Hell

At that moment, Bill said, the strangest thing occurred. In front of this group in the distance at the end of the field stood what appeared to be a large, angelic creature. An announcement was shouted from this angel's mouth: "If you are seeking rest and peace, come with me."

Drawn like a magnet to metal, the entire mass of people began moving slowly toward this supernatural being. Suddenly it was as if a veil was lifted, and Bill began seeing these people falling headlong into a very large opening that he described as a "massive pit." It was then that he observed a second angelic-looking creature casting people into this immeasurable opening located somewhere under the earth. As Bill himself was being pulled toward the edge of this canyon, he estimated this gaping opening to be many miles in circumference. He could see into the lower area, where the huge canyon contained thousands of smaller pits, all burning with fire. His ears were opened as he suddenly heard a mighty chorus of moans and cries arising from below, like millions of souls shouting from a large stadium. The voices were so many and diverse, both male and female. He observed that there were at least two people in each smaller pit. In some instances, a person would reach down into the fire and pull out a person and violently scream at that individual. There were older teenagers who were blaming their parents for being there. Bill heard one scream, "It's all your fault!"

One part of this experience that was completely unexpected was the smell coming from this area. Bill said, "There was a very depressing darkness far above the hole, and a strong odor in the air of burning sulfur." Having worked in the mines, and, on one occasion, having seen a fire break out where men were burned, Bill was familiar with the smell of sulfur and the sickening smell of burnt flesh. While Bill was hearing, seeing, and smelling this world of the lost, he began crying out to God for mercy and help.

Meanwhile, in the hospital the doctor and nurses were working on reviving Bill and were successful. In the place he acknowledges as hell, he was suddenly being drawn back upward toward the earth's surface, and everything became black again. Eventually, when he came to himself, he found himself in a hospital room, very weak and mentally overwhelmed by his experience. Shortly after he was stabilized and out of the woods, my grandfather visited Bill and was one of the first persons to hear his life-changing experience of a world that existed beyond the grave.

In 1978, I was in Granddad's church interviewing Bill—just me,

Bill, and his son. I asked Bill, "Were you attending church when this happened?"

He replied, "I would go to church, but I was not living the life I should. But after this incident, I was so shaken that I said I would serve the Lord and follow Him all of my life." Bill certainly was faithful and did follow the Lord until his death. Bill could say as David did:

> He also brought me up out of a horrible pit,
> Out of the miry clay,
> And set my feet upon a rock,
> And established my steps.
>
> —PSALM 40:2

## Now—the Rest of the Story

My grandfather John Bava built with his own hands and money the church building in Gorman, Maryland, and pastored for more than thirty years. I recall that when he retired in his late seventies, one reason he did so was because so many of his church members had passed away. Just prior to retiring, Granddad called and shared a remarkable incident with me. Bill Fishel had just passed away, and Granddad was quite sad. He was given a spiritual dream that night.

In his dream, Granddad was carried into heaven, where his spirit (or soul) was hovering over a particular area, and he could see the outlay of a portion of heaven just below him! Also below, standing near a massive, pearly-white, double gate were numerous men who had been faithful Christians and members of Granddad's church in Maryland. All of these men had passed, some many years ago, and were all together near this gate as though they were waiting for someone to arrive. Granddad saw his own father, Pete Bava, in the group. He said that Pete was talking and using his hands and pointing around (which is normal for a full-blooded Italian), and the group seemed in high anticipation of something about to occur.

Granddad described a wind that suddenly began to blow, and he observed the massive, double gate begin opening. There, outside the gate, stood Bill Fishel! When the men—all of whom had known Bill in their earthly life—saw Bill, they began to shout and praise God, hugging Bill and welcoming him into the eternal kingdom. Granddad was impressed and even laughed when he described his own father being so excited and jumping up and down at the appearing of Bill. His dad, Pete, was an Italian Catholic whom God had raised up from his deathbed and baptized in the Holy Spirit. Pete loved to rejoice in church. Nothing was different in heaven. Pete was still shouting and praising the Lord! When death arrived, Bill was prepared this time, as his soul and spirit went *up* and not *down*, and he entered his eternal "rest" in the heavenly kingdom, where he and all of the "dead in Christ" will remain until the resurrection (1 Thess. 4:16). Certainly this is what Paul meant when he said, "We are confident, yes, well pleased rather to be absent from the body and to be present with the Lord" (2 Cor. 5:8).

There are numerous men and women who have experienced a near-death or an after-death experience that convinced them there is a life beyond this life. I realize there are many good Christians whose church doctrines teach them that the soul and spirit stay in the body at death, and they do not enter either heaven or hell until after the resurrection and the judgment. They would consider this story to be the figment of someone's imagination while under medication. However, there are far too many stories similar to Bill's for this to be a coincidence or an imaginative mental journey.

Yes, there is a world of the lost. However, there is also a world where the righteous journey after their departure from this life. In the next chapter we will look *up*—to a land that is a heavenly paradise!

# Chapter 4

# WHAT DO
## the DEAD KNOW?

**W**hen the sun is rising, we seldom think of the sunset. After all, we have the entire day to look forward to. Yet the day soon passes like a morning fog melting in the heat of day. Thus it is with life. During our twenties, age thirty seems old. Then forty arrives, and fifty is viewed as over the hill. Yet after fifty, nothing seems old! For the living, the idea of dying may seem irrelevant at the moment. However, the thought of death brings a chill to the mind of every human. We all plan for the future and make every attempt to stretch the length of our days like a rubber band, until suddenly, like the snap of broken rubber, life ceases, and we lie limp in the place where our journey ended. Because death is a future and unknown experience, the thought of dying often breeds more questions than answers.

Christians often wonder, "Can we remember earthly events in heaven?" Or they ponder, "Will my loved ones know me in the same manner as I knew them in this life?" There is also the question of remembering those who did not make heaven their eternal destiny. Will believers remember the unrighteous they knew on Earth once the believer is home with Christ, or will their earthly association with us be erased from our memories once we arrive at the heavenly city?

In this chapter we hope to answer many of the questions believers have related to heaven. Before we explore what we will know in heaven, let's discover what heaven knew about Earth. We have a physical body on Earth but will enjoy a spirit body in heaven. Christ was in heaven in a spirit body, but He took on a physical body on Earth.

## What Did Jesus Know on Earth?

We know from Scripture that Christ was fully aware of who He was and what His assignment was even at age twelve (Luke 2:49). However, by clothing Himself with human flesh and human nature, it was necessary for Him to be taught and to grow as any normal young man, as indicated in Luke 2:40:

> And the Child grew and became strong in spirit, filled with wisdom; and the grace of God was upon Him.
>
> —LUKE 2:40

Theologians and Bible students understand that Christ was the Word made flesh (John 1:14) and that He preexisted with the Father prior to His incarnation (John 8:58). How much of the future did Christ foreknow, or what was He taught as He grew into a man? When did He understand His full destiny, and were there certain things hidden from Him that were not made known?

These are complicated and detailed questions and cannot be answered in one chapter. However, we can determine that Christ understood what was already revealed about Him in the prophecies. He would be born of a virgin (Isa. 7:14) in Bethlehem (Mic. 5:2), and He would live in Galilee (Isa. 9:1–2). Christ would ask His audience, "Have you not read..." speaking of the Scriptures (Matt. 12:5). Christ also had insight from information that was revealed by the Holy Spirit, as we can see in the example of His being baptized in water, when God's voice from heaven said, "This is My beloved Son" (Matt. 3:17). He also gained important information about His death from two Old Testament prophets, Elijah and Moses, on the Mount of Transfiguration.

Now it came to pass, about eight days after these sayings, that He took Peter, John, and James and went up on the mountain to pray. And as He prayed, the appearance of His face was altered, and His robe became white and glistening. And behold, two men talked with Him, who were Moses and Elijah, who appeared in glory and spoke of His decease which He was about to accomplish at Jerusalem.

—Luke 9:28–31

These two men, Moses and Elijah, were Israel's most famous prophets of God. Elijah never experienced a natural death and was transported into heaven in a chariot of fire (2 Kings 2), and after Moses died, God buried him in an unmarked grave in the plains of Moab.

So Moses the servant of the Lord died there in the land of Moab, according to the word of the Lord. And He buried him in a valley in the land of Moab, opposite Beth Peor; but no one knows his grave to this day.

—Deuteronomy 34:5–6

Upon his death, the spirit and soul of Moses would have descended into a chamber under the earth known as Abraham's bosom (Luke 16:22–23). For Moses to appear to Christ on the mountain, his spirit would have temporarily been released out of the precrucifixion underground chamber. As for Elijah, he would have descended from heaven. Here is the question: *How could Moses and Elijah speak of Christ's death, which He would accomplish at Jerusalem? Was Christ revealing to these two prophets details of His future suffering, or had these two men of God already been informed of the details of Christ's future and were making that future known to Christ?*

In the chronology of the biblical account, Jesus had begun to reveal more about His suffering at about the same time that the visitation came from Moses and Elijah:

| When Jesus Spoke of Suffering | When Moses and Elijah Appeared |
|:---:|:---:|
| Matthew 16:21 | Matthew 17:3 |
| Mark 8:31 | Mark 9:4 |
| Luke 9:22 | Luke 9:30 |

It does appear that Moses, the writer of the Law, and Elijah, the chief of the prophets, did impart vital information about Christ's future to Him. The question then becomes: How would they have known?

Moses was the first prophet who revealed the coming Messiah through the types and shadows penned in the Torah. The offering of Isaac on Mount Moriah by Abraham is a preview of Christ's crucifixion on Mount Moriah in Jerusalem (Gen. 22). The ashes of the red heifer in Numbers 19 reveals details that would happen to Christ on the cross. The brass serpent on the pole was a type and shadow of Christ, who would carry our sins to the cross (Num. 21:8–9).

Now, recall Abraham's statement to the rich man in hell: "They have Moses and the prophets; let them hear them" (Luke 16:29). Moses not only had information that was a picture of the suffering Messiah from his own experience while on Earth, but all of the Old Testament prophets—including Isaiah, Jeremiah, Zechariah, and others who had passed—were sent into Abraham's bosom and would have also continually informed Moses of their own predictions and revelations concerning the Messiah.

Perhaps Elijah would have revealed the most details of Christ's suffering. After his translation, this prophet entered a special realm of heaven and, to this time, has been preserved supernaturally for the end of days, when he will emerge on the scene in Israel as one of the two witnesses (Mal. 4:5; Rev. 11:3). At the time of the Transfiguration, Elijah had been in heaven for twelve hundred years. In fact, he had been there in heaven prior to the Incarnation, when Christ came to Earth in the form of a babe and took on flesh!

Whatever insight Christ had of His future destiny, more information was related to Him through these two Old Testament prophets. This would indicate that in eternity we enjoy an increased capability to gain previously unknown knowledge.

During this meeting on the mountain, the Bible says that Christ was transfigured. The Greek word is *metamorphoo* and means "to change or to transform." Christ was glowing in white and was surrounded by a unique glory cloud. One reason for this supernatural cloud surrounding the three men may have been to prevent Satan and his spiritual agents from hearing the conversation and the detailed plan and purpose of Christ's suffering. Much of what occurred was hidden from the general public for this reason.

> Which none of the princes of this world knew: for had they known
> it, they would not have crucified the Lord of glory.
> —1 CORINTHIANS 2:8, KJV

Do you believe that Satan would have entered Judas's heart and motivated the religious leaders to conduct an illegal trial at night condemning Jesus to death if Satan had known that the crucifixion would initiate his ultimate eternal defeat? Thus it was necessary that the information released on the mountain in the conversation between Moses, Christ, and Elijah remain known only to them.

## Twelve Legions of Angels

Move now from the Mountain of Transfiguration to Christ's sufferings in the Garden of Gethsemane. After Christ spent three hours in an all-night prayer meeting, a band of men (about six hundred Roman soldiers) was assigned to arrest Christ. Peter overreacted and sliced the ear off the head of the high priest's servant. Christ rebuked Peter, informing him that He had the power and could have called upon twelve legions of angels to interrupt this divine assignment and prevent His death (Matt. 26:53). When Christ was at the height of His physical agony in Gethsemane, an angel came to strengthen Him (Luke 22:43). This angel may have brought the news from heaven that upon Christ's request, angels were standing ready to intervene.

With all that Christ knew, there was certainly one thing that He did not know, and that was the set day and hour He would return to Earth.

> But of that day and hour no one knows, not even the angels in heaven, nor the Son, but only the Father.
> —MARK 13:32

There is a debate among theologians who believe in the return of Christ as to whether Christ now knows the timing of His return, since He is dwelling continually in the presence of His Father. Based on the pattern of the ancient Jewish engagement and wedding, the Jewish man never knew the exact time he would secretly take his bride to his father's house, as the event was solely in the control of the groom's father. The decision was often based upon the preparation of a bridal chamber, which was constructed at the house of the father. Christ had said that in His Father's house were many mansions and that He was going to "prepare a place" for us (John 14:1–2). Christ did provide us direct access to the heavenly temple by becoming the heavenly High Priest of our faith. He also has provided each redeemed believer future access to the New Jerusalem, the dwelling place of the righteous. Just as the Jewish bride was unaware when the groom would return, Christ was unaware of the exact day and hour of His return to take His bride to the Father's house. One thing is certain: the spirit world operates on a higher dimension and has knowledge of certain events.

## The Future Known in the Spirit World

In 1 Samuel 28:7–14, the biblical writer relates a very bizarre story of a witch who was asked by King Saul to make contact with the departed soul of a righteous man who had passed, named Samuel:

> Then Saul said to his servants, "Find me a woman who is a medium, that I may go to her and inquire of her." And his servants said to him, "In fact, there is a woman who is a medium at En Dor." So Saul disguised himself and put on other clothes, and he went, and

two men with him; and they came to the woman by night. And he said, "Please conduct a séance for me, and bring up for me the one I shall name to you." Then the woman said to him, "Look, you know what Saul has done, how he has cut off the mediums and the spiritists from the land. Why then do you lay a snare for my life, to cause me to die?" And Saul swore to her by the LORD, saying, "As the LORD lives, no punishment shall come upon you for this thing."

Then the woman said, "Whom shall I bring up for you?" And he said, "Bring up Samuel for me." When the woman saw Samuel, she cried out with a loud voice. And the woman spoke to Saul, saying, "Why have you deceived me? For you are Saul!" And the king said to her, "Do not be afraid. What did you see?" And the woman said to Saul, "I saw a spirit ascending out of the earth." So he said to her, "What is his form?" And she said, "An old man is coming up, and he is covered with a mantle." And Saul perceived that it was Samuel, and he stooped with his face to the ground and bowed down.

There is a controversy concerning this passage among scholars. Some suggest that the departed spirit of the prophet Samuel was brought forth from the chamber that held souls of the righteous under the earth to speak to Saul. Others believe this was a "familiar spirit" that was imitating Samuel. Let's look at the textual evidence to find clues as to which interpretation is more in line when comparing Scripture with Scripture.

First, the Spirit of the Lord had departed from Saul, and the tormented king sought a witch for information on his future. The first argument is that this apparition was a familiar spirit, because the Holy Spirit always follows the Word and will of God. As the text indicates, God refused to answer Saul by the required scriptural methods—Urim, Thummim, and dreams. Therefore God would not choose a witch to bring a message from a righteous man.

Second, consulting with the dead is forbidden in the Law of God (Deut. 18:10–12). Would God go against His own established laws to please a backslidden king and give him a message from another world? There is no other biblical record of a person asking for a message from a departed person.

Third, a witch was used to release the information. Saul had already made a threat to put all witches to death (1 Sam. 28:9). The Old Testament law required that witches, wizards, and familiar spirits were to be cut off from among the people (Exod. 22:18; Deut 18:10–11). Just as Elijah destroyed the false prophets of Baal and refused to join their allegiance, the Almighty was jealous for His people and for their righteousness.

Fourth, the witch was operating through a familiar spirit, which is a demonic power that can actually imitate the dead. Again, it was forbidden to consult or to listen to a familiar spirit, as this type of spirit uses known information involving a person, place, or thing and can deceive the living with such knowledge (Lev. 19:31; 20:6; Deut. 18:10–11). Those in the occult world who conduct actual séances often deceive grieving families by tapping into a familiar spirit that imitates the departed loved one. The same could be true concerning this witch and the spirit she conjured up.

Fifth, the witch saw "gods" going up and down in the earth (1 Sam. 28:13, KJV). I would suggest these were either the spirits of departed souls that were dying and being carried into the underworld (such as occurred when the rich man in Luke 16 died). Or these alleged "gods" were a manifestation of evil spirits that have access to the earth and the underworld. In the Book of Job when God asked Satan where he had been, the adversary replied, "From going to and fro on the earth, and from walking back and forth on it" (Job 1:7; 2:2). Angels have access to heaven, and evil spirits have access to the chambers of the underworld.

When this spirit emerged, King Saul never personally saw the person but asked the witch for a description. She described the spirit as an "old man…covered with a mantle," and Saul *perceived* it was Samuel (1 Sam. 28:14). Notice that Saul never visibly saw the spirit, because the information came from a witch with a familiar spirit. The woman would have related the information with her own mouth. This was how (as it is today) a person who allegedly consults the dead brings information to the living. The alleged departed never actually audibly speaks through the air in a voice but only through the voice of the medium or, in this case, the witch.

All of the above evidence indicates that this spirit was a familiar spirit that had specific knowledge. The main argument given that this spirit was literally the departed spirit of Samuel relates to the precise accuracy with which this being from the underworld predicted what would happen to Saul and his sons:

> Then Samuel said: "Why then do you ask me, seeing the LORD has departed from you and has become your enemy? And the LORD has done for Himself as He spoke by me. For the LORD has torn the kingdom out of your hand and given it to your neighbor, David. Because you did not obey the voice of the LORD nor execute His fierce wrath upon Amalek, therefore the LORD has done this thing to you this day. Moreover the LORD will also deliver Israel with you into the hand of the Philistines. And tomorrow you and your sons will be with me. The LORD will also deliver the army of Israel into the hand of the Philistines."
>
> —1 SAMUEL 28:16–19

The details of this prediction are:

- The Lord had departed from him.
- Saul's kingdom had been stripped from him and given to another (David).
- The reason for Saul's rejection: He did not destroy Amalek earlier in his rule as king.
- Saul would lose the battle, and he and his sons would die the next day.
- Saul and his sons would be brought to the Sheol compartment under the earth.

If this were Samuel, how would he know these details? If this were not Samuel, but a spirit, how would it know these details? First, much of the information was already known throughout the kingdom of Israel, long before this supernatural manifestation.

- The Lord had departed from Saul (1 Sam. 16:14).
- Saul's kingdom had been stripped from him and given to David (1 Sam. 15:28; 16:1–13).
- Saul was rejected for not obeying God by destroying the Amalekites (1 Sam. 15:1–28).
- Saul was preparing to go to battle.

The only detail not already publicly known was that Saul and his sons would die in the battle. When reading the entire account of what was occurring at the time, it would not take a genius to predict this was going to happen, since Saul had lost the favor of God and David was being set up by the Almighty to be the next king. David could not and would not become king until after the death of Saul.

It appears that in both heaven and the underworld, certain information about the future is known. Throughout biblical history the Almighty used angelic visitations to relate prophetic information and seal the destinies of the patriarchs and their children. Daniel was given detailed insight of future empires. An angel of the Lord related amazing insight of the future in Daniel 10–12. In summarizing what the dead know:

- They know what has been revealed in the Scriptures.
- They know what has already been revealed on Earth.
- They know what has been revealed to them when they arrive in heaven.

The only thing hidden is the exact time of the return of Christ.

In summary, those who have departed would have knowledge through the following:

- What has been revealed in the Scriptures
- What has already been revealed and spoken on the earth
- What is revealed when they arrive in the next life

The only main event whose timing was not and is still not known is the actual day and hour of the return of Christ. There are numerous stories from individuals who have returned from a near-death experience and have actually reported that family members they saw in the heavenly paradise were fully aware of many earthly events as they relate to the fulfillment of biblical prophecy.

Two days before the death of my grandmother Lucy Bava, I was standing by her bed at the hospital when she began to relate a marvelous experience she had the night before involving her departed husband and my grandfather, John Bava. She described how she saw Granddad, and he spoke to her saying, "Lucy, let me show you something!" Suddenly they were both walking through a beautiful field of high, green grass. As they walked up a hill, the scene suddenly changed, and they were both overlooking a massive hall where Grandmother described lines of tables covered with shimmering white cloths. As far as she could see, looking left and right, there were tables being prepared. In front of her in the distance were massive doors, and there were individuals coming into the room and looking at the arrangements. Granddad said, "Lucy, this is where the Marriage Supper of the Lamb will take place, and everyone is working to have everything ready. It won't be very long now." He pointed to a section of tables and said, "This is where we will be sitting with the family." The individuals who were observing the room and the preparations were, according to Grandmother, individuals who had passed away and were permitted to glimpse this glorious and wonderful banqueting chamber, large enough for countless multitudes to be seated!

Normally, Grandmother was not one to dream, and she was comforted by this vision that had occurred. There are some who believe that these types of experiences are mere images of the mind and hallucinations. However, if they were, why do they not continually occur near the time of death with all people, and why do they mostly occur with strong Christians? One man in the New Testament was given a preview of the secrets of paradise—the apostle Paul.

# Chapter 5

# SECRETS of PARADISE– ABODE of the RIGHTEOUS DEAD

What is it like in the heavenly paradise?

> It is doubtless not profitable for me to boast. I will come to visions and revelations of the Lord: I know a man in Christ who fourteen years ago—whether in the body I do not know, or whether out of the body I do not know, God knows—such a one was caught up to the third heaven. And I know such a man—whether in the body or out of the body I do not know, God knows—how he was caught up into Paradise and heard inexpressible words, which it is not lawful for a man to utter.
>
> —2 CORINTHIANS 12:1–4

Christians have been hearing about heaven for centuries. However, few have heard detailed teaching about paradise. Heaven is the place where believers from both covenants will meet in eternity, but paradise is the place the righteous dead in Christ are resting until the moment of their resurrection. Under the Old Testament, the righteous souls went under the earth in a chamber Christ called "Abraham's bosom" (Luke 16:22). After the resurrection of Christ, these righteous souls were transferred from under the earth to a new location in heaven. The apostle Paul was the first person under the new covenant to actually see this heavenly abode, which he called "paradise" (2 Cor. 12:4).

Paul was writing this revelation in the third person when he said, "I knew a man." Scholars indicated Paul was speaking of a personal experience but was writing in this journalistic form so as not to boast about the many visions and revelations he was receiving from the Lord. Paul wrote that the incident of seeing paradise occurred fourteen years earlier from the time he penned this letter to the Corinthian believers.

If we go back fourteen years, Paul would have been in the city of Lystra, where he was stoned and left for dead:

> Then Jews from Antioch and Iconium came there; and having persuaded the multitudes, they stoned Paul and dragged him out of the city, supposing him to be dead. However, when the disciples gathered around him, he rose up and went into the city. And the next day he departed with Barnabas to Derbe.
>
> —ACTS 14:19–20

A Jewish stoning was not intended to intimidate or simply put a few bruises on the victim—it was intended to kill a person. It was permissible punishment for certain crimes, according to the Law of Moses (Exod. 21:28–32; Num. 15:30–36). Paul wrote that "once I was stoned" (2 Cor. 11:25), alluding to this event in Lystra. The remarkable fact is that as the disciples gathered around the bruised body of Paul and began to pray, he not only got up but also was physically strengthened to go into the city and travel the following day!

Paul said he was "caught up" into the third heaven into paradise. This heavenly chamber is where the souls and spirits of the righteous go at death. Paul was uncertain if he was "in the body," meaning that he had a supernatural vision of paradise while he was unconscious, or if he was "out of the body," a term used to identify the departing of the soul and spirit at the time of death. If it was a vision, what Paul saw was so dramatic that he refused to reveal details in his letter to the church at Corinth. If he was stoned to death (the accusers thought he was dead) and his soul and spirit departed his body, then Paul was literally taken into heaven. The saints standing near his lifeless body actually prayed life (his soul and spirit) back into his body, and he was raised from the dead! If Paul was uncertain of what actually happened, then I refuse to speculate which of the two actually occurred.

Whatever happened, he was taken into the heavenly paradise. When was this heavenly garden called paradise made accessible to the souls of the righteous departed? Based upon Luke 16, prior to the resurrection of Christ the souls and spirits of all people, both the righteous (those in covenant with God through Abraham) and the unrighteous, were carried into the Sheol compartment under the earth. The righteous were placed in one section, and the unrighteous grouped in another. Christ informed us there was a "great gulf" that separated the two groups. The word *gulf* in the King James translation is the Greek word *chasma*, from which we get the word *chasm*, or "a great impassable opening or canyon."

When the early patriarchs died, the Bible says they "gave up the ghost" and were "gathered unto his people" (Gen. 25:8, 17, KJV; 35:29, KJV). *Giving up the ghost* is a phrase used to describe the departing of the soul and spirit from the physical body. The dying were gathered to their people, which is a term used in the departing of Abraham, Isaac, Jacob, and Aaron (Gen. 25:8; 35:29; 49:33; Deut. 32:50). This same phrase is recorded by three Gospel writers the moment Christ breathed His last breath. He cried, "It is finished," and He "gave up the ghost" (Mark 15:37, KJV; Luke 23:46, KJV; John 19:30, KJV). Some suggest that this phrase simply means they ceased to be or quit physically breathing. However, let's examine what occurred with Christ after He died.

## Paradise Transferred

First, one of the two thieves dying beside Christ prayed to Jesus that Jesus would remember him when He entered His kingdom. Christ replied, "Today you will be with Me in Paradise" (Luke 23:43). Both Christ and the thief died before the sun set that day. Christ had informed His disciples that "as Jonah was three days and three nights in the belly of the great fish, so will the Son of Man be three days and three nights in the heart of the earth" (Matt. 12:40). Some who do not believe that the soul and spirit leave the body at death say this phrase *heart of the earth* means Christ would be in the grave for three days and nights. However, other scriptures tell you what Christ actually did when His "ghost" (soul and spirit) departed from His body. He descended to the paradise chamber (Abraham's bosom) to preach to those spirits imprisoned under the earth!

> (Now this, "He ascended"—what does it mean but that He also first descended into the lower parts of the earth? He who descended is also the One who ascended far above all the heavens, that He might fill all things.)
>
> —EPHESIANS 4:9–10

What was the purpose of Christ's descent into the lower chambers of the earth? Peter wrote:

> For Christ also suffered once for sins, the just for the unjust, that He might bring us to God, being put to death in the flesh but made alive by the Spirit, by whom also He went and preached to the spirits in prison.
>
> —1 PETER 3:18–19

We are certain that after Christ cried, "It is finished," from the cross (John 19:30), His Spirit descended into the righteous chamber, and He preached to the spirits of the righteous dead. We must remember that these spirits in Abraham's bosom would include Abraham, Isaac, Jacob and his sons, David, the prophets, and all who had died in a covenant relationship with God. Many of these individuals would have lived and died under the Law of Moses during a fifteen-hundred-year period. Thus, Christ would have preached a three-day message of God's plan of redemption and revealed what He had accomplished on Earth. One man, a repentant thief, was with Him in paradise, confirming the plan was true! After all, this unnamed former thief was the first to be crucified under the Law but to die under grace, since Christ died before he did!

The proof that Christ was ministering in this subterranean "prison" was what would occur the morning He rose from the dead. Christ brought these righteous souls out of this underground chamber when He arose from the dead! This is recorded by Matthew:

> Then, behold, the veil of the temple was torn in two from top to bottom; and the earth quaked, and the rocks were split, and the graves were opened; and many bodies of the saints who had fallen asleep were raised; and coming out of the graves after His resurrection, they went into the holy city and appeared to many.
>
> —MATTHEW 27:51–53

These "saints" were Old Testament saints whose souls and spirits joined their bodies, and they were resurrected and seen in Jerusalem. The Bible is not clear if all believers under the old covenant were raised, or if just a selective number were raised to be seen in Jerusalem. These individuals did not continue to live on Earth in their bodies, as they would still be walking among us today. (A resurrected body lives on without dying.) This brings up two questions: will there be other Old Testament saints resurrected at the second coming of Christ, and what happened to these saints who were raised at Christ's resurrection?

## Firstfruits of the Dead

Christ was crucified prior to Passover, buried at the time of Unleavened Bread, and was raised the Sunday (first day of the week) that began the Feast of Firstfruits. Paul said, "But now Christ is risen from the dead, and has become the firstfruits of those who have fallen asleep" (1 Cor. 15:20). "Those who have fallen asleep" would refer to the Old Testament saints. During the Feast of Firstfruits, the high priest marks the first ripened grain of barley in the field, and on the day after the Sabbath (Sunday) he presents the firstfruits at the temple along with a lamb (Lev. 23:10–12).

Offering the firstfruits makes the remaining field holy before God.

In the Gospels, several women arrived just before sunrise on the first day of the week (Sunday) at the tomb to anoint Christ's body (John 20:1). To their shock, Christ was risen and was preparing to ascend to His Father in heaven. Christ told Mary not touch Him, as He was preparing to ascend to His Father.

> Jesus said to her, "Do not cling to Me, for I have not yet ascended to My Father; but go to My brethren and say to them, 'I am ascending to My Father and your Father, and to My God and your God.'"
>
> —JOHN 20:17

This event of Christ ascending to heaven is far deeper than most Christians realize. First, it was necessary that He ascend into the heavenly temple to purify the heavenly articles in the heavenly temple with His own blood. This was necessary because in ages past Lucifer led a rebellion in heaven, and the presence of sin had defiled the very temple in the heavens. Each year during the Day of Atonement, at Moses's tabernacle and later at Solomon's temple in Jerusalem, the high priest would take the blood of an ox, a goat, and a lamb, sprinkling the blood on the sacred furniture in a symbolical act of expediting sin and providing access to God. The same pattern was necessary for the sacred furniture that rests in the temple of God in heaven. Thus, it is recorded in Hebrews:

> Therefore it was necessary that the copies of the things in the heavens should be purified with these, but the heavenly things themselves with better sacrifices than these. For Christ has not entered the holy places made with hands, which are copies of the true, but into heaven itself, now to appear in the presence of God for us.
>
> —HEBREWS 9:23–24

> But Christ came as High Priest of the good things to come, with the greater and more perfect tabernacle not made with hands, that is, not of this creation. Not with the blood of goats and calves, but with

His own blood He entered the Most Holy Place once for all, having obtained eternal redemption.

—Hebrews 9:11–12

This act of preparing the heavenly temple was not just to purify the temple from the rebellion of Lucifer and his angels (Isa. 14:12–15), but it was also for the purpose of allowing the souls and spirits of the righteous to have a new resting place separated from the Sheol compartments under the earth. These souls who had been confined from the time of Adam's death to the Crucifixion (about thirty-five hundred years) were not given direct access to appear in heaven following their death until the purification by the blood of Christ and the sealing of the plan of redemption.

Matthew revealed that many "saints who had fallen asleep were raised" (Matt. 27:52). When did these resurrected saints ascend into heaven? While there is no scriptural indication as to when these firstfruit saints were presented in heaven, some suggest, based upon the firstfruits pattern, that when Christ departed from Mary and ascended to heaven, He took these saints with Him as the visible firstfruits of the dead.

Others observe a particular phrase when Christ ascended forty days after His resurrection from the Mount of Olives. We read:

Now when He had spoken these things, while they watched, He was taken up, and a cloud received Him out of their sight.

—Acts 1:9

We assume that this *cloud* that received Him out of their sight was a normal, visible, white cloud that we see on any cloudy day. However, the same Greek word is used in the following passage:

Therefore we also, since we are surrounded by so great a cloud of witnesses, let us lay aside every weight, and the sin which so easily ensnares us, and let us run with endurance the race that is set before us.

—Hebrews 12:1

This "cloud of witnesses" consists of the many saints from the Old Testament listed in Hebrews chapter 11, such as Abel, Enoch, Noah, Abraham, Jacob, and others. These witnesses are a "cloud" of people who have finished their race and are observing us as we are running our own race to win the prize.

It is possible that when Christ ascended to heaven to take His seat at the right hand of the Father (Heb. 12:2), He was joined with a great cloud of saints whom He had brought forth from under the earth when He came out of the tomb. Whatever and whenever these saints went to their permanent eternal home, paradise was moved from Abraham's bosom under the earth to the third heaven. Now when the righteous pass away, their souls and spirits are separated from their bodies by angels of the Lord, and they are carried instantly to paradise.

## The "Harpazo" Effect

Paul said he was "caught up" into the third heaven (2 Cor. 12:2). This phrase *caught up* is the Greek word *harpazo* and alludes to being seized or plucked up by force. It is the same word found in 1 Thessalonians 4:16–17, where Paul reveals the "removing" of the church to heaven and says that the living believers will be "caught up" in the clouds to meet the Lord in the air. This event will occur suddenly, and we will be changed from mortal to immortal "in a moment, in the twinkling of an eye" (1 Cor. 15:52).

When Christ returns, the living saints are changed from mortal to immortal and instantly caught up to heaven to appear before the throne of God in a moment of time. In like manner, when a believer dies, that person's soul and spirit can be transported from the earthly realm to the heavenly realm in a fraction of a second of time.

I am uncertain if all of the Old Testament saints were raised when Christ came forth out of the grave, or if there are some who were taken to the heavenly paradise and others who must be raised at the Rapture of the church. We are informed, however, that at the next resurrection, the "dead in Christ shall rise first," then the living will follow them

(1 Thess. 4:16–17). Because of those who are identified with the phrase "the dead in Christ," this would allude to all who died from the time of Christ's resurrection to the time of the gathering together of the church.

This would imply that the next resurrection would be for those who have died under the new covenant and not under the old covenant. If the next resurrection is for those "in Christ," then the Old Testament saints have all been removed from Abraham's bosom and have already been taken into heaven, and we will meet them there when we arrive.

The important point is that we know what happens to believers at their departure. Death for a believer is not finality or the end of the road. It is only the beginning of a wonderful journey that will never end.

# Chapter 6

# MORE SECRETS of the THIRD HEAVEN

The apostle Paul speaks of being caught up into the third heaven. Among many of the ancient beliefs and religions, it was taught that there were seven levels of heaven. This concept may have originated with the fact that the ancients believed there were seven major lights in heaven, or seven objects that could be seen with the naked eye. These were the five main planets, along with the sun and moon. The Jewish menorah in the temple had seven golden branches, which, according to Josephus, was a picture of the seven heavenly planets.[1]

Among the early Jews, the days of the weeks were not named but were numbered. Sunday was the first day, Monday the second, and Saturday was the seventh day. Later, the Jewish method of numbering the days was changed by the ancient pagans. Eventually the days of the week were given names dedicated to the seven great lights of heaven:

- *Sunday* was dedicated to the sun.
- *Monday* was dedicated to the moon.
- *Tuesday* was dedicated to Mars.
- *Wednesday* was dedicated to Mercury.
- *Thursday* was dedicated to Jupiter.

- *Friday* was dedicated to Venus.

- *Saturday* was dedicated to Saturn.[2]

Jewish mystics have taught that there are seven levels of heaven. Each level is given a specific name and is allegedly ruled by a specific archangel. Each level also has a central feature, such as the level of wicked spirits, the level of paradise, the realm of God's throne, and so forth:

| The Level | The Hebrew Name | Ruled By | Central Feature |
|---|---|---|---|
| First level | *Shamayim* | Gabriel | Closest to Earth |
| Second level | *Raquia* | Zechariel and Raphael | Fallen angels imprisoned |
| Third level | *Shehaquim* | Anahel | Eden and the tree of life |
| Fourth level | *Machonon* | Michael | The heavenly Jerusalem |
| Fifth level | *Machon* | Samael | A dark servant angel |
| Sixth level | *Zebul* | Zachiel | Just under the throne of God |
| Seventh level | *Araboth* | Cassiel | The throne of God |

The belief in the seven levels of heaven, as recorded in the Hebrew Midrash, can be summed up in this statement:

> When Adam sinned, the *Shechinah* departed to the First Heaven. The sin of Kayin [Cain] forced it to the Second Heaven; the Generation of Enosh to the Third; the generation of the Flood to the Fourth; the generation of the Dispersion to the Fifth; Sodomites, to the Sixth; Egypt of Avraham's [Abraham] day, to the Seventh.[3]

Even Islam picked up upon this tradition of seven heavens:

> Don't you see how Allah has created the seven heavens one above another, and made the moon a light in their midst, and made the sun as a (Glorious) Lamp?
>
> —SURAH 71:15–16

While these traditions may seem interesting, the inspired Scriptures only indicate three specific levels of heaven. Genesis 2:1 mentions heaven in the plural form, "the heavens and the earth." Heaven is alluded to in the plural form one hundred fourteen times in the Old Testament and nineteen times in the New Testament. The phrase *heaven of heavens* is mentioned five times in the Old Testament, such as in Deuteronomy 10:14 (KJV). This plural form indicates more than one division of heaven.

The idea of three regions of heaven can be seen in such examples as Isaiah 14:13–14. Lucifer made the following statements:

- ☛ "I will ascend into heaven..."
- ☛ "I will ascend above the heights of the clouds..."
- ☛ "I will exalt my throne above the stars..."

The clouds are identified as the first level of heaven, the stars and planets are the second level, and above the stars would be the region of the third heaven. Man was given dominion over the first heaven, where the birds fly and the clouds produce rain (Gen. 1:28). The second heaven is dominated by the various spirit rebels mentioned in Ephesians 6:12—principalities, powers, rulers of the darkness, and spiritual hosts of wickedness in the heavenly places. The first and second heavens are where God's angelic army battles Satan and his angels (Rev. 12:7). The third heaven is at the edge of the galaxy and is located above the stars of God (Isa. 14:13). According to Isaiah 14, the heavenly territory above and beyond the stars is where the throne of the Almighty is positioned.

## The Three Regions in the Third Heaven

When we think of heaven, we all have a different mental picture. As children, we imagine floating on a cloud while playing a golden harp and of being able to jump from cloud to cloud like bouncing on a trampoline. As teens we may picture heaven as a rather boring place where old people with white beards and long, flowing gowns walk around with staffs, reminiscing about the past and getting answers to questions that have always bugged them! As we age, heaven becomes the place where many of our loved ones have gone and are waiting for our arrival. Time soon passes, and we too await our departure.

When we carefully look at the Scriptures, heaven consists of several major parts.

1.  The heavenly temple of God
2.  The heavenly New Jerusalem
3.  The heavenly paradise

The Book of Revelation is the account of a vision experienced by the apostle John while an exile on the island of Patmos. John gives the reader the most detailed description of the secrets in heaven of any biblical author.

John is "caught up" in the spirit into the heavenly temple (Rev. 4:1–2). This heavenly temple is the center of all activity in heaven. The central feature is the throne of God. The radiance of God is said to be like "a jasper and a sardius stone" (v. 3). These two stones are the last (jasper) and first (sardius) stones of the twelve stones that covered the breastplate of the Old Testament high priest (Exod. 28:17–20). The first stone is for Reuben, Jacob's firstborn, and the last stone is for Benjamin, Jacob's last son. The Hebrew name for Reuben means "Behold a son," and Benjamin in Hebrew means "son of my right hand." The stones are a picture of Christ, who is "the First and the Last" (Rev. 1:17). Also, while Christ was on Earth, the Almighty addressed Him as "My beloved Son"

(Matt. 3:17), and in heaven He is the Son who "sat down at the right hand of the Majesty on high" (Heb 1:3).

The number twenty-four is found in the Old Testament in connection to the temple priests, who numbered twenty-four thousand. In the New Testament, John saw twenty-four elders sitting on thrones (Rev. 4:4). The twenty-four elders in Revelation 4:4 are believed to be the twelve sons of Jacob from the Old Testament and the twelve apostles of Christ from the New Testament (Luke 22:30).

The original sacred gold furniture that Moses saw in a vision and replicated in his tabernacle was seen and recorded by John for the first time (since Moses) in the Apocalypse. John saw seven candlesticks, which is the imagery of the golden menorah (Rev. 1:12–13). He saw a golden altar where incense was offered (Rev. 8:2–4), and the sacred ark of the covenant (Rev. 11:19).

When the resurrection of the dead in Christ and the gathering together of the living saints occur, we will all be gathered together at the temple in heaven, where we will worship God and sing new songs to the Lamb, Jesus Christ. (See Revelation chapters 4 and 5.) God instructed Jewish men to appear three times a year at the temple in Jerusalem—Passover, Pentecost, and the Feast of Tabernacles. We too will appear first at the temple before entering the city.

## The Holy City

In Hebrews 11:10 we read where even Abraham "looked for a city which hath foundations, whose builder and maker is God" (KJV). The patriarch understood that God lived in a heavenly city. However, outside of Moses seeing into heaven and building the tabernacle furniture according to the pattern of God (Heb. 8:5) and David receiving a revelation of the patterns for the future temple built by Solomon (1 Chron. 28:19–21), after nearly four thousand years of human history, John was finally permitted to see and describe the heavenly city, called the New Jerusalem.

John wrote:

> I, John, saw the holy city, New Jerusalem, coming down out of heaven from God, prepared as a bride adorned for her husband.
>
> —REVELATION 21:2

> The city lies in a square, its length being the same as its width. And he measured the city with his reed—12,000 stadia (about 1,500 miles); its length and width and height are the same. He measured its wall also—144 cubits (about 72 yards) by a man's measure [of a cubit from his elbow to his third fingertip], which is [the measure] of the angel.
>
> —REVELATION 21:16–17, AMP

The New Jerusalem is fifteen hundred miles wide and long at the base and fifteen hundred miles across at the base. There are twelve levels of precious stones that extend from the base of the city to the top. The New Jerusalem has twelve outer walls garnished with twelve different types of stones.

| The Foundation Level | The Stone | The Main Color |
|---|---|---|
| The first foundation | Jasper | Dark green |
| The second foundation | Sapphire | Dark blue |
| The third foundation | Chalcedony | Greenish blue |
| The fourth foundation | Emerald | Bluish green |
| The fifth foundation | Sardonyx | Red and white |
| The sixth foundation | Sardius | Bright red |
| The seventh foundation | Chrysolite | Golden yellow |
| The eighth foundation | Beryl | Blue green |
| The ninth foundation | Topaz | Yellow green |
| The tenth foundation | Chrysoprase | Apple green |
| The eleventh foundation | Jacinth | Blue |
| The twelfth foundation | Amethyst | Purple |

It is interesting to note how these colors blend from a dark green foundation all the way to a purple on top. A rainbow consists of a progression of colors—red, orange, yellow, green, blue, indigo, and violet. Many of these stones on the city walls are also the stones found on the breastplate of the Old Testament high priest (Exod. 39:10–13). Each foundational stone has the name of an apostle carved into the actual walls.

The city has twelve gates at the foundation with twelve angels stationed at each gate. There are three on the north, three on the south, three entrances on the east, and three on the west. Above these twelve gates are carved the names of the twelve tribes of Israel (Rev. 21:12). Each of the huge gates is made with one large pearl (v. 21). Christ gave a parable about one pearl a merchant found that was so valuable he sold all his possessions to purchase the pearl. This parable was a parable of the kingdom (Matt. 13:45–46). The pearl is the gospel, and the twelve gates are a picture of the gospel that came through Christ and His twelve apostles.

## Heaven May Be Shaped Like a Pyramid

Ministers and scholars have always assumed that the New Jerusalem is a giant square, a multicolored gem-covered cube. This is because the city is as high as it is wide. However, the city may actually be in the form of a pyramid. The base would be fifteen-hundred-miles square, and from the center of the base to the top of the capstone would be fifteen hundred miles. The pyramid concept has some support in the fact that the pyramid is one of the world's oldest geometrical forms. Pyramids were constructed in Egypt and are also found in other places. Where did this idea and form originate among the ancients? The pyramids were used among the Egyptians to bury their pharaohs, with the belief they entered an afterlife from the pyramid.

In a pyramid the capstone is positioned on the top. If a line is drawn from the center of the capstone, the line would fall directly in the center of the base. Consider the following. In the New Jerusalem the Lamb is the light of the city. From a pyramid form, the light (or glory) of the Lamb could radiate from the top center and cover the entire city.

We are also informed by John:

> And he showed me a pure river of water of life, clear as crystal, proceeding from the throne of God and of the Lamb. In the middle

of its street, and on either side of the river, was the tree of life, which bore twelve fruits, each tree yielding its fruit every month. The leaves of the tree were for the healing of the nations. And there shall be no more curse, but the throne of God and of the Lamb shall be in it, and His servants shall serve Him.

—REVELATION 22:1–3

The water of life flows out of the throne. In the earthly Garden of Eden there was one main river that parted into four divisions, and the tree of life was in the "midst of the garden" (Gen. 2:9). In the heavenly city, the river of life provides life-giving water to the inhabitants of the city. John gives the first insight into the tree of life as a special tree that produces twelve types of fruit each month on one tree! We continually see the number twelve associated with the Holy City—twelve gates, twelve angels, twelve foundations, twelve types of fruit, and so on. The biblical number twelve is associated with divine order and government. Thus the Holy City is the perfection of divine order.

## The Location of Paradise

Paul taught that paradise was in the third heaven, but where in the third heaven? Obviously it is linked either with the heavenly temple or the Holy City. It is certainly not some orb or platform floating in vast space like a *Star Trek* spaceship. Paradise is the resting place of the righteous dead. The only New Testament location for departed souls resting in heaven is recorded in Revelation chapter 6.

When He opened the fifth seal, I saw under the altar the souls of those who had been slain for the word of God and for the testimony which they held. And they cried with a loud voice, saying, "How long, O Lord, holy and true, until You judge and avenge our blood on those who dwell on the earth?" Then a white robe was given to each of them; and it was said to them that they should rest a little while longer, until both the number of their fellow servants and their brethren, who would be killed as they were, was completed.

—REVELATION 6:9–11

Three statements or words are important in this passage:

1. They were "the souls of those who had been slain" on Earth—their souls were in heaven.

2. "A white robe was given" to each of them.

3. They were told to "rest a little while longer" in this region of heaven.

These three facts tie into what occurs when righteous people die. They are carried into heaven (paradise), they are given a white robe, and they rest until the time of their resurrection. These particular souls are located "under the altar of God" in heaven.

As stated, the throne room is actually the heavenly temple. John described the floor as "a sea of glass, like crystal" (Rev. 4:6). The word *sea* implies a very large area, much like looking at the ocean from a beach. In almost every instance, the New Testament word *sea* means "the waters on Earth." The same Greek word used for "seawaters" is used for "the sea of glass." The floor is clear, and a person can look though this crystal floor and see the souls that are "resting" under the sea of glass. Since the floor is like a crystal and crystal is similar to glass, these souls under the heavenly altar could be seen by John, who was standing *on* the sea of glass looking at what was a large area *under* the sea of glass.

I know of no greater location for paradise than to be placed under the sea of glass where the heavenly Father sits upon His eternal throne.

## Heaven in the North

If I were to ask you to step outside on a clear night and point to where God dwells, most would point either outward or directly upward. Depending upon where you live, someone at the South Pole would actually be pointing downward (south), and those at the equator would be looking outward (east or west). Only those standing at the North Pole would actually be pointing upward (north) from the positioning of our planet. North is always up, and south is always down.

When exploring the actual direction in the heavens where the throne of God sits, most believers would say, "No one knows. It's just out there somewhere!" As a teenage minister, I became curious as to the location of heaven, and when a skeptical high school colleague challenged me to *prove* heaven existed, I took the challenge. I eventually concluded that it was located in the northern section of the heavens.

The first reference I found was in Isaiah 14, where Lucifer threatened a rebellious takeover of God's throne. We read where Satan said:

> How you are fallen from heaven,
> O Lucifer, son of the morning!
> How you are cut down to the ground,
> You who weakened the nations!
> For you have said in your heart:
> "I will ascend into heaven,
> I will exalt my throne above the stars of God;
> I will also sit on the mount of the congregation
> On the farthest sides of the north;
> I will ascend above the heights of the clouds,
> I will be like the Most High."
>
> —Isaiah 14:12–14

Lucifer said he would ascend into heaven "above the stars of God." He then believed he would "sit on the mount of the congregation on the farthest sides of the north." The mount of the congregation is the holy mount where the heavenly temple is. This mountain is called "Mount Sion" in Hebrews 12:22 (kjv) and Revelation 14:1 (kjv). Hebrews 12:22 says there is "an innumerable company of angels" on this mountain. The word *congregation* in Isaiah 14:13 is the Hebrew word *mowed*, the same word used to identify the appointed times when Israel came together for the feast and, specifically, when the men ascended to Jerusalem to worship the Lord during the three feasts. The common word for "congregation" in the Hebrew Scriptures is *qahal*, which means "an assembly or a multitude." Lucifer knew this mountain was the mountain for special assemblies designed to worship and exalt God.

Lucifer was attempting to make his move against God "on the farthest sides of the north." The word *side* in Hebrew is *yerekah* and figuratively alludes to the rear or the recess. Today we would say, "He was attempting to sneak in the back door!" The location of God's eternal throne and of the mount of the assembly is in the "north."

The north is also identified by the prophet Ezekiel, where the prophet saw "a whirlwind was coming out of the north, a great cloud with raging fire engulfing itself" (Ezek. 1:4). Out of this heavenly whirlwind came the throne of God, being transported upon the shoulder of four angelic creatures called *cherubim* (Ezek. 1:1–28).

The psalmist must have recognized the significance of the north when he wrote:

> For exaltation comes neither from the east
> Nor from the west nor from the south.
> But God is the Judge.
>
> —PSALM 75:6–7

By the omission of the north, one could deduct that the Judge, the Lord, sits in the northern part of the heavens assigning His promotions.

## The Empty Space—the North Star

There are two unique features about the north from a scientific view. The Book of Job tells us:

> Sheol is naked before Him,
> And Destruction has no covering.
> He stretches out the north over empty space;
> He hangs the earth on nothing.
>
> —JOB 26:6–7

The writer states there is an "empty space" in the north. From our visibility on Earth, it appears that every *inch* of the heavens contains stars. While this is true, there is an empty place, void of stars, in the northern part of the heavens. However, one of the most unique facts about the stars in heaven concerns the famous *North Star*. The Creator placed one special star, two degrees off true north, in the heavens. This star is located in the arm of the Big Dipper and is the brightest star in the heavens from our view on Earth. The North Star, also called Polaris, is globally recognized as the directional star that has assisted ships and travelers for centuries in marking their directions when using the stars as a guide. When a captain at sea identifies the North Star, he can identify the other three directions: south, east, and west.

With the heavenly temple being in the north and an empty space created in this region and the brightest star to the human eye being placed in the northern part of heaven, the message appears to be that when you need direction and help, look to the north!

When a person who has a redemptive covenant through Christ breathes his or her final breath, angels are present to release the soul and spirit from the physical body of the redeemed and carry the eternal spirit into paradise, where others who have passed before await the arrival.

I recall a very stirring dream I had related to my own father, which I wish to share. While the majority of dreams are not from the Lord and are simply the subconscious mind projecting images while we sleep, there are times a person is certain that a dream was a true spiritual revelation. A spiritual dream with a spiritual meaning always has symbolism that can easily be interpreted, using the same symbols found in the Scriptures. For example, a dream of a serpent is a warning of trouble (as Satan's symbol in Scripture is a serpent), sheep allude to believers, and wolves to people who are false teachers and hinder the church. In a dream that reveals the future, biblical symbols are used or the meaning is made clear in the dream.

## A "Waiting Room" of Family and Friends

In 2009 I dreamed that I was walking with my beloved father, Fred Stone. In the dream Dad had become quite feeble, walking with a cane, and I was helping him keep his balance. I assisted him into a large building that was quite dark and empty. In the distance appeared a young woman with a clipboard in her hand. She gently spoke up saying, "Please come with me." I was very impressed with her clothing. It was very bright in color and looked tailored. In fact, it looked very expensive. I assisted Dad into a very large and creatively decorated room where other female attendants were working to process individuals into this place we were entering. I recall each was dressed in the most magnificent, colorful clothing, and it looked as through a personal seamstress had worked with expensive material and carefully sewed the dresses for each worker.

At that moment one of the women requested, "Mr. Stone, please come this way," speaking to Dad. I was joining him, and the woman held up her hand like a traffic policeman and said, "I'm sorry. You cannot come here yet." I released Dad and watched him walk down a long hall that suddenly appeared in front of us. He walked alone, limping and slightly stooped in the shoulders. I knew we were being separated, and Dad was about to enter into eternity. I was very sad in the dream, yet excited because I knew that through all the years of Dad's ministry, he had waited for this moment—to see the Lord he loved. He had preached for almost sixty years!

I stood, watching him move down the hall, when suddenly something came rising up out of the floor. Dad stopped, and I saw it was a large weight scale—the kind a person would stand upon to weigh themselves, but much larger than normal. This scale was a large square, and it gently lifted Dad from the floor about twelve inches. As he stood there, a most remarkable metamorphosis occurred. Dad's gray hair began to change to the original coal black that he had in his twenties. His stooped shoulders went straight, and suddenly the most beautiful black suit was covering his entire frame. I never saw his face, but he looked the way he did in his late twenties and early thirties!

Then another exciting thing occurred. The hall led into a large room that suddenly became white, like white marble. The scales disappeared back into the floor. Dad had been "weighed" for his life's work and ministry and was found worthy to enter this heavenly paradise. I suddenly observed a room off to the right side in front of Dad. At that moment my beloved grandfather John Bava peeped around the corner to see where Dad was! I then realized there was a waiting room full of people whom Dad had personally known throughout his life and had already passed on who were awaiting his arrival. I immediately thought of how Granddad had seen a gathering of men in heaven right after Bill Fishel passed away. Dad entered the room, never looking back. The dream, however, did not end.

At that moment, everything in front of me turned a pearly white. The floors, walls, and ceilings were all covered in the most radiant white color. As I was admiring the beauty that was before me, a lovely black woman approached me and asked, "Will you please come with me?" She too was dressed in a remarkably lovely dress that was full of the brightest matching combination of colors. She then said to me, "I was killed on 9-11, the day the planes flew into the World Trade Center." I was amazed to hear this. She said, "My job was dealing with insurance." She then said this: "You cannot imagine how many people arrived here that day [speaking of heaven]. People were praying and repenting, and many, many souls arrived here that day!" She escorted me to a door, and I awoke.

I have often wondered why the Lord gave me this dream in the form I saw it. I did not see people in white robes, and the rooms with the workers were beautiful, yet quite normal looking. I do believe the black woman speaking to me gave me that word to comfort someone who lost a loved one on 9-11.

The idea of a waiting room where your arrival has been announced should not come as a surprise. When the patriarchs died, they gave up the ghost and were "gathered to [their] people" (Gen. 25:8; 35:29). These were individuals the departed knew while living on Earth who had died prior to the departed and were awaiting him or her beyond the grave.

For the believer, death is not the end but only the beginning. When our earthly journey ends, our eternal journey is only beginning. Christ made this all possible through His death and resurrection. Because He lives, we can live also. Because He transferred the righteous out of Abraham's bosom to the third heaven, we will never have to spend eternity near the edge of hell.

Chapter 7

# MAN IS a THREE-pART BEING— ONE pART DIES, and TWO pARTS LIVE

**D**on't ever believe you were a *birth accident*. According to the inspired writers of the Bible, God foreknew you before your birth (Jer. 1:5). It was the Almighty who created you in your mother's womb (Ps. 139:13). God also ordained the season in which you would live (Esther 4:14). The Creator has also numbered your days (Ps. 90:12). God has also created you a tripartite being with a body, soul, and spirit:

> Now may the God of peace Himself sanctify you completely; and may your whole spirit, soul, and body be preserved blameless at the coming of our Lord Jesus Christ.
>
> —1 Thessalonians 5:23

When God formed you, He made you one of a kind. You have a distinct set of fingerprints, footprints, and a unique design in your eyes. Even your teeth have imprints that are distinctly yours, and when you speak, your voice tone and inflection have a pattern that distinguishes your voice from all others. Each human being has a gene pool in his or her DNA that marks that person as a single human being, different from all others. This uniqueness can only be explained as the work of a divine Creator who has the ability to design you as one distinct person among more than seven billion people.

Doctors can effectively explain the miracle of conception, the formation of the fetus within the womb, and life development, but they have difficulty explaining death. Why do we age and eventually die? Human cells can reproduce themselves every seven years, yet death is the conclusion of life. While it may be a mystery to science, it is not a secret to God. The first man, Adam, was created without sin and sickness; however, when he rebelled against God and God denied Adam access to the tree of life, then sin led to physical decline, which eventually concluded in physical death. By one man sin entered the world and death by sin (Rom. 5:12). Adam was 130 years of age when his son Seth was born; he lived to be 930 years of age. Thus he experienced a spiritual separation from God, a death in his spirit, long before he died physically (Gen. 5:3, 5).

When we attend a funeral, we all see the physical shell of the person lying in a coffin. What most unbelievers are unaware of is that the *real* person departed from the shell at the moment of death. The Bible is very specific in revealing that each human being is a tripartite being, consisting of a body, soul, and spirit.

The body is simply the physical flesh part of the person. The soul and spirit are interconnected, and at times it is difficult to explain the difference between the two. In the Old Testament Hebrew, the word *soul* is *nepesh* and alludes to the life force. According to Leviticus 17:11, the life (Hebrew, *nepesh*) of the body is the blood. The common Hebrew word for "spirit" is *ruach* and can be translated as "wind," "breath," and "spirit." Thus, when God formed man, He molded a physical body. When God breathed into man's nostrils, Adam became a living soul (Gen. 2:7, KJV). God did not call Adam a *living body*, although he had a physical body, but a *living soul*. This is because God intended Adam to remain faithful and forever partake of the tree of life and live forever with Him in Eden (Gen. 3:22).

In the Hebrew language, the word *ruach* has about nine different meanings! In the realm of the spirit world, there are three different types of spirits:

1. The Spirit of God and the angels, who are spirits
2. The spirit of Satan and the evil angels and evil spirits
3. The spirit of mankind, the eternal spirit that dwells in their bodies

When describing the difference between the soul and the spirit, I have often said that the soul is linked to the mind, the brain, the five senses, and the emotions of a person. The soul can be either carnal or spiritual, depending upon how you feed it! The real spiritual struggle among all humans is the battle of the mind, between choosing what is right and what is wrong.

The soul and spirit are a part of the breath of God, which gives us life in our bodies and life eternal. The spirit of a man is the eternal part of all humans that will never die but will spend eternity either with God or separated from God. I compare the spirit to the air in a balloon. If the shape of the balloon is round, the air in the balloon fills up the round shape. If it is a pear form, the air fills the pear shape. If the balloon is long like a hot dog, the air that was blown in the balloon will fill the form of the balloon. Our spirit takes on the same form as our body. In fact, if our spirit would depart out of our body—and we could physically see it—our spirit would look like our twin! This is why Paul could say, "But then I shall know just as I also am known" (1 Cor. 13:12).

> But there is a spirit in man,
> And the breath of the Almighty gives him understanding.
> —Job 32:8

> The spirit of a man is the lamp of the Lord,
> Searching all the inner depths of his heart.
> —Proverbs 20:27

The Book of Job tells us about death and how the spirit departs and the body returns to the dust:

> Who gave Him charge over the earth?
> Or who appointed Him over the whole world?
> If He should set His heart on it,
> If He should gather to Himself His Spirit and His breath,
> All flesh would perish together,
> And man would return to dust.
>
> —JOB 34:13–15

Physical death is not simply when the heart stops beating or we cease breathing and shut our eyes for the last time. People have been revived from a heart attack or restored after they were not breathing for several minutes, having been brought back from the brink of eternity. So when is a person actually deceased? At what point can we truly say, "They are gone"?

I remember seeing a movie when I was a child of a person who lived at the turn of the century and was believed to be dead but was buried alive. There was not a medical doctor present to examine the body. Although the person was actually in a coma, his heartbeat was so weak that it could not be detected. The man was buried but revived in the coffin. The discovery was made when some old graves were being moved to another location. The coffin lid on the old pine box was opened, and the skeleton's hands had clawed the inside of the box. Trust me, that *is not* the type of movie you want your children to see!

According to numerous scriptures, physical death only occurs when the soul and spirit are separated from the physical body. The next question is: How does this separation actually occur? A very unusual passage of Scripture, written by King Solomon, one of the wisest men ever to live, may hold a clue to how this separating of the spirit from the flesh occurs.

> For man goes to his eternal home,
> And the mourners go about the streets.
> Remember your Creator before the silver cord is loosed,

Or the golden bowl is broken,
Or the pitcher shattered at the fountain,
Or the wheel broken at the well.
Then the dust will return to the earth as it was,
And the spirit will return to God who gave it.

—ECCLESIASTES 12:5–7

A full reading of Ecclesiastes 12:1–7 reveals that the writer is describing death, mentioning that a "silver cord" is loosed. Then man shall return to dust and the spirit returns to God who gave it. For many years I was intrigued with the meaning of this silver cord. I understood that when an infant is growing in its mother's womb, the fetus is connected to the mother's placenta with an umbilical cord. All nourishment the unborn receives comes through this cord for nine months during a normal pregnancy. Once the birth time arrives, the baby exits the womb, and a trained medical physician cuts the cord. At that moment the child begins a life of his own, but only after the umbilical cord is severed.

I suggest that this "silver cord" is something rather mysterious to us that connects the human spirit to the physical body in the same manner that an umbilical cord maintains life for an infant until the moment of the cord being severed. This invisible yet very real connector must be severed before the spirit can depart from the body. I believe it is at the conclusion of this *separation process* that a person actually experiences death.

When Paul was stoned, he was unsure if he was "in the body or out of the body." Obviously, if his experience was an out of the body experience and his soul and spirit had departed and later returned to his body, then Paul experienced an actual resurrection from the dead as his spirit returned into his body and he revived.

There are various beliefs related to the soul and the spirit, including the belief (called soul sleep) that at death the soul and spirit remain in the place where the body is laid to rest. For example, if you have loved ones who have passed and they are buried in the community cemetery, the soul sleep doctrine teaches that the soul and spirit do not depart from the body at death and do not go either to heaven or hell, but they remain in the body "sleeping" until the time of the resurrection and the judgment. However, there are far too many scriptures that teach the departing of the soul and spirit into another afterlife at death.

Two examples of the soul departing the body are in the life of Rachel and the son of the Shunamite woman. In Genesis chapter 35, Rachel was pregnant and entered into hard labor. We read:

> Then they journeyed from Bethel. And when there was but a little distance to go to Ephrath, Rachel labored in childbirth, and she had hard labor. Now it came to pass, when she was in hard labor, that the midwife said to her, "Do not fear; you will have this son also." And so it was, as her soul was departing (for she died), that she called his name Ben-Oni; but his father called him Benjamin.
>
> —GENESIS 35:16–18

The departing of her soul indicated she was dying. The soul was the force that gave her life, yet the soul could depart.

Another example is when a young boy had passed away and Elijah was called upon to raise him from the dead.

> And he stretched himself out on the child three times, and cried out to the LORD and said, "O LORD my God, I pray, let this child's soul come back to him." Then the LORD heard the voice of Elijah; and the soul of the child came back to him, and he revived.
>
> —1 KINGS 17:21–22

The child had died, and the prophet prayed the life back into the little fellow. Some "soul sleepers" suggest that the terms *her soul was departing* and *the soul came again* simply mean Rachel felt herself dying and that the boy's life returned to him. Yet notice the scriptures that teach God will preserve your soul and keep you from the "pit" (Job 33:18, 28, 30). When David wrote about the Messiah's resurrection, he said, "For You will not leave my soul in Sheol, nor will You allow Your Holy One to see corruption" (Ps. 16:10). In the New Testament, Peter quotes this verse when he speaks about the resurrection of Christ when He came forth from the chambers of hell after three days (Acts 2:27, 31). The word *hell* in these passages is *hades* and refers to the underworld where the souls of men were carried prior to the resurrection of Christ. The soul departing is the same as when Lazarus died and the angels carried him (his soul) to Abraham's bosom.

One more example is found in Genesis 37. Jacob was handed the bloodied coat of his young son Joseph with the word that a wild beast had killed him. The father was being deceived, as Joseph's brothers had sold Joseph to a band of nomads (Gen. 37:28). After many days of mourning, Jacob told his sons:

> "For I shall go down into the grave to my son in mourning." Thus his father wept for him.
>
> —GENESIS 37:35

To a casual reader, the father seems to be saying that he was going to die and be buried (go to the grave) as his son did. However, the father said he would "go down," and in that time the souls and spirits went down under the earth to "Abraham's bosom" (Luke 16). Jacob would go down into the "grave." When someone says "grave," we picture a cemetery or a graveyard. However, the Hebrew word *Sheol* indicates the subterranean world of departed spirits. The father was saying that he would mourn for his son as he would go down to meet him ("go down...to my son") in Sheol. Jacob believed his son was dead but knew he was in Sheol. He also knew he would die of grief but would meet his son in Sheol.

Some who are *pro-choice* do not believe that an infant in the womb has an eternal spirit. However, the inspired Word of God teaches otherwise. When Job had lost his wealth, ten children, and his health, he wrote:

> Why died I not from the womb? Why did I not give up the ghost when I came out of the belly?
>
> —JOB 3:11, KJV

It is pointed out that the Hebrew word *ghost*, used in the 1611 King James translation, is the Hebrew word *gava*, a primitive root that means "to breathe out or expire."

When the New Testament used the same term for Jesus "giving up the ghost," the word *ghost* is the Greek word *ekpneo*, which is also to "expire." Those who do not believe that the spirit departs the body use these two words to say, "These verses simply indicate that at death the people quit breathing and expired." However, if this was all that occurred and they simply died without going to paradise or hell, then how can we explain Abraham's bosom, the rich man and Lazarus, Christ preaching in the heart of the earth to the spirits in prison, Paul's being "out of the body," and Paul saying that when we are absent from the body we are present with the Lord (2 Cor. 5:8)? Then, what about those who were martyred and are in heaven being told to rest until their fellow servants are killed (Rev. 6:11)?

Death is not just breathing your last breath and expiring. It includes a separation of the soul and spirit from the body and a gathering together either with the righteous in a heavenly paradise or with multitudes of the unrighteous in a subterranean chamber under the earth.

## Is Cremation Wrong for a Christian?

The question of DNA being altered by fire and heat leads to a very important and somewhat controversial question that many people have asked: Is it biblically wrong for a Christian to be cremated?

Usually at least once a week I receive an e-mail or letter from a Christian family asking a question about cremation. The process of cremation is when heat reduces the bodily remains of an individual to gasses and bone fragments. The remains given to a family are not the ashes, as some suggest, but are actually the fragments of the bones. The remains are white in color and are usually placed in an urn either to remain in the possession of the family, to be buried in a cemetery or other location, or to be scattered in a special place.

There are various reasons why families choose cremation. At times it is at the request of the departed loved one. At other times it is simply the choice of the family members who are making the final arrangements. There are times—as with a fire, extreme accident, or other circumstance—when the physical body is unable to be viewed in a traditional manner. Most commonly, however, cremation is a cost issue, and the family is unable to afford a traditional interment involving a funeral home, a coffin, and burial costs. The average funeral—including service charges, embalming, viewing in the funeral home, hearse, casket and vault, and burial costs—now averages $6,130.[1] Families struggling with finances and without burial and death insurance often choose cremation not as a first choice but as the only option.

The question is: From the biblical and Christian perspective, is it ever wrong to cremate a fellow believer? First, the entire Bible is clear on how the patriarchs, the Hebrew people, and the New Testament believers buried their loved ones. Abraham purchased a cave in Hebron, the cave of Machpelah, to bury his wife, Sarah (Gen. 23). Later, Abraham, Isaac, Jacob, Sarah, and Leah were all buried in the same cave (Gen 25:9; 49:30; 50:13). Joseph was embalmed in the traditional Egyptian method, and his body was laid in a golden coffin and placed in a special vault in Egypt (Gen. 50:26). At the time of the Exodus, Moses entered the vault and removed the golden coffin with Joseph's bones, and they were transferred from Egypt to the Promised Land (Exod. 13:19) and later buried by Joshua in the land of Joseph's inheritance (Josh. 24:32). This burial process was requested by Joseph before his death. He wanted to be brought back to the land of his fathers when Israel returned to the land (Gen. 50:25).

Those who completely oppose cremation point out the following: In Joshua 8, after Achan sinned by stealing the gold and the garments from Jericho, his sin was exposed, and the people stoned him and burned his body, leaving a pile of stones as a reminder of God's anger being turned from Israel (Josh. 7:24–26). Also, it is noted that the pagan city of Jericho was to be "burned with fire" (Josh. 6:24) after it was conquered by the Hebrews. There is, however, a practical (not just a spiritual) reason for burning the dead remains of people, animals, and the city with fire.

Jericho was located in a hot desert region. There were thousands of bodies of men and animals lying in the streets of the city. The Hebrew men were told to take the land, and they did not have the time to bury the remains of the dead, as touching a dead carcass would also make them unclean according to the Law of Moses (Lev. 5:2; 7:19–21). If these dead, bleeding corpses were permitted to lie in the sun for days, disease would spread to the living and could spread among the Hebrew people, eventually taking the lives of the Israeli warriors. Thus the simplest explanation for burning the city was to prevent deadly plagues from being passed on.

The sin of Achan was so great that when Israel engaged their second city, Ai, in battle, this smaller city defeated the Israelite soldiers! Usually God permitted His people to hold on to the spoil of a city after the battle. However, Jericho was the first of thirty-one cities Israel was to conquer and was a *firstfruits city*. It was taken during the Feast of Firstfruits, and the spiritual principle mandated that all possessions in the city belonged to the Lord and to the treasury in the tabernacle built by Moses. Achan actually stole from the Lord!

There is no clear scripture either promoting or discouraging cremation. This is actually a spiritual and moral issue with some, but it probably falls under the scripture that teaches, "Work out your own salvation with fear and trembling" (Phil. 2:12). Some people believe that in some way cremation impacts God's ability to resurrect that person from the dead, since the crematory fires have consumed the entire remains, except the powder of the bones. This cannot be true, for consider the number of Christians who were unable to escape from and died in burning planes, homes, or large buildings. Their departure from this life in a tragic fire will not impact their future with Christ because their souls and spirits are already with the Lord. Cremation does not affect the soul and spirit; these two eternal life forces exit the body at death.

Often after death, a major autopsy is performed. Also, many people have stipulated in their wills that their organs should be donated for medical research or to assist a person who needs a kidney or some other life-giving organ. The fact that the remains of the person has undergone the knife of a specialist searching for the cause of death or to harvest organs for donation has absolutely no influence upon the person's future resurrection.

## The Jewish Burial

In the Jewish tradition, there are two principle considerations at the time of death. The first involves *kevod ha-met*, or the treatment of the dead. This tradition enables the Jewish community to show "respect for the body of the deceased as the vessel which housed the soul in life."[2] The second consideration is *kevod ha-chai*, the concern for the living.[3]

The Jewish process of burial during the time of Christ was to bury the person the same day that he or she died. The Jews bury the body without any form of cremation or embalming, believing the body must revert to its original state and return to the earth. To ease the anxiety of the family, the burial takes place promptly. In Jerusalem, the Orthodox community performs the funeral and burial the same day of death when possible. This is based upon the instruction from Deuteronomy 21:23:

- "You shall surely bury him that day."
- "His body shall not remain overnight."

If it is not possible to bury the person on the same day, the burial must occur within three days unless circumstances do not permit.

The body is wrapped in linen, a custom initiated nearly two thousand years ago by Rabbi Gamaliel to indicate that the rich and poor are equal before God. The shroud is a garment with seven layers made with muslin, cotton, and linen, with the outer garment (since the sixteenth century) being a large white sheet that the corpse is wrapped in. Shrouds have no pockets, which indicates that a man takes nothing with him into the afterlife.

At the time of Christ, the body was laid in a cave-like structure with large niches cut inside to lay the body. After the decaying process, the corpse was unwrapped, and the bones were washed and placed in a small, stone-cut ossuary. These small boxes holding the bones were then laid inside the cave in one of the niches. The cave, called a sepulchre, became a family tomb for many generations and could hold numerous stone boxes that could be stacked one upon another in the cave-like opening. This is what Jesus referred to when He said to the Pharisees: "Woe unto you, scribes and Pharisees, hypocrites! for ye are like unto whited sepulchres, which indeed appear beautiful outward, but are within full of dead men's bones, and of all uncleanness" (Matt. 23:27).

We read about a Jewish process of burial in the four Gospels, when Joseph of Arimathaea and Nicodemus joined together to care for the body of Christ after His death. Nicodemus purchased one hundred pounds of linens and spices, wrapping the body of Christ in a linen death shroud and laying Him in a new tomb (John 19:38–42). At Christ's resurrection, His body slipped through the linen, and He left the cloth on the stone slab inside of the tomb (John 20:7). Thus, from the beginning, the traditional method of burial was to place the body in a tomb that was designed for the entire family's use for several generations.

Later it was a custom to place the body in a coffin made of wood. The reason for wood, according to a Rabbi Levi, was based on the fact that Adam and Eve hid in the trees in the garden from the presence of the Lord (Gen. 3:8). Also, wood would eventually decay and return to the earth along with the body, as required in Genesis 3:19: "And to dust you shall return." Some individuals drill holes in the bottom of the coffin to allow air in to better assist in the decomposition of the body.

Among some Jews a coffin is not used, since in a Jewish cemetery (as in Israel) the remains are placed above the ground and the body is encased in a stone covering (rectangular box) above the surface, with the remains wrapped in the shroud and touching the earth itself.

When a physical body remains in the earth long enough, the remains will return to dust. Eventually even bones will become dry and brittle and become a form of powder, which mixes back into the earth. Those who have been dead since the time of the early church have already gone though a decaying process. Will the fact that their physical remains are mixed with the dust of the earth impact their resurrection? Certainly not in any way.

The physical remains of the person are only the outer shell, which will return to the dust of the ground from which the original man, Adam, was created and to which all men will return (Gen. 2:7). The *real* believer is with the Lord. I recall being with some close family members as we were relating humorous stories at the funeral of a loved one who had passed and was now with the Lord. I said, "Well, you know, the departure of a believer reminds me of a person who has just eaten a peanut."

Everyone looked at me as if to say, "Where did that concept come from?"

I continued, "The shell is still here, but the nut is gone!"

My granddad laughed until he was almost crying.

Someone may say, "That was distasteful!" Well, you didn't know my Italian grandparents and their relatives. They loved life, they loved the Lord, and they loved to laugh. The departed relative would have "split his sides" upon hearing that comment. We knew he wasn't in that funeral home in his coffin—but he was actually with Christ at that very moment. Therefore we can rejoice, for as the Bible says: "Precious in the sight of the LORD is the death of His saints" (Ps. 116:15).

My father, who pastored a small church in rural southwestern Virginia, took me as a child with him occasionally when he preached a funeral. I sat near the front as believers passed the coffin for the viewing. They would comment, "Praise God, he is not here; he's with the Lord!" Remember, I was only about five or six years old, and I thought to myself, "Are you blind? He is lying in front of you!" I didn't understand until years later that the saints meant that the believer's soul and spirit had long departed, and the real person was not in the wooden box.

It is true that the DNA can fall apart and eventually be destroyed by fire. Would this fact hinder the resurrection and recreation of a new body of a person, since the Bible teaches, "But then shall I know even as also I am known" (1 Cor. 13:12, KJV)? The human spirit has the same exact appearance as the human body; therefore, the features of the person would be recognized in paradise just as they would be recognized by those living on Earth. Thus the spirit form is the same as it was on earth, and the DNA is not needed to bring forth the original appearance of the person. The spirit is a mirror image of the person.

In ancient times religious articles like Torah scrolls and prayer books that were no longer usable (such as the ink becoming unreadable on a Torah scroll) were placed in hiding in special rooms in a synagogue. Later it was customary to bury religious articles in a cemetery. A Torah scroll is considered a living thing since it holds the Word of God, and the Word of God is eternal and has the power of life. Thus, just because the scroll becomes unreadable in places as the ink fades does not take away from the sacredness of the scroll. Because of this reason, there are records of Jewish men running into a burning synagogue to rescue a scroll. The scroll is treated like a living human.[4]

The custom of placing a grave marker over the grave is based upon Genesis 35:20. When Jacob's wife Rachel died on the road to Bethlehem, he placed a pillar upon her grave. The original reason was to honor the departed, but marking a grave was also done so the priests (*Kohanim*) would avoid contact and remain ceremonially clean.

Other nations have their own methods of burial, which we will not take the time to examine. In America, the traditional funeral process is to contact a funeral home and director and permit them to make the arrangements based upon the family's personal desires or financial ability. In years gone by, a homemade casket was prepared, and the friends and relatives gathered in the home of the departed. This was called a *wake*. Food was provided for the family, and at times the home was filled with conversations of wonderful memories and stories about the departed. The coffin was placed in the living room, open for all to see. Of course, the following day men carried the departed to a family cemetery or church burial grounds for a final interment.

The custom of a two- to three-day process of embalming, preparing the body, and arranging the viewing and church funeral eventually emerged as children moved to other states and grandchildren were scattered at colleges or at different regions of the country. It took time to drive or catch a flight to honor Mom, Dad, Grandma, Granddad, or, in some instances, a sibling. Today in North America, we have developed a traditional form of burial for our dead. There are some, however, who cannot or choose not to follow the traditional form and choose cremation.

## Four Main Beliefs About Death

There are four main beliefs about what occurs after death. The first theory teaches there is *annihilation*, meaning that after death there is no life beyond this life. This is the belief of atheists and many agnostics. The second and very popular belief, especially among those of the Hindu religion and those in the New Age movement, is *reincarnation*. This nonbiblical theory teaches that after death a person's inner self transmigrates into other forms, and this process of death to reincarnation continues in a nonstop cycle from one life form to the next. The third theory is *soul sleep*, a teaching promoted by certain churches that the soul and spirit exist, and at death they "sleep" in the physical body until the resurrection. The fourth belief is that the eternal parts of a human, the soul and spirit, are removed from the body of the departed and will enter into one of two realms, heaven or the underworld of the lost.

Among Christians, there is a disagreement between soul departure and soul sleep, or the teaching that at death the soul departs to paradise or hell, or the soul remains in the area of death and "sleeps" until the resurrection.

According to the early father Eusebius, the idea of soul sleep was invented in the third century by heretics.[5]

One argument for soul sleep is the use of the word *sleep* in the Bible. Paul used this word extensively when speaking of believers who had died. Matthew spoke of those Christ raised with Him as the "saints who had fallen asleep" (Matt. 27:52), and Paul spoke of the resurrection and those who were asleep (1 Cor. 15:20). When alluding to the return of Christ, Paul said, "We shall not all sleep, but we shall all be changed" (1 Cor. 15:51). The idea among some is that the soul and spirit are sleeping in the body, as proven by the usage of the word *sleep*.

However, other scholars point out that the word *sleep* is simply a metaphor for death. The following notes explain the controversy:

This metaphorical use of the word *sleep* is appropriate, because of the similarity in appearance between a sleeping body and a dead body; restfulness and peace normally characterize both. The object of the metaphor is to suggest that, as the sleeper does not cease to exist while his body sleeps, so the dead person continues to exist despite his absence from the region in which those who remain can communicate with him, and that, as sleep is known to be temporary, so the death of the body will be found to be...

The early Christians adopted the word *koimeterion* (which was used by the Greeks of a rest-house for strangers) for the place of interment of the bodies of their departed; thence the English word *cemetery*, "the sleeping place," is derived.[6]

The Jewish commentary, the Midrash, teaches:

The word *sleep* is used to describe the body at rest, awaiting the resurrection while the soul is conscious in the afterlife (Mid. Gen. 549).[7]

The Jewish historian Josephus reported about a group of men who lived in Qumran, a village near the Dead Sea. According to him, the Essenes believed in the immortality of the soul.

For their doctrine is this: That bodies are corruptible, and that the matter they are made of is not permanent; but that the souls are immortal, and continue for ever.[8]

Other early fathers spoke about the consciences of the soul after death:

We affirm that the souls of the wicked, being endowed with sensation even after death, are punished, and that those of the good being delivered from punishment spend a blessed existence.[9]

—JUSTIN MARTYR

## The Purgatory Belief

There is a very popular belief among those in the Roman Catholic Church that is defined as purgatory. *The Catholic Fact Book* gives the reader a definition of *purgatory*:

> Purgatory is held to be a place or condition of temporal punishment for those who, having died, are in venial sin or have not satisfied God's justice for mortal sins already forgiven....The doctrine of purgatory is a teaching...that may be defined as an intermediate place or state after death where souls who die in God's Grace make atonement, or satisfaction, for past sins and thereby become fit for heaven. This satisfaction is in the form of temporary punishment which afflicts the soul until demands of God's justice are fully met.[10]

This teaching identifies two types of sins: mortal sins, which will damn the soul, and venial sins, which will not damn the soul but will confine the person to purgatory. It is very clear the doctrine of any form of purgatory is not found in either the Old or New Testaments, but it gradually emerged as a Roman Catholic Church teaching due to a question of what happens to a believer baptized in water who willfully sins after conversion and dies.

At the Council of Trent in 1547 and 1563, purgatory became an official doctrine. Below is a quote explaining the purpose for purgatory:

> If any one saith, that, after the grace of Justification has been received, to every penitent sinner the guilt is remitted, and the debt of eternal punishment is blotted out in such wise, that there remains not any debt of temporal punishment to be discharged either in this world, or in the next in Purgatory, before the entrance to the kingdom of heaven can be opened (to him); let him be anathema.[11]

Below is the Council of Trent's twenty-fifth-session decree on purgatory in 1563:

> Whereas the Catholic Church, instructed by the Holy Ghost, has, from the sacred writings and the ancient tradition of the Fathers, taught, in sacred councils, and very recently in this ecumenical Synod, that there is a Purgatory, and that the souls there detained are helped by the suffrages of the faithful, but principally by the acceptable sacrifice of the altar.[12]

*The Dictionary of the Christian Church* explains that the leaders in the early church from the first to the fourth century began teaching prayers for the departed.[13] Tertullian (160–220) was the earliest father to refer to prayer for the dead. He also admitted that there was no direct biblical basis for praying for the dead. Clement of Alexander (150–220) spoke of sanctification of deathbed patients by purifying fire in the next life. In the early third-century church there was much debate over the consequences of post-biblical baptismal sin. A suggested solution was the idea of a purgatorial discipline after death. This concept was discussed at Alexandria, Egypt, at the time of Clement.

Augustine (354–430) taught purification through suffering in the afterlife. The concept of purgatory spread to the West, which was the Roman branch of the church, and into West Africa through the influence of Augustine and Gregory the Great. Gregory (540–604) was the bishop of Rome and therefore pope from 590–604. He popularized and developed the doctrine of purgatory, aiding its spread throughout the western branch of the empire.

We must note here that early writers of history and philosophy mention various religions who prayed for the dead and even paid their own "priest" to pray for their departed loved one. Plato (427–347 B.C.) wrote of Orphic teachers in his day:

> Who flock to the rich man's door, and try to persuade him that they have a power at their command, which they procure from heaven, and which enables them by sacrifices and incantation…to amends for any crime committed by the individual himself, or his ancestors.…Their mysteries deliver us from the torments of the other world, while the neglect of them is punished by an awful doom.[14]

Chinese Buddhists believe it is necessary to pray their loved ones out of places of fire similar to purgatory. They have special shops set up for prayer to be offered to deliver their loved ones from the place of fire. The Zoroaster religion believes that the souls of the dead pass through twelve stages before they are sufficiently purified to enter heaven. Even in the Islamic religion, the Muslims teach that the angels Munkar and Nakir question the dead as to their religion and their beliefs after they die. Many who are unprepared will go into a type of purgatory.

## Paying for Their Release

There is a very lengthy history in the Roman Catholic Church of conducting masses for the purpose of praying souls out of the fires of purgatory. This is one of the major doctrinal differences between the Roman Catholic Church and the mainline Protestant denominations. Among traditional Protestants, there is a clear teaching that the act of redemption releases a repentant sinner from the future punishment of hellfire, as long as the person continues in the faith. The belief stems from understanding the finished work of Christ on the cross and how His precious death and suffering replaced our need to suffer and die in sin. Having great-grandparents whose roots were from Italy and having a great love for the Catholic people, I know it is often difficult to challenge traditional doctrines that are inbred from youth. However, the great news is that redemption has been paid, and the Scriptures, not the traditions of men, reveal that a person should never give money for the dead. Only the blood of Christ redeems!

## What Does the Bible Say?

Many sincere individuals will readily accept their church's tradition as being equal with the inspired Scriptures. However, if and when any man-made tradition of any church contradicts the full revelation of the Bible, then the tradition must be recognized as the opinions of men and not the direct revelation from God.

As far as giving money on behalf of someone who is dead, God strictly forbade the activity.

> I have not eaten any of it when in mourning, nor have I removed any of it for an unclean use, nor given any of it for the dead. I have obeyed the voice of the LORD my God, and have done according to all that You have commanded me.
>
> —DEUTERONOMY 26:14

> You were not redeemed with corruptible things, like silver or gold...but with the precious blood of Christ, as of a lamb without blemish and without spot.
>
> —1 PETER 1:18–19

> Those who trust in their wealth
> And boast in the multitude of their riches,
> None of them can by any means redeem his brother,
> Nor give to God a ransom for him.
>
> —PSALM 49:6–7

On one occasion, an occult leader from Samaria saw a visible manifestation of the power of God as Peter and John prayed for the new converts in the city. This city sorcerer offered money to receive a transfer of this power in his own life. The problem was that this man, named Simon, was not converted to Christ and was operating through familiar spirits. Peter rebuked him and said:

> Your money perish with you, because you thought that the gift of God could be purchased with money!
>
> —ACTS 8:20

## Christ, the Final and Complete Redemption

Your redemption is in Christ alone and is a completed work. Christ is your High Priest in heaven and is your Intercessor before God:

For by grace are ye saved through faith; and that not of yourselves: it is the gift of God: Not of works, lest any man should boast.

—Ephesians 2:8–9, kjv

If any man sin, we have an advocate with the Father.

—1 John 2:1, kjv

If we confess our sins, he is faithful and just to forgive us our sins, and to cleanse us from all unrighteousness.

—1 John 1:9, kjv

But Christ being come an high priest of good things to come…he entered in once into the holy place, having obtained eternal redemption for us.

—Hebrews 9:11–12, kjv

But this man, after he had offered one sacrifice for sins for ever, sat down on the right hand of God.

—Hebrews 10:12, kjv

Who gave himself a ransom for all.

—1 Timothy 2:6, kjv

I heard one man suggest that Christ's sacrifice was not enough and only through our works of righteousness can we be guaranteed salvation. According to his upbringing, this was the reason for souls to enter a purging chamber prior to going to heaven. However, notice this prophecy about the Messiah:

He shall see of the travail of his soul, and shall be satisfied: by his knowledge shall my righteous servant justify many; for he shall bear their iniquities.

—Isaiah 53:11, kjv

When a person receives forgiveness of sins and accepts the final and complete sacrifice of Christ, there is an assurance of salvation and our final destiny. There is no work of man that can make us worthy to enter the kingdom of heaven—only the sacrifice of one man, Christ Jesus, gives us access to eternal life.

At times throughout the history of the Christian church, certain church fathers and biblical teachers initiated their own personal interpretation of Scriptures, which stretched their meanings beyond the scope of the original intent or understanding revealed to the prophets by the Almighty and to the apostles by Christ Himself. Certain doctrines that persist to this day are never found in the Scriptures but were developed for either spiritual convenience or to answer some question that was unclear in the Scriptures. If and when any doctrinal teaching or church doctrine does not line up with the inspired Word of God, it must be considered a man-made tradition and interpretation, and it should not be treated equal to the inspired Word of God.

Imagine the sheer terror of someone who lived his life in a completely sinful manner, avoiding the convicting power of the Holy Spirit, believing that those surviving him could eventually pray him into heaven and out of the underworld, only to discover he is in hell for eternity. It is not worth the risk! Believe the gospel, serve the Lord, follow His Word, and receive assurance of your future destination!

Chapter 8

# The MYSTERY of NEAR-DEATH EXPERIENCES

Steve Lofty has worked with the emergency medical services (EMS) in the area where I live. In May of 2008, on a Saturday, he returned from work tired, fell asleep, and suddenly awoke with a funny feeling in his chest. After drinking water brought no relief, his experience with heart attack patients indicated to him that he was having a heart attack. He was rushed to the hospital in Chattanooga, Tennessee, where he underwent emergency bypass surgery to relieve the heart pressure.

After regaining consciousness in his room, he began to notice certain people appearing near his bed. He was amazed to see people who were deceased stepping through the wall and watching him. They would smile at him, and he could actually communicate with them. They answered questions that were in his mind—without his audibly communicating with them.

One of the first questions he asked was, "Am I going to die?"

The response was, "No. You are not done. There are still things you have to do."

He asked this question twice and both times was told he would live and not die. He was amazed at how he could simply think of a question, and the answer would come, just as when two people communicated with each another. As hours and a few days passed, he was fully awake and would see others who had departed pass into his hospital room. At times they would smile at him and say nothing. He saw two very special people: his grandmother and a past friend—rescue chief for West Park Fire Rescue, Roy L. Rogers. They looked exactly as he remembered them while they lived on Earth, except they had a rather *translucent* appearance, almost like a full-color hologram. When nurses entered the room, the nurses walked right past the visitors—and through them at times— and never realized they were there!

When asking his grandmother and Roy how they were, they replied they were fine. After several days of seeing many friends who had passed appear in his room, he realized that two people were missing from this group: his father and his grandfather. When he inquired of Roy and his grandmother about the two missing men, they simply looked at each other and ignored his question, never responding. After this occurred several times, he then realized that these two men were *not* in the same heavenly place that his Christian grandmother and Roy were. He recalled that his father had passed away with severe unforgiveness and with an unrepentant heart. He also recalled that his grandfather was a very wicked man in many ways. Both men suffered before their deaths. They never went to church, never asked for forgiveness, and allowed pride to hinder them on their deathbeds.

Some would suggest that Steve was simply hallucinating from his heart problems or *tripping out* on medicine. The following incident proves this theory incorrect.

A man appeared to Steve and revealed an important incident concerning a mutual close friend. He asked Steve when he returned home to speak to this friend and give him this information. After returning home, Steve called the man to his house and revealed what the departed fellow had told him. The fellow ran out of the house, later returning, and said, "You really did see him. Only two people on Earth knew about that incident—me and him!"

Steve and I have discussed these events, and we are uncertain if these individuals appeared to him in the same manner as Moses and Elijah did to Christ or if this was an actual vision given to him in the manner

John saw the events of the Apocalypse. However, such strange events are a part of what some term *near-death experiences*. Steve said prior to this experience, he was always afraid to die, as he had seen many people die over the years. After this, however, all worry and fear of death have departed from him.

During my many years of ministry, I have read articles and books on the subject of near-death experiences and met individuals who have had one. In some instances the individual had been in a major accident and was in a comatose condition for some time. One friend from Alabama who is now a minister was in a terrible car accident and spent months in the ICU hooked up to machines. He was in a complete coma, yet he could hear all of the conversations, including one from a nurse who cussed him out because she was required to work in ICU on New Year's night and was missing a big party. He also left his body on one occasion, walked to the chapel where his mother was praying for him, and heard her entire prayer! Imagine the shock to this nurse when he awoke and rebuked her for complaining about working on New Year's. His mother told him of praying in the chapel when, at one point, she remembered feeling a presence in the room. She even turned to see who was behind her, but she saw nothing. The man recalled his mom turning, as he had placed his hand on her shoulder while she was praying!

These incidents are amazing, but all prove what the Scripture teaches: there is an inner person who is more real than the physical person, and this spirit person departs the body at death and can experience all five senses even when the physical body is dead.

## Four Things That Commonly Happen at Death

In all of the material I have read and personal information I have collected, there seem to be four common things that happen at the moment a person is dying or encounters an afterlife experience.

The first common occurrence is at the moment the heart stops, or the moment of impact in an accident. The person may hear a loud, strange, and at times rather uncomfortable *buzzing noise* in his or her ears. All other surrounding sounds become faint, except for perhaps the voices of those who may be near (especially in a hospital emergency room).

What usually follows is that the person is suddenly alert, fully awake, and can clearly see his or her surroundings, even though his or her physical eyes may be closed. He describes seeing the accident scene and himself lying on the bed, with doctors and nurses working on him. He may be outside his body, looking at himself. At this point he can see and hear all that is taking place near his physical body. Believers have a sense of a clear mind, are very alert, and have a sense of being *free*. This is refreshing for them, especially if they have been in some form of physical pain because of a heart attack or painful accident.

The third process separates believers from unbelievers. At this point, some believers describe seeing an angelic being waiting to escort them. Others can identify relatives and close friends in the distance, who appear to be waiting for their arrival. The person who lived in spiritual rebellion and sin or who rejected the gospel often senses a blanket of gloom and oppression, and darkness encloses him. A foreboding feeling of fear overwhelms that person. From this point on, believers begin moving upward toward a bright light or multicolored lights at a very rapid speed. Unbelievers begin moving downward. Often both describe being inside some type of tunnel—one filled with light and the other with darkness.

The fourth process commonly begins when a person exits the *tunnel* or finally reaches his destination of light or darkness. Believers conclude their journeys in a beautiful field of grass and flowers or beside a large crystal river inside an area of heaven with loved ones with or near them, or they find themselves in some area where there is bliss, joy, and freedom. The unbeliever, on the other hand, may see a tunnel of fire, people in dark chambers or individuals who appear in dread, and a feeling of being lost or hopelessness.

## A Medical Doctor's Experience

One of the first books I read documenting life after death was written by Dr. Maurice Rawlings and is called *Beyond Death's Door*. Dr. Rawlings is a specialist in internal medicine and cardiovascular disease in Chattanooga, Tennessee, and has resuscitated many people who were clinically dead. He considered all religions as "hocus-pocus" and "death nothing more than a painless extinction." In 1977 his opinions changed as he revived a man who had a heart attack. Rawlings wrote:

> Each time he regained heartbeat and respiration, the patient screamed, "I am in hell!" He was terrified and pleaded with me to help him. I was scared to death....His pupils were dilated, and he was perspiring and trembling—he looked as if his hair was on end. He said, "Don't you understand? I am in hell....Don't let me go back to hell."[1]

On page 85 of this book he writes:

> This place seems to be underground within the earth in some way...

When a person clinically dies, for example, with heart failure, and has an out-of-body experience, some of the most unusual things are reported to happen from time to time. At times a person's watch quits working at the very time they *expired*. The battery simply quits. The quartz batteries placed in common watches are manufactured to endure a certain amount of voltage. However if the watts of electricity exceed the standards, the battery will fail.

Others observed later that all of their credit cards had been demagnetized in their wallets for no apparent reason. Some returned saying that their memory was sharper and their knowledge was increased after the experience. These simple yet unusual phenomena, which are occasionally reported among "after-deathers," cannot be explained in a medical sense or in a laboratory experiment. For batteries to quit and magnetic strips on bank cards to be demagnetized would require an extremely powerful surge of electricity in the body or some type of electromagnetic activity.

## The Image on the Shroud

This is similar to one of the explanations given about the famous Shroud of Turin, a 14.3 by 3.7 foot linen cloth that bears the image of a man who has been physically beaten. It appears consistent with the description of the scourging and crucifixion of Christ. The mysterious cloth has been on public display throughout the centuries, and small segments have undergone critical examinations by specialists, some attempting to prove the cloth is the burial shroud of Christ and others maintaining it is a remarkable forgery from the Crusader period of medieval times.

The image of the suffering man became clear on May 28, 1898, when an amateur photographer made a black-and-white negative of the shroud. Clearly the face and body of a man was seen with what appeared to be small bloodstains on the forehead, holes in the wrists, and long furrows on the back—again, consistent with the biblical account that Christ was scourged on His back, had a crown of thorns placed upon His head, and was crucified using nails in His hands and feet.

I personally have no opinion one way or another concerning the authenticity of the shroud, as my faith and confidence do not rely upon a linen cloth but in Christ, who is my High Priest in the heavenly temple (Heb. 9:11). However, let us assume that the image is actually of Christ. How could His entire body be imprinted on a herringbone twill cloth? The only explanation would be that the power of the resurrection was so great that the energy around Christ's body was imprinted in the cloth in the same manner that light passing through a lens of a camera would imprint the images (a negative) on photo film. A "great earthquake" shook the entire area at Christ's resurrection, and an angel whose appearance was like lightning rolled the stone away. The guards were lying on the ground like "dead men" (Matt. 28:2–4). Imagine the global implications the moment that Christ raises the dead and returns to gather the living saints to Himself (1 Thess. 4:16–17).

The point is: if the departing of a spirit from the body or the energy that is released at the moment of death is this tangible, then it should come as no shock that batteries, magnetic cards, and other objects would be affected in the process.

## Death of My Wife's Best Friend

During the 1980s, my wife had a very dear friend named Tracy Davis who lived in Forestdale, Alabama. In March of 1990, Tracy was driving in Birmingham, and an eighteen-wheeler accidentally came over into her lane, causing Tracy's car to go under the huge semitruck. Eyewitnesses told the EMS that when Tracy passed them in her car, there were two people—Tracy and a man in the passenger's seat. However, Tracy was the only one in the car. Pam always believed that God sent an angel to take her *home*.

My wife, Pam, was very sad and grieved about her death. Tracy had been with Pam when the doctor did an ultrasound and told Pam she was having a boy. Tracy always said, "I'm going to move and be the nanny for the family!"

Many months after Tracy's departure, I was spending the night with some ministers, preparing for an early morning fishing trip at the mouth of the Mississippi River outside of New Orleans. We arrived at a small hotel at about one thirty in the morning, and I immediately went to sleep. Sometime during the early hours of the morning, I had a most marvelous experience. I am uncertain if it was a dream or a vision. I actually thought I had experienced a heart attack and had passed away! I found myself in a wonderful place, which I will attempt to describe in human words.

As I stood in this large area, I looked to my left and saw flowers growing in a rock flower bed. Instead of being just one color, such as red or yellow, each flower was a specific color, but multihued like a rainbow. The blue flower started as a pale blue and went to a dark blue. The reds went from an orange to a fiery red. The colors were bright, crisp, and clear. I looked around and saw in the distance various types of architecture.

To the right was a massive white stone building that reminded me of the Greco-Roman buildings we see in drawings and paintings. It looked as if it could seat as many as a huge sports stadium. I asked a passerby, "What is that building?"

The individual replied, "That is a worship center, where people from the Roman period continually worship and sing to God." The entire area was covered with buildings of Greco-Roman style.

As I looked, directly in front of me I saw a different type of structure. This section of heaven was a massive, very contemporary city with large skyscrapers, some forming spirals twisting upward into the atmosphere. The entire city was an emerald green. I have seen real emeralds, and this was certainly an *emerald* city. I was told that this area was for those who had passed away and had lived in major cities during their lives. They loved the large buildings where they lived, and the Lord allows them to live in the greenish-clear city.

As I was admiring the diversity of this place, I looked to my left and recognized a young man who had been converted to Christ in my ministry. During his lifetime this young man wore a back brace; he had been deformed from birth. He shouted out at me and said, "Perry! Perry! Look at me...I no longer wear that brace! I can bend and move without pain! Look at me!" I hugged him, and we rejoiced together. I had no idea until I shared this dream a few years later that this very young man had passed away and was actually dead at the time I was having this experience!

There was much activity in this area. However, for some reason I asked my friend about Tracy Davis—if he knew her and where she was. He pointed to the left and said, "You'll find her if you go that way." Suddenly, the scene changed, and I was in what I would describe as a children's paradise. To my right I saw the cutest little houses. They were built just for children between the ages of about five to twelve (this was the age that came to me in the dream). These were all constructed on the side of a hill and looked just like the homes I saw on a trip I had made to Romania. They all had orange tile roofs and reminded me of a large playhouse that would hold several children. Even the doors were half the size of a normal door. Each little house was personally designed for a child who had passed away. In my spirit I heard these words:

God created various types of land and structures in heaven to appeal to individuals who lived on Earth in these same types of places. There are mountains for those who love mountains, rivers for those who love water, and various plants and trees of all types that all people enjoy. This area is where the spirits of children were and is designed in the same form, pattern, and likeness to where the children lived and were familiar with on Earth, except there are no tears, sickness, or death. All is perfected!

At that moment, I heard the most beautiful singing coming from the direction to my left. I turned to see a large, round structure open at the top. All of the voices were those of children singing a song I had never heard. As I entered this mini-arena, it was filled with children of all ages. I knew these were children from various places who had passed away and joined other children in what I would term a children's paradise. They were all so happy and were singing and clapping. To my amazement, standing in the center of the group was Tracy Davis! I was so excited to see her that I yelled out, "Tracy! Tracy, it's me, Perry!" She neither saw nor heard me, and she continued with her ministry of leading these children in worship.

The scene began to fade, and I found myself with my eyes open lying on a bed in the hotel room. I was glad I had not passed away, but I was thrilled about the revelation about Tracy. Several months later I ministered in Alabama, and Tracy's mother and sister attended the meeting. After the service I requested to speak with them and brought them into a room with my wife. I said, "I want to tell you an experience I had," and I proceeded to detail each part of this dream/vision. As I got to the part about Tracy, we were all in tears. Before I told them what I saw, I asked them both, "If Tracy could do one thing in life, what would it have been as far as ministry?" Without pausing to ponder an answer, both said, "She would be working with and ministering to children. She absolutely loved children!" Well, the tears really began to flow when I described her leading worship among children who had passed away!

For some reason we have a mental impression that when we arrive in heaven, we are all wearing white robes (which, of course, we will—Rev. 19:8, 14), and we are sitting on green grass with our feet soaking in the water of life! I've told folks not to put their feet in that river, because I plan on drinking the water from it!

Heaven, however, is as real as what we see on Earth. Just as Earth has diverse landscapes; plant life; and a variety of tree, hills, mountains, and valleys, so heaven has a variety of appearances to appeal to all believers from around the world.

I am certainly a mountain lover. From ages three to ten, I lived in southwestern Virginia in a small town surrounded by rolling mountains. On the outskirts of the town were farms with rolling hills carpeted in green where cattle roamed freely. My favorite time of the year has always been the fall months, when God splashes His bright colors on the leaves and the crisp, cooler air blows gently across your face. By God's grace, when I arrive in heaven I hope to spend time in an area with mountains and a place where the trees are multicolored and never change.

## The Waiting Period for the Resurrection

When I came to the full realization that a person's soul and spirit continue to live outside of the body at death and that there are *holding places*, one in Sheol (hell) and the other in the third heaven (paradise), I began to imagine what this intermediate state is like for those who have departed—especially those who have gone to be with the Lord.

As a young child, I visualized people floating around in the atmosphere like ghosts, blanketed in a white, misty vapor and sort of hovering over some special location in heaven. I did not visualize them with clothes but saw them in my mind as covered with light. I didn't think they actually communicated but lived in this intermediate zone until the resurrection. As a teenager the image changed, and I realized they could communicate and actually lived in a realm similar to what we have on Earth, except in a realm of perfection.

Paul makes it clear that if he were absent from his body he would be "present with the Lord" (2 Cor. 5:9). We know from the incident in Luke

16 that both the rich man in hell and the beggar in Abraham's bosom had all five senses in the afterlife. Now the righteous are dwelling in the land of light in the third heaven in the paradise of God. Paul wrote that "to live is Christ, and to die is gain" (Phil. 1:21). He wrote that to die and be with Christ was far better, but to remain in the flesh and minister to the saints was more needful at the time (vv. 22–24). Certainly Paul did not believe that at death his soul went to sleep in the grave until the resurrection. If our souls slept when our bodies do, it would be impossible to experience a vision or to have a spiritual dream. As God pours out His Spirit at the time of the end, the "old men shall dream dreams" and the "young men shall see visions" (Joel 2:28).

## The State of "Resting"

In Job 3:17 we read, "There the wicked cease from troubling, and there the weary are at rest." The word *rest* is used extensively when describing the righteous in the afterlife. In Hebrews chapter 4, the writer consistently mentions the danger of a believer falling into unbelief, as the Hebrew people did in the wilderness, and falling short of his or her eternal rest. In Hebrews 4, the word *rest* is mentioned nine times; eight times the word means "to repose, sit down, and relax." It is a word used to describe the position of a person after working long hours, when that person returns home to repose, sit down, and, as I would say, *chill out*. In Hebrews 4:9, the writer uses a different word for rest: "There remains therefore a rest to the people of God." The Greek word here for "rest" is *sabbatismos* and refers to a Sabbath of rest that God's people will receive if we remain faithful in this life to follow the Lord.

Revelation 6:11 refers to numerous martyrs in a special region of heaven who are given white robes and commanded to "rest for a season." This word *rest* is *anapano* and alludes to "repose, to take ease and to refresh." Those who have lived in a redemptive covenant and died in the faith will enter into a time of refreshing and rest in the heavenly realm prior to their resurrection. During the future tribulation, there will be a multitude who will die. These souls are alluded to in Revelation 14:13, when John wrote, "'Blessed are the dead who die in the Lord from now on.' 'Yes,' says the Spirit, 'that they may rest from their labors, and their works follow them.'" The word *blessed* is similar to saying *happy*. Just as the poor beggar was "comforted" in the afterlife (Luke 16:25), those who die in Christ will also be comforted and happy when they enter the heavenly dimension.

When we speak of resting on Earth, we are usually sitting or lying down. Our rest in heaven is to cease from our earthly work and labor and to enjoy the presence of other saints, the holy angels, and the presence of God. The writer to the Hebrews describes a believer who enters heaven as follows:

> But you have come to Mount Zion and to the city of the living God, the heavenly Jerusalem, to an innumerable company of angels, to the general assembly and church of the firstborn who are registered in heaven, to God the Judge of all, to the spirits of just men made perfect.
>
> —HEBREWS 12:22–23

If soul sleep were true, then the soul and spirit would not be conscious, awake, or able to operate in all five senses. As indicated in Revelation 6:11, after a believer dies on Earth, that person's soul and spirit are taken under the golden altar in heaven, given white robes, and commanded to rest for a season under the altar of God.

## Can't Tell You Everything

When Paul experienced his visitation of paradise, he said he heard "inexpressible words, which it is not lawful for a man to utter" (2 Cor. 12:4). Either he was saying that God forbade him to tell the numerous secrets or that God knew those hearing his story would find it hard to believe everything Paul saw. However, we can have confidence in God's promises for our future, as it is written:

But as it is written: "Eye has not seen, nor ear heard, nor have entered into the heart of man the things which God has prepared for those who love Him." But God has revealed them to us through His Spirit. For the Spirit searches all things, yes, the deep things of God.

—1 Corinthians 2:9–10

At times a somewhat skeptical person will ask me how I know that what I believe about the future, especially heaven, is true. The easiest answer is to say, "Because the Bible says so." However, there is another reason why it is easy to believe in these eternal truths—the Holy Spirit! He is a living witness of all heavenly and eternal realities. He is not an *it* or a *force* or a mystical, divine energy of light, but He is a person. When a living human being is truly converted to Christ, that person first encounters the Holy Spirit, for it is the Spirit who draws that person to Christ (John 15:26–27; 16:13). The Holy Spirit also introduces the power of God to the believer (Acts 1:8). Christ said, "He [the Spirit] will tell you things to come" (John 16:13). As a believer, there is this *inner knowing*, this deep feeling that comes after receiving a spiritual revelation from the very person who has been with the Almighty from the beginning—the Holy Spirit! He confirms to us that these truths are established.

# Chapter 9

# The GREATEST HOMECOMING EVER KNOWN

**M**any years ago the mother and father of a U.S. soldier received a visit that no military parent ever wants to receive. They were informed that their son had been killed in the line of duty. The shock and feeling of grief were unbearable. They waited for more information and for the set time that the remains of their son would be returned home for his final rest and his military burial. That is when a most bizarre twist of fate occurred.

A second visit brought the shocking and unexpected news that the military had made a mistake. It was not their son but a young man with the same name who had been killed. Because of the grief the mistake had brought them, the military was sending their son home on a special flight to rejoin his mother and father. The plans were finalized, and the date was set. That morning the crowds gathered at the airport, along with a military band, civic leaders, and the mother and dad waiting in high anticipation. Suddenly, the giant iron beast of a plane landed on the runway, and the plane door was opened. There were other important people on the plane, but the soldier exited first. There he stood at the top of the stairs, overlooking a cheering crowd, while the band played to a fevered pitch. The mom and dad stood there, crying tears of joy.

Suddenly the mom could take it no more. She threw down the flowers in her hand and began running down the red carpet. The son ran down the steps, and suddenly the dad was running behind the mom. She grabbed her son, kissed him all over his face, and rubbed his hair as the crowed cheered and the parents cried tears of joy. This was a homecoming unlike most—but nothing to compare to the homecoming we will experience one day![1]

The greatest homecoming ever known will occur on a set day that is known to no one except to God Himself (Matt. 24:36). At an appointed time, those dwelling in paradise will return with the Lord, as their bodies will be resurrected and joined with their spirits to form an immortal body. Those of us living will be changed in a moment of time, and we will be caught up to meet the departed saints in the air. Forever we will be with the Lord (1 Thess. 4:16–17).

> But I do not want you to be ignorant, brethren, concerning those who have fallen asleep, lest you sorrow as others who have no hope. For if we believe that Jesus died and rose again, even so God will bring with Him those who sleep in Jesus.
> —1 Thessalonians 4:13–14

The departed souls of men and women who have died in Christ are now in heaven in paradise. These individuals will receive the first notification that Christ is returning to Earth to catch the living up to be with Him, and they will return with Christ in the air. At that moment there will be a mysterious resurrection of the "dead in Christ." This raising of the dead is not raising the soul and spirit from the ground, but raising from the ashes of the dead a new body that joins with the spirit and soul.

How can God bring the dead with Christ at the moment He returns for the church? Just as He brought the Old Testament saints out of their resting place under the earth at His resurrection, so He will bring the dead in Christ out of their heavenly resting place to be given a resurrected body and meet the living saints. The Bible says we will be "caught up together with them in the clouds" (1 Thess. 4:17). The departed righteous return from heaven with Christ, but we are then caught up together with them. Is this a contradiction? They come out of heaven, and then we read that "together" we meet Him in the air. So are they in heaven or Earth?

The answer is that they are presently in heaven. However, at the resurrection, their spirit and soul will leave the heavenly paradise and follow Christ in the air at His appearing. Christ will then conduct a supernatural, mysterious resurrection, and they will be joined with a new resurrected body, as we who are living will be "changed—in a moment, in the twinkling of an eye" (1 Cor. 15:51–52), and together, with new immortal bodies, we will meet in the air!

## Why Do We Need a New Body?

During one of my conferences in West Virginia, I was asked a question that I had never studied or read an answer to. The person asked, "Perry, if our souls and spirits are already eternal, then why would we need a body that is raised from the dust?" I thought for a moment and then replied, "All spirit beings, whether it be God, angels, demons, or even the spirits of departed loved ones, are normally invisible to the human eyes." (See 1 Timothy 1:17.)

Many people have stood at the bed of a dying loved one and watched him or her breathe his final breath. At that moment, angels entered the room and took his soul and spirit from his body (Luke 16:22). Many people feel a peaceful presence or sense the atmosphere becomes charged, but no one actually sees the angels or the spirit of the person as it leaves the body. In the Bible, in order to see in the spirit realm, either the angel must take on human form and appear as a human (Gen. 19:1–5; Heb. 13:2), or the eyes of the human being must be opened and the veil removed to see the spirit world (2 Kings 6:17).

If at Christ's coming both the dead saints and those living who were caught up only return to Earth in a *spirit body*, then all earthly men and women who survive the Tribulation would never be able to see us, as we would be, as all spirits are, invisible to their eyes. However, with this new, resurrected body, all men will see us, and we will be as Christ was after His resurrection: He could travel from one place to another at the speed of thought and could walk through a door (Luke 24:31; John 20:26). This is perhaps one of several reasons for a having a body that is not just a spirit but is a new body.

Paul pens one of the most interesting discourses on the resurrection of the dead in his letter to the church at Corinth:

> All flesh is not the same flesh, but there is one kind of flesh of men, another flesh of beasts, another of fish, and another of birds. There are also celestial bodies and terrestrial bodies; but the glory of the celestial is one, and the glory of the terrestrial is another. There is one glory of the sun, another glory of the moon, and another glory of the stars; for one star differs from another star in glory. So also is the resurrection of the dead. The body is sown in corruption, it is raised in incorruption. It is sown in dishonor, it is raised in glory. It is sown in weakness, it is raised in power. It is sown a natural body, it is raised a spiritual body. There is a natural body, and there is a spiritual body.
>
> —1 Corinthians 15:39–44

Some argue that since *flesh and blood cannot inherit the kingdom*, it is impossible for there to be any form of flesh on a resurrected body. Thus they believe the statements in this passage of Scripture are a metaphor or some mysterious allegory pointing to a different meaning. I would answer, "Did Jesus have the same *body* when He came out of the grave three days later, and was this the same body that He was clothed in when He ascended to heaven?" The answer, of course, is yes.

Eight days after His resurrection, Christ appeared to "doubting" Thomas. When Thomas saw Christ, he thought He was a mere spirit being. Jesus said, "Reach your finger here, and look at My hands; and reach your hand here, and put it into My side. Do not be unbelieving, but believing" (John 20:27). Thomas saw and felt the prints and the slit in Christ's side where the Roman lance had sliced open His side at the crucifixion (John 19:34). Christ presently has the same *body* but in a resurrected form. There is a reason that Christ must always bear the scars of His suffering.

When Christ returns to rule on Earth, the scars will be evidence of the fact He is the promised Messiah of prophecy:

> And one will say to him, "What are these wounds between your arms?" Then he will answer, "Those with which I was wounded in the house of my friends."
>
> —ZECHARIAH 13:6

I would also go as far as to say that the adversary is always attempting to discredit the Word of God. In time to come, the righteous will one day judge the angels, and this will include Satan (1 Cor. 6:3). At the judgment of Satan, this lying adversary would love to say that redemption never really happened! For example, there is a major world religion today, Islam, with approximately 1.5 billion followers, that denies that Jesus is the Son of God and teaches that He was never really crucified. However, Christ's scars on His hands, feet, and side are visible indicators of the fact of redemption! Satan will never say, "The crucifixion was a hoax," as Christ will have the evidence on His own body of His redemptive covenant with mankind!

Christ doesn't have a *normal* body, however, since His resurrection. A normal body cannot appear and disappear, walk through closed doors, and travel at the speed of thought—all of which Christ could do following His resurrection. Therefore, the flesh-and-blood body we now have cannot inherit the kingdom in its present form. A spiritual body will not need blood, as the "life of the flesh is in the blood" (Lev. 17:11). A body with normal human blood would be unable, in the natural, to travel at high speeds, such as the speed of light (although with God all things are possible; remember Elijah in his chariot ride in 2 Kings 2). Traveling in a flesh-and-blood body at high speeds would melt the flesh and boil the blood until there would be nothing remaining!

## DNA and the Resurrection

An amazing discovery was made in 1953. Researchers studying human cells discovered a nucleus within the nucleus, a tiny dark spot in the middle of the human cell. After detailed study, this spot was identified as deoxyribonucleic acid, or abbreviated as DNA. This DNA was a complex molecule containing life's instructions and has been determined to be the most important part of our human makeup. DNA looks like a twisted ladder called a double helix. It is the biochemical recipe in the body for creating proteins—thus cells, tissues, and organs.[2]

For many years medical and genetic researchers identified up to 90 percent or more of our DNA as junk DNA. The term *junk DNA* was originally coined to refer to a region of DNA that contained no genetic information. Scientists are beginning to find, however, that much of this so-called junk plays important roles in the regulation of gene activity. No one yet knows how extensive that role may be.[3]

In his book *In the Beginning*, Walt Brown, PhD, gives the most amazing details about DNA. There are about one hundred trillion cells in your body. Most of your cells have forty-six segments of DNA, twenty-three from the mother and twenty-three from the father, which all contain coded genetic information about you that will determine your eye and hair color and so forth. If these forty-six segments of DNA information could be uncoiled, they would be seven feet long! The string would be so thin that it could not be detected under an electronic microscope.[4]

If the information from one cell from one person was written in books, it would fill four thousand books. If the DNA in your entire body was placed end to end, it could stretch from here to the moon five hundred thousand times. In book form, all cells of DNA from a human body could fill the Grand Canyon more than seventy-five times. Yet one set of DNA from one cell from every person on Earth in a pile would weigh less than an aspirin![5]

This amazing DNA is found in every part of the human body, including your fingernails, hair, blood, bones, semen, skin, and saliva. DNA testing now makes it possible to identify who the father of a child is by simply swabbing the inside of an infant's mouth and testing it with the DNA of the man presumed to be the father. This DNA discovery has also assisted in having criminals arrested who left their DNA in a tiny spot of blood, a miniscule piece of skin under the fingernails of the victim, or in male semen. Special DNA testing has also assisted in the release of men from prison after examiners tested the DNA samples from crime scenes and discovered the blood in no way matched the accused.

The DNA discovery also has unlimited possibilities. The discovery of the bones and remains of ancient dinosaurs has anthropologists drooling with the idea that DNA from certain remains may one day be used to actually re-create a dinosaur in a laboratory. After examining the amazing details of DNA, it has been called the "Genetic Book of Life," as it encodes every detail about an individual.

The prophet Daniel wrote about the resurrection of the dead by saying:

> And many of those who sleep in the dust of the earth shall awake,
> Some to everlasting life,
> Some to shame and everlasting contempt.
>
> —DANIEL 12:2

I have heard well-meaning Christians say, "Once the body decays and goes back to dust, there is nothing left for a resurrection. This is just a metaphor about sleeping in the dust." This word *dust* in Hebrew is *aphar*, and it is used in the Old Testament as literal dust, clay, and earth. This word is the same word used when Moses wrote that God created man from the dust of the ground (Gen. 2:7) and the same word used after Adam's fall when God said he would return to dust (Gen. 3:19). Every human body placed in the ground will, over many years, deteriorate and return to the dust. Within each speck of human dust is DNA.

DNA smaller than the head of a pin has information encoded in it. Researchers can actually take cloth and other objects that are two thousand years old and find DNA on the cloth! Years ago you may have heard of the discovery of a set of tombs in Israel that the archeologist claimed were the *tombs of Jesus's family*. The archeologist used dust particles from the remains found in each tomb to match the DNA with samples from the other tombs and identified them as family tombs. Obviously, he didn't believe in the resurrection of Jesus, because Jesus took His body and bones with Him when He got up from a borrowed stone slab in the tomb!

Another interesting point about DNA is how it is being used in connection to the Dead Sea Scrolls. These ancient scrolls and thousands of small parchments were discovered in jars and caves in the Qumran community. They were believed to have been written by a group of religious men called the Essenes. In order to determine which small piece of parchment linked with other pieces, the researchers tested the DNA on the animal skins the ink was written on, and thus they have matched certain pieces of small parchment with their counterparts, indicating they came from the same animal![6]

At the resurrection, will God re-create from the dust another person, and the body be raised to join the spirit of the dead that Christ brings with Him? Will the spirit that comes from paradise head toward the location of the dust of the dead and rejoin a new body and then return to the air where we who are living will rise to meet them? It is interesting to note that one small speck the size of the head of a pin from a hair follicle, fingernail, or a decayed piece of dust can actually hold the genetic information of a person. Thus, one speck of DNA from the dust has all the information needed to re-create someone who has passed!

Years ago I did a study to show how one speck of DNA can hold enough information to re-create a person. I was criticized for this statement by someone who pointed out that under certain circumstances DNA can be altered, changed, or destroyed. One way DNA can be destroyed is through intense fire and heat. Thus the critic asserted that my DNA theory could not possibly apply to someone whose DNA was destroyed.

Paul called the resurrection a mystery: "Behold, I tell you a mystery: We shall not all sleep, but we shall all be changed" (1 Cor. 15:51). If the apostle Paul—who penned thirteen dynamic New Testament books, made known revelations that had been hid in ages past, and revealed several mysteries to the church for the first time—says the resurrection is a "mystery," then how can I—or anyone else—explain the mysteries linked to the raising of the dead?

## Will You Know Your Loved Ones?

Someone asked, "If it is true that we will be known at the resurrection as we were before we died, then why didn't Mary recognize Christ after He was raised from the dead?" When the women arrived at the tomb and found it empty, they assumed someone had broken the Roman seal, moved the massive rolling stone, and stolen the corpse. Here is the conversation, recorded in John 20:11–17 (KJV):

> But Mary stood without at the sepulchre weeping: and as she wept, she stooped down, and looked into the sepulchre, and seeth two angels in white sitting, the one at the head, and the other at the feet, where the body of Jesus had lain. And they say unto her, Woman, why weepest thou? She saith unto them, Because they have taken away my Lord, and I know not where they have laid him. And when she had thus said, she turned herself back, and saw Jesus standing, and knew not that it was Jesus. Jesus saith unto her, Woman, why weepest thou? whom seekest thou? She, supposing him to be the gardener, saith unto him, Sir, if thou have borne him hence, tell me where thou hast laid him, and I will take him away. Jesus saith unto her, Mary. She turned herself, and saith unto him, Rabboni; which is to say, Master. Jesus saith unto her, Touch me not; for I am not yet ascended to my Father: but go to my brethren, and say unto them, I ascend unto my Father, and your Father; and to my God, and your God.

Christ had only been dead three days. How could this woman, Mary, who was with Him throughout His ministry, not recognize Him? Remember, she actually thought He was still dead, and the corpse was missing, so she was not expecting this man to be Christ. Also, Christ was buried without garments or cloths (only a loincloth). He was now appearing fully clothed, and she thinks He is a gardener. Where did Christ get the clothing he was wearing, considering He was buried immediately after being removed from the cross? I suggest that just as the high priest had to remove his garment of beauty and wear four linen garments on the Day of Atonement when he entered the holy of holies, so too Christ was wearing special *priestly atonement garments* that were brought to Him by the two angels who rolled the stone away and were later seen by the women after His resurrection. At the moment Christ saw Mary, He was preparing to ascend into the heavenly temple to present Himself and His blood to seal the final atonement for mankind.

The Torah reveals the four garments a priest wore on the Day of Atonement. Using the imagery in the Scriptures, Christ would be wearing linen pants, a linen belt, a headdress, and a linen coat (Lev. 16:4). As Christ stood in the garden, Mary had never seen Him in these garments and assumed He was a gardener.

Another reason she may have not known Him after His resurrection may have been a change in His outward appearance. While we have no description of the physical height, weight, or hair color of Christ in the Bible, He did have a Jewish mother and father. Historically, most Jewish people were olive skinned and have dark hair. The shock of the crucifixion and the mental pressure He endured was so great that His sweat became drops of blood, and that may have changed certain features such as His hair color. As I child, I knew a minister who was driving in the fog one night and almost hit a train. The shock was so great that his hair changed color from dark black to grey within a few days. The trauma of the crucifixion may have affected the very hair color of Christ. Based on John's vision, which occurred more than sixty years after the resurrection, we know His hair color now:

> ...and in the midst of the seven lampstands One like the Son of Man, clothed with a garment down to the feet and girded about the chest with a golden band. His head and hair were white like wool, as white as snow, and His eyes like a flame of fire.
>
> —REVELATION 1:13–14

After His resurrection, Christ's hair was white. If a physical change in His appearance took place within three days, then Mary would not have immediately recognized Him. Christ was standing in the garden fully clothed and with white hair.

It was also a "great while before day" when she saw Him, meaning prior to the sun completely rising, which is the simplest explanation—it was dusk and not as visible as it would be later on. Any one of these factors, or a combination of all three, could be the reason Mary did not recognize Him until she heard His voice! Then she knew by His voice that He was Christ!

A person cannot use this example to affirm, "If Mary did not recognize Jesus, then we will not be recognized as we were on Earth in heaven." After Christ was raised, ascended to heaven, and sat down on the throne of majesty, Stephen, the first martyr of the church, saw Jesus standing on the right hand of God. He said, "Look! I see...the Son of Man [Jesus] standing at the right hand of God!" (Acts 7:55–56). Stephen knew Christ while He was on Earth and recognized Him after Christ's ascension into heaven!

There is a second reference used by skeptics to say that we will not know our loved ones in heaven. After Christ's resurrection, two men were walking on the road toward a town called Emmaus. One was Cleopas (Luke 24:18). They were discussing the events of Christ's death, when Christ suddenly joined them and overheard their conversation. Many scholars believe the second man was Luke himself, who was the only gospel writer to report this event. As these two men walked and explained their confusion concerning recent events in Jerusalem, Christ expounded on the prophecies of the Messiah's sufferings from Moses and the prophets. Christ entered their home and was still not known to them until He took bread, blessed it, broke it, and gave it to the men. Suddenly their "eyes were opened and they knew Him" (v. 31). He then vanished from their sight.

The biblical reason they did not recognize Christ was "their eyes were holden that they should not know him" (v. 16, KJV). The word *holden* means that their eyes were "restrained" from seeing him. Later their eyes were opened. The biblical expression of a person having physical eyes and not being able to see is often used for individuals who lack understanding: "And their eyes they have closed, lest they should see" (Matt. 13:15).

In the Old Testament there is one example that illustrates this point. The prophet Balaam was headed to curse Israel, and an angel stood in front of this compromising prophet's donkey. The donkey could see the angel and refused to go forward, but Balaam saw nothing and began to beat the donkey. Later the Lord opened Balaam's eyes to see into the spirit realm. He had eyes but could not see into the invisible world of angels until his "eyes were opened," or the scales were removed, to see into the realm of the spirit. (See (Numbers 22:22–34.)

In the case of the two men on the road who met Christ, their eyes were supernaturally restrained from knowing Him. However, on the occasion when Christ suddenly appeared to His disciples behind locked doors, they knew it was Him. Thomas, who was not present, later thought that when he saw Christ He was only a spirit being and not physical. This belief was later disproven when Thomas touched the nail prints and the side of Christ, which had been pierced (John 20:25–29).

The veil over our eyes is compared to seeing through a dim mirror. Paul said it this way:

> For now we see in a mirror, dimly, but then face to face. Now I know in part, but then I shall know just as I also am known.
> —1 Corinthians 13:12

When Paul said, "Then I shall know," he was alluding to the time when perfection comes and we are with Christ. In heaven I will know Paul, recognize Moses, and know all my family members. Even at the Transfiguration, Peter knew that the two men beside Christ were Moses and Elijah without being told who they were. When the three sleeping disciples awoke and saw three men glowing on the mountain, Peter did not whip out an old poster of Moses crossing the Red Sea and say, "Hey fellows, look; it's Moses!" Neither did he have a copy of a press release with Elijah waving good-bye from his fiery chariot. He knew who they were without being told (Matt. 17:1–4).

Part of the departing from the body and being with the Lord includes the unusual ability to gain knowledge that was missing about things while living on Earth. Many people who have had a near-death experience comment on being able to communicate in heaven by simple thoughts without ever opening their mouths. This is logical, considering that God could—but seldom ever does—speak audibly to humans. We hear His voice by the inward leading of His Spirit. At times there is a sudden impulse or thought that comes to our minds, and we are aware of a divine link with the heavenly realm. The speed of sound and light can be measured. However, the speed of thought has never been measurable. You can only think about what you know or have heard, and can only imagine a location after you have been there. If I have never seen heaven, I can only imagine what it's like from what I read in the Bible or hear from others.

After the dead are raised and the living are changed from mortal to immortal (1 Cor. 15:53–54), what type of changes will have occurred? What type of bodies will we be given? Events after Christ's resurrection give us the clues.

## Four Things a Resurrected Body Can Do

The same supernatural abilities Christ had after His resurrection will be abilities every resurrected believer will enjoy. The Bible indicates that after Christ arose, He was seen alive for forty days (Acts 1:3). On one occasion, at His ascension, more than five hundred men saw Christ at one time as He was taken up into heaven (1 Cor. 15:6). During the forty days in His resurrected body Christ could do the following things.

### 1. Christ could walk through a door that was locked (John 20:19).

Following Jesus's crucifixion, the disciples were fearful for their own lives and, for fear of the Jews, went into hiding in a house with the doors and windows completely shut (John 20:19). Huddled like a group of orphaned boys who had just lost their dad, they were stunned when Christ walked through the locked door and appeared in the same room. Christ did not knock but actually moved from outside to inside the house, passing through a solid door. I can understand angels, which are spirits created from a different dimension than flesh, being able to transport themselves through a solid object. But if Christ has a body with visible scars, then how did His body (He called it "flesh and bone" in Luke 24:39), move through a solid object? I would break my bones trying to run through any closed door!

This is one of the most unique mysteries in the New Testament. Remember that Paul called the reality of the resurrection and the new body the dead will receive "a mystery" (1 Cor. 15:51–52). However, if Christ was enabled in His new, raised body to pass through solids, then all future resurrected saints will be able to do the same. John wrote:

> Beloved, now we are children of God; and it has not yet been revealed what we shall be, but we know that when He is revealed, we shall be like Him, for we shall see Him as He is.
>
> —1 JOHN 3:2

## 2. Christ could reappear and disappear at will (Luke 24:31, 36).

At the tomb in the early morning, Christ told Mary:

> Touch me not; for I am not yet ascended to my Father: but go to my brethren, and say unto them, I ascend unto my Father, and your Father; and to my God, and your God.
>
> —JOHN 20:17, KJV

The phrase "touch me not" may allude to the fact that on the Day of Atonement when the high priest was ministering in the holy of holies (only once a year), no one was permitted to touch him physically due to defilement. The Greek in John 20:17 can read, "Do not cling to me."[7] Some suggest Christ was speaking about His ascension to the Father forty days later. However, the way the statement is worded, Christ was saying, "I am preparing now to ascend—so do not delay Me right now."

Again, His purpose for ascending was to cleanse the articles in the heavenly temple and fulfill the pattern in the Torah for presenting a lamb (Himself) and the firstfruits (Himself) at the temple.

This encounter with Christ and Mary happened early in the morning. Christ would have made His appearance in the heavenly temple, then returned the same day, for we read that He later appeared to His disciples on the same day "at evening" (John 20:19). The Jewish day begins at six in the morning and concludes at six in the evening, a total of twelve hours. Mary saw Him early in the morning, and the disciples saw Him later in the evening. Between those two appearances, Christ journeyed to the heavenly temple and back. He would have about ten hours between the morning and evening appearances.

Later, Christ is on the road to Emmaus, and in the evening He broke bread with His followers. While sitting in a chair at the table, He suddenly vanished out of their sight (Luke 24:31). Years ago I was thinking about this amazing feat and began laughing when I thought to myself, "What would it be like for some children to be playing hide-and-seek in heaven? Every time you thought you had found them, they could just zap themselves to a new location!" Then I thought, "I'm glad there will be no anger and frustration in heaven. Imagine looking for a child who just got mad and *ran away* for a while. You wouldn't know what planet in the universe that child had slipped away to." (Trust me—your mind thinks this way when you have kids of your own, as I have, who ask imaginative questions all the time!) In His new body, Christ was not limited to time and space and was able to travel to and from distant locations without hindrances.

If an angel can be in heaven one moment, the next moment be ministering on Earth, and then, minutes later, be back in heaven...and if Christ ascended to heaven and weeks later Stephen saw Him "standing on the right hand of God in heaven" (Acts 7:56, KJV)...then clearly Christ was able to travel in the same manner as angels—without limitations. I believe Christ was transported from the earthly dimension to the heavenly and back through mind travel or thought travel. This may explain why people who have experienced a visitation in heaven always mention that the conversations were not with words but with thoughts.

### 3. He could eat food with His disciples (John 21:13).

This is one of the most amazing events after Christ's resurrection. He ate fish with His disciples at the Sea of Galilee (John 21:12–13). For some reason, we think of a spirit being (such as an angel) never needing food. However, the manna that fed Israel for forty years in the wilderness was called "angels' food" (Ps. 78:25); it arrived from out of heaven each morning and was laid on the ground, where the Israelites could gather up the small white wafers and prepare their meal (Num. 11:6–9). If manna came from heaven and is the food eaten by angels, then we ourselves will eat in our resurrected bodies.

There is food in heaven. The Scriptures tell us there is a tree of life with twelve types of fruit in the New Jerusalem (Rev. 22:2). Believers will also enjoy the marriage supper of the Lamb in heaven (Rev. 19:7–9). Christ mentioned that He would not break bread and drink from the cup again until He did so with His followers in the future kingdom (Matt. 26:29). Considering that a resurrected body can eat, we should have no difficulty comprehending Christ eating with His disciples.

The eating-in-heaven concept presents interesting questions from children. I had a child ask me a question that I had pondered but would never publicly address because of the mental impression people received if it were asked. The child asked, "When we go to heaven and eat, will we need to go to the bathroom the way we do now, and will the commodes be made of gold?" Oh boy, talk about putting a minister on the spot! The child assumed that if the streets we walk on are made of transparent gold (Rev. 21:21), then why wouldn't the porcelain seat on Earth be created into gold in heaven?

The answer was: I don't know! Most of the time I can at least give scriptures, a particular word, or a quote from a historical source to give at least some idea or direction or a logical speculation. Christ has flesh and bones, but no blood, as His blood was removed at the Crucifixion. Flesh and *blood* cannot inherit the kingdom. Food was created for enjoyment and nourishment, and the blood is central in carrying the vitamins and nutrients into the organs of the body. Without blood and physical organs, the breakdown of the food is not necessary. However, how could a person eat without teeth, a mouth, and a stomach? Thus it is a mystery. As for the gold toilet, well…I won't go there! (Oh, the questions children can ask!)

### 4. Christ could be touched by His disciples (Luke 24:39).

This may not seem significant, but Christ could be touched by His disciples. When I think about seeing my dearest loved ones or closest friends who have gone to be with the Lord, it would be sad if we could only *see them* in heaven, like a three-dimensional image, but never hug them. To me, heaven would not be complete if we only existed as a ghostly image that could communicate and yet never hug and hold someone's hand. I am aware that "in the resurrection they neither marry nor are given in marriage" (Matt. 22:30); however, I deeply love my wife of almost thirty years and enjoy hugging her and just holding her hand. I imagine that one day she and I will be able to walk though a beautiful section of heaven while holding hands and talking with some of the patriarchs and enjoying our children and family members.

This may be the most remarkable aspect of eternal life with Christ. When we lose a companion to death who was in a redemptive covenant with Christ, the sadness overwhelms us and the sorrow continues for weeks. However, the thought of seeing that loved one again and spending eternity with him or her is the greatest comfort to a believer. This is why Paul wrote:

> For if the dead do not rise, then Christ is not risen. And if Christ is not risen, your faith is futile; you are still in your sins! Then also those who have fallen asleep in Christ have perished. If in this life only we have hope in Christ, we are of all men the most pitiable.
>
> —1 Corinthians 15:16–19

We as believers have so much to look forward to. I believe we will be amazed at how much God has hidden from us that will surprise us in heaven. Just imagine our arrival (Rev. 4–5) when we see God on the throne and the worshiping angels with the faces of a man, a lion, an ox, and an eagle (Rev. 4:7–8). Then we will view the seraphim with six wings on each side of their backs flying above our heads. Imagine a floor of crystal like a giant ocean reflecting the light of God's glory and changing colors like the rainbow or the colors in a prism. Then, to see Christ Himself as He reaches for the seven-sealed scroll—just the thought of seeing these things is exciting!

For a believer, the best is yet to come!

# Chapter 10

# The TIME-LIGHT MYSTERIES and ETERNITY

Adam lived to be 930 years of age (Gen. 5:5). He has been dead for about 5,080 years. Abraham died at age 175 (Gen. 25:7) and has been gone now for 3,500 years. The apostles were all martyred (except John) from about A.D. 34 to about around A.D. 69; thus they have been in paradise for more than 1,850 years. This seems like a very long time to be in one place. However, eternal time is far different from normal earth time.

With the creation of the sun, moon, and stars, day and night, months and years became our time measure. Our time is set as the sun determines the day, the moon cycles the month, and the earth orbiting the sun gives us our solar year. One of the best arguments favoring a divine Creator is that earth is positioned in the heavens in the perfect location. If we were farther from the sun, we would freeze to death, and if we were closer we would all burn. Plant life would cease in either case, as would all life on Earth. The positioning is miraculous!

Another reason for the sun, moon, and stars is for "signs and seasons, and for days and years" (Gen. 1:14). The ancient Hebrews divided the day between twelve hours and twelve hours. The day began at six in the morning and concluded at six in the evening. This is why Christ asked, "Are there not twelve hours in the day?" (John 11:9). The month was determined by the four-phase cycle of the moon: from dark to half, from half to full, from full back to half, and finally back to darkness, which was called the "new moon" (Ps. 81:3, KJV).

If we were living in a realm where there was no sun, moon, or stars, there would be no concept of time. This is the realm of heaven, the dwelling place of God. The Bible tells us that God dwells in "unapproachable light" (1 Tim. 6:16), which is of His own glory. The heavenly Jerusalem has no need of the sun, moon, and stars, because the Lamb (Christ) is the light of the city (Rev. 21:23). The region of heaven where God, the holy angels, Christ, and the departed saints dwell is lit by the very illumination of God Himself. This glory is pure light and divine energy—very bright—and humans are unable to approach it in their natural forms. This is the same glory that Moses experienced when he saw only the "back parts" of God (Exod. 33:23, KJV) and when he spent so much time in God's presence that his own face had to be veiled (Exod. 34:29–35). This glory was manifested on the Mount of Transfiguration, where Moses and Elijah conferred with Christ and the glory of God caused Christ to glow in a bright light:

> And He was transfigured before them. His face shone like the sun, and His clothes became as white as the light.
>
> —MATTHEW 17:2

Because earth time is set by the cosmic powers of the sun and moon, and these two lights are absent in God's eternal kingdom, *time* is measured differently in heaven than it is on Earth.

First, the Bible teaches that spirit beings need no rest. Those dwelling in paradise have no physical limitations and are spirit forms. Some would disagree and say that at the original Creation, God "rested" on the seventh day (Gen. 2:2). Yet God created *all things*, including forming man in six creative days, and there was nothing more to create! The word *rested* in Hebrew does not mean that God became tired and had to take a break or "chill out," as some would believe. It is the word *shabath* from which we derive the word *Shabbat* for the seventh day that is set aside for ceasing from our work. There are other words in the Old Testament for "rested," and these allude to lying down, to being quiet and physically resting. God did not rest because He was wore out and tired. The Word says, "Behold, He who keeps Israel shall neither slumber nor sleep" (Ps. 121:4).

The Creator rested to initiate a Sabbath of rest as a pattern to His own people. After departing from Egyptian slavery, the Lord instructed Israel to work six days and to rest (*shabath*) on the seventh day (Exod. 23:12). For centuries of time, the religious Hebrew people have ceased from working on the seventh day (which is Saturday on the Jewish calendar) and have continued this weekly day of rest pattern that the Lord set in motion at Creation.

Although spirit beings need no sleep or rest, our earthly physical bodies center on a twenty-four hour time period called a day. The average person sleeps eight hours, works eight hours, and eats two hours, with the remaining time for activity up to the person (usually it's the television or the Internet). We need rest to continue our daily activities. Our bodies are created with a chemical called melatonin. When darkness arrives, this chemical is secreted to help the body to sleep. When the light appears, there is no secretion of this substance.[1]

The Bible reveals how time is perceived by the Lord.

> For a thousand years in Your sight
> Are like yesterday when it is past,
> And like a watch in the night.
>
> —PSALM 90:4

> But, beloved, do not forget this one thing, that with the Lord one day is as a thousand years, and a thousand years as one day.
>
> —2 PETER 3:8

How can one day be as a thousand years, but a thousand years as one day? If Abraham has been dead for four thousand years, it only seems like a few days. There may also be an interesting scientific explanation as to the time mysteries in heaven.

Light travels at 186,400 miles per second. The earth is a globe that is about 25,000 miles in circumference. Light can circle the planet about 7.2 times in one second. The prophet Ezekiel described angelic creatures that were moving like "lightning" (Ezek 1:13–14). This speed "as lighting" suggests that an angel moving with such speed could travel around the planet more than seven times in one second.

One of the theories of Albert Einstein was the special theory of relativity, which stated that no objects would travel faster than the speed of light. Concerning the theory of time, it was called the *time dilation* theory, wherein the faster an object travels, the slower its perception of time becomes. Thus if an object could suddenly travel the speed of light, the perception of time would become zero, as perception of time slows down infinitely. Space becomes the second important aspect of time travel. According to Einstein's theory, once an object reached the speed of light, the object's size will become zero, and it will disappear.[2]

## Amazing Research on Light

According to an article that was released June 4, 2000, Dr. Lijun Wang of the NEC Research Institute in Princeton claimed to have broken the speed of light. A special chamber had been created, and a particular gas was used within the chamber. To the amazement of all, when the scientist sent a pulse of light into the chamber, before it entered it went completely through and traveled 60 feet farther across the laboratory. It was reported 300 times faster than light, traveling at 55,8000,000 miles per second. This research indicates that in the future, information could one day be transmitted faster than light.[3]

I find this theory interesting in light of the scripture where the Almighty said, "Before they call, I will answer; and while they are still speaking, I will hear" (Isa. 65:24).

The secret to increasing the speed of light was the light passing through the chamber of gas. We know from science that the cosmic heavens consist of numerous types of gases that help hold together and form the numerous nebulas and stars in the heavens. Not only are angelic beings spirit, but they also consist of light (there are chariots of fire, 2 Kings 2) and can pass through the entire universe much faster than the normal speed of light.

## Key to Invisibility

In another unique article dated August 23, 2000, scientists professed to have discovered the key to invisibility. Scientists allegedly found a way to make flesh transparent for a few minutes of time. According to the University of Texas, the scientists "created a tissue window" in an area of two to three inches. The experiment was to manipulate the way light passes through tissue. During the test, the small area of the skin became transparent.[4]

## From Three to Eleven Dimensions

There is a gentleman on my ministry Board of Directors, Wayne Penn, who, among other things, is a researcher and is quite knowledgeable in physics, being a laser scientist. At times we have engaged in discussions that are very deep and often mind boggling, especially to my simple mind. One of the interesting theories about the spirit world and time travel has to do with the levels of what we call *dimension*.

We all live in a three-dimensional world. Everything created on the planet and built by men consists of filling existing space in three dimensions: height, width, and length. Every object can be measured by using all the combinations to determine its size. Some suggest that a fourth dimension is added to the earthly realm, which is faith. Faith enables a person to pray, believe, and bring into existence those things that are not (Rom. 4:17). This fourth dimension of faith is used on Earth by believing in the unseen.

God, however, dwells in at least seven different dimensions. The first three are height, width, and length. The New Jerusalem can be measured with these three combinations, and we know the base (1,500 miles across), the length (1,500 miles), and the height (1,500 miles). (See Revelation 21.) God dwells in absolute light without the sun, and light can be measured at a speed of 186,400 miles per second. This would be the fourth dimension. God also can travel into the past, see the present, and go into the future and make what He has spoken in the past come to pass in the future. These are the seven spiritual dimensions that exist in the spirit realm.

When we begin to include the body, soul, and spirit and angels into the equation, we could theoretically tap into eleven different dimensions. Of course this would be considered theoretical physics, but some in the physics community believe in what is called *super strings* and an eleven-dimensional theory of super gravity. If it were possible for earthly men to enter a level of six dimensions, then theoretical physics says it would then be possible to eat an orange from the inside out.

Because we live our lives in a three-dimensional world, we cannot go back and undo wrongs we have done, and we cannot see what tomorrow will bring. However, the Almighty can reach back and remove sin and can prepare your future today. We are unable to stop the aging process, as linear time always moves forward in a straight line. Once outside of our bodies, there is no longer an aging process. (Good news, ladies—no more wrinkles!) When Adam ate from the tree of the knowledge of good and evil, God placed an angel at the tree of life to prevent Adam from partaking of the tree and living forever (in his sin condition, Gen. 3:22). God intended for Adam to live forever in Eden and to populate the planet, continually eating from this special tree whose very leaves could continually bring health (Rev. 22:2).

At death, we depart the world of three dimensions and enter a realm of at least seven dimensions. Travel is possible at immeasurable speeds, and there is no time to count, other than how God uses earth time to fulfill prophetic events.

## Wormholes—Entrances Into Heaven?

As angels release the soul and spirit from a believer on Earth and carry them into the heavenly paradise, is there a specific entrance into the heavenly city? While on the island of Patmos, the apostle John was suddenly "in the Spirit," meaning he was instantly placed into a trance or a vision of heavenly things (Rev. 1:10). He wrote:

> After these things I looked, and behold, a door standing open in heaven. And the first voice which I heard was like a trumpet speaking with me, saying, "Come up here, and I will show you things which must take place after this." Immediately I was in the Spirit; and behold, a throne set in heaven, and One sat on the throne.
>
> —REVELATION 4:1–2

John saw a "door…in heaven." The Greek word for "door" is *thura* and is used metaphorically of Christ (John 10:7, 9), of the opportunity of preaching (1 Cor. 16:9; 2 Cor. 2:12), and of the entrance into the kingdom at the return of Christ (Matt. 25:10). John used this word to describe a gate or a portal that was opening in the heavens above him where he was on the island of Patmos. Immediately he was "caught up," and the scene changed from the vision of Christ on the desolate island to John actually standing in the heavenly temple, which is also the throne room of God. Just as Paul wrote, was John "in the body, or out of the body"? Was he seeing an open vision, or was his spirit caught up in heaven? His phrase "I was in the Spirit" indicates that he was experiencing a vision in which his soul and his spiritual eyes were being unveiled, and he was literally seeing into the invisible realm in the same way that Elisha's servant's eyes were opened to see the chariots of fire (2 Kings 6:17).

Some suggest the door is a metaphor, but I believe there are portals into the next world that are located somewhere in the galaxy. Such portals may be linked to research on "wormholes." In physics, a wormhole is considered a hypothetical "shortcut" though space. A wormhole is considered a space tube where movement is faster than light. It is theorized that a wormhole connects the distances between time and space and serves as a shortcut in time-space travel. The theory is that if a person could enter a wormhole at normal space time, that person could move faster than a beam of light. Cambridge astrophysicist Stephen Hawking is one of the first scientists to research their existence. He concluded that something fundamental in the laws of physics would prevent wormholes being used for time travel.[5]

However, there is still support for the idea of traversable wormholes in the scientific community. The idea is that once you enter the bottom or the entrance in our galaxy through a wormhole, you would exit it at about the same moment you entered it. This is generally the type of travel we are speaking of where the spirit of a departed person is carried from Earth and suddenly arrives in heaven in a moment's time.

Perhaps this is the type of *tunnel* that people describe when having a near-death experience. To the rational mind, the very concept of a person traveling from Earth to a heavenly realm not visible in our own galaxy is ludicrous. However, the ability to transport a person from Earth to heaven has been tested on three occasions during the past five thousand years of history.

The first was Enoch, the seventh man from Adam, who walked with God for 365 years and was suddenly translated to heaven. Moses wrote, "And Enoch walked with God; and he was not, for God took him" (Gen. 5:24). The Hebrew word *took* is *laqach*, meaning "to take or carry away." This does not mean God took him in death, but He translated Enoch without seeing death. This is the clear meaning from Hebrews 11:5:

> By faith Enoch was taken away so that he did not see death, "and was not found, because God had taken him"; for before he was taken he had this testimony, that he pleased God.

The second prophet to be caught up to heaven was Elijah. In 2 Kings 2:11 we read:

> Then it happened, as they continued on and talked, that suddenly a chariot of fire appeared with horses of fire, and separated the two of them; and Elijah went up by a whirlwind into heaven.

Both of these men have never experienced physical death, thus defying the law of Hebrews 9:27: "And as it is appointed for men to die once, but after this the judgment." Both men are believed by many scholars to be the two witnesses who will lead a restoration of faith among Jewish men in Israel during the Tribulation and later be killed by the Antichrist in the middle of the Tribulation (Rev. 11:3–8). Thus, they will eventually experience death.

The third person to make a translation from Earth to heaven was Christ, in Acts 1:9: "Now when He had spoken these things, while they watched, He was taken up, and a cloud received Him out of their sight."

There is biblical evidence that all three of these individuals made it to heaven and have been seen in heaven by other prophets. Zechariah saw the heavenly temple and identified the two olive tress and golden candlesticks standing before God (Zech. 4:1–14). The imagery of these two olive trees is the same imagery painted by John in the Apocalypse (Rev. 11) of the two future prophets who will come to Earth for forty-two months and perform miracles and announce judgments on the earth. The two men who have never died are Elijah and Enoch. Elijah will return as predicted in Malachi 4:5, and the fact that Enoch was the first prophet in history to predict the return of the Lord with ten thousands of his saints (Jude 14) causes many prophetic students to identify the two olive trees, or two witnesses, as these two Old Testament prophets who were taken alive into heaven. Enoch was translated five thousand years ago, and Elijah was caught up about thirty-five hundred years ago. Yet John saw them in heaven more than nineteen hundred years ago, meaning both men made it to heaven—and it didn't take thousand of years to get there! Both Stephen and Saul of Tarsus saw the resurrected Christ in heaven, and Saul heard the voice of Christ calling to him out of heaven (Acts 7:55; 9:4–5).

A secular scientist would point out three scientific facts. First, any person who would be *transported* from Earth to heaven would still be traveling from Earth to heaven even after five thousand years, even if they were moving at the speed of light, since the heaven where God dwells is in the third heaven and at the edge of the galaxy. The second fact is that once a person leaves the earth's surface, the temperature in the clouds becomes colder, and any human would freeze to death. (Perhaps this is the reason for the "chariot of fire"!) The third point is that all living creatures must breathe oxygen to exist, but the second heaven lacks this life-giving substance. For these reasons, liberal scholars consider the translations of Enoch and Elijah as a myth, metaphor, allegory, or as some story that has been embellished.

The answer is that God is certainly able to alter the cosmos and the human body in whatever manner He chooses. The fact that three individuals in Scripture were translated from Earth to the third heaven without any major disruptions and today dwell in the presence of the Almighty should encourage any believer that the method of catching away the living to heaven has already been tested—and it works!

When John was on the island of Patmos and experienced the vision of the Apocalypse recorded in the Book of Revelation, he said, "I was in the Spirit on the Lord's Day, and I heard behind me a loud voice " (Rev. 1:10). John eventually heard a voice like a trumpet saying, "Come up here" (Rev. 4:1). At this moment, he said, "Immediately I was in the Spirit; and behold, a throne…" (v. 2). John went from being on the barren, rocky, desolate island to standing on the crystal floor of the throne room of God. The transition occurred as fast as the blinking of an eye.

When Paul wrote about our own transition from a mortal to an immortal body, he wrote: "In a moment, in the twinkling of an eye…we shall be changed" (1 Cor. 15:52). The events John recorded in Revelation 4:1–2 demonstrate the swiftness in which the living saints will be snatched suddenly from off the earth and translated to heaven. The travel route has been tested by three men in the past and will be experienced by millions in the future.

# Chapter 11

# WHO WILL BE in HEAVEN, and WHO WILL BE MISSING?

According to Buddhist tradition, the entrance to hell exists at Fengdu, China, which is located on the Yangtze River, a four-day boat ride from Shanghai. In this rather depressing city, there are forty-eight temples covering the entire village, all depicting hell and the sufferings of hell. One is called "The Tower of the Last Glimpse of Home." High upon a mountain overlooking the entire area is the Ghost King, a temple carved with a gigantic, frightening face. When entering the temples, one sees hundreds of statues depicting all forms of demons tormenting and punishing men and women. Some are being boiled in blood, and others are being cast into a lake of fire, where they are supposed to suffer until a cycle concludes and they have been purged.[1]

In the nation of China, Buddhists point out that their religion is much older than the Christian faith. However, long before Buddha, the first man to enter into a covenant with the true God was Abraham, and Christ was the seed of Abraham. Believers are the spiritual seed of Abraham through Christ.

An important question to consider is this: Who taught the Buddhist that a place called *hell* exists? I have heard it argued that the concept of hell was begun by the Christian faith and that the Roman Church developed a detailed teaching of hell to frighten people into converting and joining the church. Even if a person believed this, it does not explain why every major world religion, including those that existed prior to the Christian faith, believed in an afterlife and a place of fire or hell.

All of the world's major religions—Christianity, Islam, Judaism, Hinduism, and Buddhism—have a belief in the afterlife, and all believe in some form of heaven and a place of punishment. All major religions believe in a place of fire and a place of "light." The religions of Judaism, Hinduism, and Buddhism all existed prior to Christianity. However, they did not exist before God made a covenant with Abraham! Thus, the true God, true faith, and true revelation come through the seed of Abraham and the Word of God.

Among many Chinese Buddhists, the belief in an afterlife is so inbred that at set times during the year, family members will purchase a small cardboard car, television, or some other object and burn it, believing it passes into the afterlife for the use of their ancestors! Buddhists also have "hell money," which is printed and purchased to help to pay for a person's escape from hell.[2]

Religions that preceded Christianity boast that their beliefs are the correct beliefs and all others are wrong. However, if any other form of belief or religion had been sufficient to provide redemption and eternal life to mankind, then it would not have been necessary for God to send Christ to the earth to suffer in man's place and to establish a new covenant of eternal life through Christ if humanity received Him and His sacrifice.

## Who Will Be in Heaven?

In today's politically correct culture, there is a common belief that all people from all nations who are good people, follow good works, and try to help people will be in heaven. In some extremes, heretical teaching called universalism teaches that all those in hell will eventually be taken out, forgiven, and allowed into heaven.

However, from a more practical perspective, most Christians have three major questions:

1. Will there be aborted spirits of infants in heaven?
2. Will my pet be in heaven?
3. Will people who have never heard the gospel be in heaven?

What does Scripture reveal about children? For centuries there has been a debate about the age at which a child becomes accountable for his or her own sins and decisions. As a child growing up, I heard that this *age of accountability* was five, ten, twelve, thirteen, and even older. Among those of the Jewish faith, religious Jews recognize the significance of the age of thirteen in the life of both boys and girls. When a Jewish child turns thirteen, the family celebrates with a bar mitzvah, meaning, "son of the commandments," or a bat mitzvah, meaning, "daughter of the commandments." Prior to the age of thirteen, the father of the children is responsible for the moral and spiritual instruction of his sons and daughters. Age thirteen is the age when most young people experience the physical and emotional changes we call *puberty*.

The Bible does give insight into the fact that children are special to the Lord and are brought to Him at death. One prime example is David's adultery with Bathsheba, which resulted in Bathsheba becoming pregnant with David's child. The child was a son, and after he was born, he was stricken with a sickness as a judgment against David's sin. The newborn lived seven days, then died. During those seven days, David fasted for the child's healing, and when he passed, David said:

> But now he is dead; why should I fast? Can I bring him back again?
> I shall go to him, but he shall not return to me.
>
> —2 SAMUEL 12:23

The child had died, and its tiny spirit was taken out of its body and taken to the paradise chamber. David knew he could not bring the infant back, but that he would one day go where the infant was! In the New Testament, Christ continually blessed the children, and on one occasion Christ revealed how children have their own personal angels:

> Take heed that you do not despise one of these little ones, for I say
> to you that in heaven their angels always see the face of My Father
> who is in heaven.
>
> —MATTHEW 18:10

The setting of this verse is the occasion when the disciples asked Christ who was the greatest in the kingdom. Christ brought a little child before Him and spoke of "their angels." Children are assigned angels, and these angels are continually before the throne of the Lord. Christ made it clear that heaven is made of children.

> But Jesus said, "Let the little children come to Me, and do not forbid
> them; for of such is the kingdom of heaven." And He laid His hands
> on them and departed from there.
>
> —MATTHEW 19:14–15

If a person cannot receive Christ in the simple faith of a child, that person will miss entering the kingdom of heaven.

> Assuredly, I say to you, unless you are converted and become as
> little children, you will by no means enter the kingdom of heaven.
> Therefore whoever humbles himself as this little child is the greatest
> in the kingdom of heaven. Whoever receives one little child like this
> in My name receives Me.
>
> —MATTHEW 18:3–5

There is also a firm and dangerous warning given to anyone who would ever hinder a child from following Christ or physically harm a child.

> Whoever receives one little child like this in My name receives Me.
> But whoever causes one of these little ones who believe in Me to sin,
> it would be better for him if a millstone were hung around his neck,
> and he were drowned in the depth of the sea.
>
> —MATTHEW 18:5–6

David knew his infant child was with the Lord. God has assigned angels over children, and the kingdom of heaven is made up of children. I believe that all children who pass away are taken into the presence of the Lord in perhaps a *children's paradise*.

## What About Abortions?

There is a theological disagreement among Christians as to when the soul and spirit enter a fetus. It is obvious that life begins at the moment of conception, for without the life force the fetus would never grow or develop. But is this when the eternal spirit enters the little human? The four main beliefs are:

1. The fetus has a soul and spirit from the moment of conception.

2. The fetus has a soul and spirit from the time the blood flows through it (five weeks).

3. The fetus has a soul and spirit after about six months.

4. The fetus has a soul and spirit at the moment the umbilical cord is cut.

This is an important issue, for if the soul and spirit enter at the moment of conception, then the willful termination of the fetus would be taking a life. If the soul and spirit come at the moment the umbilical cord is cut, then abortion, for those who believe this, would only be a medical procedure. The inspired Scripture must be our source of knowledge on this subject.

Man has been given a unique honor above all other of God's creation. Only of man, did God say: "Let us make man in our image, after our likeness" (Gen. 1:26, KJV). Man alone is a tripartite being, with a body, soul, and spirit (1 Thess. 5:23). The animal kingdom was created with a life force called a *nephesh* (translation "soul" in the King James Version) and to have a distinct personality. But animals lack an eternal spirit, and this is what sets man apart from the animal kingdom. As it is written:

> Who knows the spirit of the sons of men, which goes upward, and the spirit of the animal, which goes down to the earth?
> —ECCLESIASTES 3:21

Another God-given gift to mankind that separates him from even the angels of heaven is the ability to procreate another human being with a never-dying soul and spirit! "Children are a heritage from the LORD…" (Ps. 127:3). "Children's children are the crown of old men, and the glory of children is their father" (Prov. 17:6). Children are a gift, a joy, and an honor. Yet millions of mothers have aborted their own seeds—created in their own likenesses—and have destroyed their own futures in the process.

Twenty-two percent of all pregnancies (excluding miscarriages) end in abortion. In 2005, 1.21 million abortions were performed, down from 1.31 million in 2000.[3] There are various reasons that women have an abortion. "Three-fourths of women cite concern for or responsibility to other individuals; three-fourths say they cannot afford a child; three-fourths say that having a baby would interfere with work, school, or the ability to care for dependents; and half say they do not want to be a single parent or are having problems with their husband or partner."[4]

The psalmist wrote a fantastic word about his own conception and development in his mother's womb:

> For You formed my inward parts;
> You covered me in my mother's womb.
> I will praise You, for I am fearfully and wonderfully made;
> Marvelous are Your works,
> And that my soul knows very well.
> My frame was not hidden from You,
> When I was made in secret,
> And skillfully wrought in the lowest parts of the earth.
> Your eyes saw my substance, being yet unformed.
> And in Your book they all were written,

The days fashioned for me,
When as yet there were none of them.

—PSALM 139:13–16

## What God Says About Those in the Womb

In Genesis 25:21–22, Rebekah was pregnant with twin sons. As the little fellows wrestled in their mother's womb, Moses wrote, "The children struggled together in her" (Gen. 25:22). Between the conception and the birth, these twins are being identified as "children." When a child dies in the womb due to what is termed a miscarriage, that child is still called a person (infant):

Why was I not hidden like a stillborn child,
Like infants who never saw light?

—JOB 3:16

The word *infant* is the Hebrew word *'owlel* and always refers to a human being (Ps. 8:2; Hosea 13:16). In Luke 1:43, Elizabeth was calling Mary the "mother of my Lord" nearly nine months before Christ's birth. Even when the child is not yet born, the woman is called *mother*. Also in Luke 1:41–44, when Elizabeth was speaking about her baby in her womb, she said, "The babe leaped in my womb for joy" (v. 44). The Greek word *babe* here is *brephos* and is the second most common word used for "babe."

Throughout the Scriptures God calls future children the "seed"—even before they are conceived in the womb. Abraham and his sons were circumcised in the flesh of their foreskins, and all Hebrew infant sons were to be circumcised on the eighth day after their birth as a sign of their covenant with God (Gen. 17:1–14). When a Hebrew son grew into a man, married, and consummated the marriage with his wife, his seed (sperm) would pass through the "sign" of the covenant (the mark of circumcision on his flesh), and the seed would enter the woman. Thus, the seed was "marked" for blessing by the Lord before the infant was ever conceived.

This same principle is found in the account where Abraham paid tithes to Melchizedek in Jerusalem. (See Genesis 14.) In Hebrews 7:1–10, the writer wrote that Abraham paid tithe for Levi, who was still in his father's loins when Abraham met Melchizedek! At the time, Isaac, Jacob, and his son, Levi, had not been born, and yet an act of faith by Abraham was impacting three generations that were still seeds in Abraham's loins.

For someone to state that a child only becomes a human when the umbilical cord is cut shows severe lack of knowledge and understanding of Scripture. In the Bible the *moment of conception* is the mark of the birth; it is not merely the birth process that comes with the labor pains nine months later. In the King James Version of the Bible, Scripture continually speaks of a "son" being conceived:

- "Children…" and "sons in the womb…" (Gen. 25:21–22; Ruth 1:11, 2 Kings 19:3).
- "A male child is conceived" (Job 3:3).
- "Elizabeth…has also conceived a son…" (Luke 1:36).
- "Elizabeth…brought forth a son" (Luke 1:57).
- "The babe leaped in her womb" (Luke 1:41, 44).

One of the most important facts is that God foreknows the child while the infant is still in the womb, or as Jeremiah explains, before the infant is ever conceived God knows that child's destiny:

Before I formed you in the womb I knew you;
Before you were born I sanctified you;
I ordained you a prophet to the nations.

—JEREMIAH 1:5

For You formed my inward parts;
You covered me in my mother's womb.
I will praise You, for I am fearfully and wonderfully made.

—PSALM 139:13–14

Notice the special occasions when God foreordained the names of the sons who were to be born:

- Abraham and Sarah would have a son named *Isaac* (Gen. 17:19).

- Elizabeth and Zacharias would name their son *John* (Luke 1:13).

- Mary's son would be called *Jesus*, for He would save His people from their sins (Matt. 1:21).

In certain instances, the sexual identity of the child was known, the name of the child was given in advance, and the purpose or plan for the child was made known before the birth. In two instances, the names of great leaders were given hundreds of years before their births: one was Josiah (1 Kings 13:2), and the other was Cyrus (Isa. 44:28). The foreknowledge of God would indicate that God knows the name, the sex of the child, and the child's destiny before the child is ever conceived in the womb.

I believe that the soul-spirit of the child begins its life force the moment that actual conception occurs. Life can only come from a Creator who has given His creation the power to reproduce. I believe that the life force creating the soul-spirit of a child begins at the moment of conception. After all, how could the fetus even grow if there was not a special force of life behind the joining of the egg and seed of the parents? Consider numerous couples who for varied reasons are unable to conceive a child. At times the reason why conception does not occur is a mystery. However, life must come from the giver of life, and the Almighty was—and still is—the originator of life. He is also able to cause the barren womb to bring forth.

In the Bible, many important Israelites were birthed out of the wombs of barren women:

- Sarah was barren until, at age ninety, she conceived Isaac.

- Rachel was barren until she conceived Joseph and later Benjamin.

- Rebecca was barren until she conceived twin sons, Jacob and Esau.

- Hannah was barren until she gave birth to Samuel, followed by six other children.

- Elizabeth was barren until she gave birth to John the Baptist.

In certain instances, these barren mothers began crying out to God and interceding to give birth, and the Lord "opened her womb." Mary was actually a virgin, but God chose her to carry the future Savior of the world and proclaimed that all the nations would call her blessed (Luke 1). Conception begins the life force and the actual count of the nine months of a standard pregnancy. All indications in the Bible of God's foreknowledge, all biblical words used to describe the infant in the womb, and the fact of a growing fetus are indications of *life*.

When Gabriel told Mary that she would have a son, he said, "That holy thing which shall be born of thee shall be called the Son of God" (Luke 1:35). In the King James translation, the word *thing* is used 116 times. There are numerous words that may be translated as "thing." However, this word in Greek is *hagios*, which is the word for "holy, sacred, and blameless." The angel was not calling Jesus a thing—an object growing in Mary—but was identifying the holiness of the thing she was going to carry.

Other believers theorize that the soul and spirit are placed within the infant at about six months when the fetus has developed certain abilities. They base this concept upon statements made by Elizabeth concerning John the Baptist. When Mary visited her cousin Elizabeth, she was already six months pregnant with her son, John. As Elizabeth and Mary began talking, suddenly the baby "leaped" in Elizabeth's womb. The mother cried out, "The babe leaped in my womb for joy" (Luke 1:44). The Bible says that John was "filled with the Holy Spirit, even from his mother's womb" (v. 15).

According to all New Testament scriptures that speak of the infilling of the Spirit, He comes into your human spirit to abide. The New Testament speaks of a prayer language or praying in unknown tongue, and Paul wrote, "If I pray in a tongue, my spirit prays" (1 Cor. 14:14). Since the Holy Spirit is a spirit, and He enters the human temple and dwells in the holy of holies of the human spirit, then John obviously had a soul and spirit at six months. He could not have been "filled from his mother's womb" if he were only a piece of solid tissue developing into a person. These passages would eliminate the next theory completely.

The third theory that is believed by some politicians who accept partial birth abortion is that the soul and spirit are not in the infant until after the umbilical cord is severed and the infant breathes on his or her own outside of the womb. The supposition is that the baby only breathes *on its own* outside of the womb. This notion gives a person the "freedom" to abort a child up until the time of birth, as the eternal soul and spirit are not in the body before birth. I cannot accept this at all, either from a scriptural or medical point of view.

Recently a member of Planned Parenthood resigned after seeing an MRI of an actual abortion being performed. It was noted that the infant actually appeared to be attempting to protect itself from the intrusion of the outside force.[5] Little ones can be seen moving, jumping, sucking their thumbs, and doing other *human activities* in the womb.

Under the Law of Moses there were penalties for harming the unborn in the mother's womb:

> If men fight, and hurt a woman with child, so that she gives birth prematurely, yet no harm follows, he shall surely be punished accordingly as the woman's husband imposes on him; and he shall pay as the judges determine. But if any harm follows, then you shall give life for life, eye for eye, tooth for tooth, hand for hand, foot for foot, burn for burn, wound for wound, stripe for stripe.
>
> —EXODUS 21:22–25

There are ample Scripture references to prove that the eternal soul and spirit are a part of the development of the child in the womb of its mother.

Thus, if an infant dies in the womb or shortly after birth, the eternal spirit returns to the Lord, and we will one day join that spirit in heaven!

## Those Who Have Lost a Young Child

Those who have lost an infant or a young child often wonder whether the soul and spirit will remain in an infant or childlike state in heaven, or if the soul-spirit of the infant grows to a certain age appearance and remains at that size for eternity. Scripture is silent on this particular aspect of infants' and children's soul-spirit. I have, however, gleaned from the unique experiences of very godly men and women.

In an interview on our *Manna-fest* telecast in 2006, a ninety-year-old minister of the gospel related a most marvelous story that occurred to his wife. The minister, Theo Carter, and his wife, Thelma, had a nine-year-old son, Charles Edward Carter. It was on Halloween day in 1947 that the lad was playing in the street in front of the home in Kentucky, shooting off fireworks. The lad accidentally ran in front of a truck and was killed. Of course, the sadness was overwhelming, but this strong Christian family believed that their son, who loved Jesus, was in the presence of the Lord.

It was forty-three years later in 1990 that Thelma had heart surgery in Louisville, Kentucky. During the surgery, Thelma suddenly passed away. Instead of being taken to the recovery room, she was covered with a sheet and wheeled toward the hospital morgue. Doctors estimate that she was dead for twenty-one minutes, but she suddenly revived and stunned the hospital workers. Later, to her husband, she related that while she was dead, she was taken to heaven and actually saw their nine-year-old son.

Thelma and the boy recognized each other! The little lad related to his mother that he and other children enjoyed playing games on the *streets of gold*. Thelma recalled how she could see her reflection on the streets of gold. As she spoke to her son, he looked exactly as he did when he passed, forty years prior! She also noticed several saints whom she had known for years and had worshiped with in church who had also passed away many years ago. One of the main individuals, a fellow minister, was standing with the boy in heaven. The lad said, "Momma, he is my guardian angel!" Later, as they discussed the incident, the Carters realized that when a child passes, that child is not lonely in heaven but enjoys the friendship of children his or her own age, and there are also people who knew that child or his or her family on Earth who are there with them! This should be a comfort to anyone who loses a child. Thelma also saw her godly parents, who had died, but never spoke to them—she only saw them. She saw many people she had seen being baptized in the river many years ago who had also passed.

Not many people die more than once and experience both paradise and hell, but I know one man who has. Bishop Curtis "Earthquake" Kelley was a guest on *Manna-fest* when we aired the series on paradise. Bishop Kelley was once a heavyweight boxer, which is where he acquired the nickname "Earthquake." While his mother was a Spirit-filled believer, his father, who had Haitian ancestry, was a voodoo priest who was training Earthquake in voodoo from the age of five with the intent to send him to Haiti to work under Papa Doc. Earthquake became a drug user who died at age fifteen after consuming a mixture of marijuana, cocaine, pills, and alcohol.

Earthquake left his body at death and was pulled into a place within the earth, where he was mocked and tormented by evil spirits. Here demonic spirits beat him and laughed as they said, "You did voodoo for us. You were a sorcerer. You sold drugs for us. We tricked you! Now you are in hell. You can't get out of here. You belong to us now. You are lost forever!"

In his book *Bound to Lose, Destined to Win*, Earthquake wrote, "It seemed that every bad thing I had ever done, every good thing I had ever heard about Jesus, every Sunday school lesson I'd been taught, and every prayer I'd heard my mother pray came back to me. But there was not one thing I could do about it now. I was in hell."[6]

Then he described how that suddenly, two hands that were a golden color and brighter than the noonday sun reached into the room where he was being tormented. When the demonic spirits saw the hands, they screamed, "No! No! He belongs to us! You can't have him! No!"

The golden hands placed him back in his body. He heard a voice say,

"Because of your mother's prayers, and because you have been chosen by God, you were spared." Earthquake's mother prayed fervently for him and the rest of her children, often speaking the Word of God over their lives. Although paralyzed from the waist down after the experience, God miraculously healed him. Soon after, Earthquake received salvation and deliverance.

Years later, Earthquake briefly died of a brain aneurism as he lay in a hospital bed hooked to machines. Angels that were so bright they were almost difficult to look upon appeared in his room, along with a beautiful golden, boxlike vessel. The angels carried him to paradise, where they invited him to step out of the vessel and walk around.

In his book, Earthquake wrote of beauty that was indescribable. Grass was lush, green, and perfectly manicured. Blades of grass and branches of trees swayed to the music as they appeared to be praising God. The music was more outstanding than any he had heard on Earth, and it permeated his entire being. Flowers on Earth seem to be painted with crayons compared to the flowers in paradise. There was a fragrant aroma that surpassed anything imaginable.

Earthquake wrote, "God's presence was not only around me but in me. The beauty is spectacular, and there is an overflow of abundant peace and joy. I felt like I would burst because I was filled with so much joy. I wanted to dance and do handstands. I had never been able to do handstands on Earth, but I knew I could do one now. In fact, it seemed that I had the ability to do anything. I wanted to run and leap into the air shouting, 'Thank You, Jesus!' It also occurred to me that I was no longer sick and in pain."

As he stood gazing at a crystal river that shimmered like liquid diamonds, he thought about his son Scott who had been killed a few years earlier by a carjacker in South Central Los Angeles. He looked across the crystal river and saw a figure walking toward him. It was his son—as handsome as ever with his big locks of curly hair. Earthquake cried out, "Scott, it's you! It's you! You're alive!"

Scott replied, "Yes, Dad, I'm alive."

When Earthquake asked if there was a boat or something that he could use to cross the river, Scott replied, "There's no boat coming for you, Dad. You can't cross this river because you must go back and finish the work God has for you to do. You must go back. Remember when you made me that promise? You're still helping the poor, aren't you? Remember, Dad, you gave me your word."

Along with Scott, Earthquake saw many other men and women of God whom he had known on Earth. Other faces were unknown, but they all were telling him that he had to return to Earth and finish the work God had for him to do.

Before returning to his body, where he once again was sick and in his hospital bed, he received from God messages of repentance and holiness to bring back to the church.[7]

## Animals That Are Pets

Throughout the Bible, living creatures such as birds, fish, and four-footed beasts are given to men for various purposes. Prior to the creation of Eve, Adam lived in the garden with the animals and gave each creature its name (Gen. 2:19). While this zoo in a garden was lovely, the companionship of animals was not enough for Adam, and God made an intimate helpmate, Eve, for him.

The animals were given for labor, such as oxen and donkeys for plowing; or to be given as sacrifices on the altar, such as rams, lambs, goats, and birds; or to provide milk (cows, goats, and camels) and food for people. The priests were permitted to eat portions of the meat offering at the tabernacle and the temple. Animals also provided protection and companionship. The most common animals for companionship are dogs and cats. Both of these creatures have their own personalities, and dogs are people oriented.

After the flood of Noah, men were permitted to eat meat, although it was required not to eat it with blood (Gen. 9:3–4). There are some Asian nations that eat both dogs and cats. This is repulsive to those living in the West. Even in parts of Europe, horse meat is a high-priced meal. Of course, for most Americans, the idea of eating a horse is a real *turnoff!*

Because people love their pets, there has recently been a rise in interest and a theological debate concerning the beloved pets that are owned by believers. There are many wonderful Christians who have a dog, cat, or some type of animal that is very dear to them. When a companion is taken in death, especially for the elderly, a personal pet often becomes the companion for fun and fellowship. To some pet owners, their pets are just like children, especially to a couple who has never been able to conceive. The thought of the pet dying and the owner never seeing that pet again is hard to bear, and it has created a question: Is it possible that my pet will be in heaven?

The fact that God created all animals and that Adam gave them all their names is amazing in itself. This was prior to Eve being formed, so apparently the animals served as *friends* to Adam. Of course Eve provided far better companionship than Adam laying his head on a lion or hugging a little bear! A dear hug (not *deer*) from this two-legged beauty called Eve was far better for this handsome first man than Adam stroking the finest four-legged animal in the garden!

## Pets in Heaven?

Several years ago a teaching emerged that said a person's pet will join them in heaven. I was personally listening to a man I know and have always admired in his Bible knowledge as he explained to his audience that when the Rapture occurs, Christians' pets would be raised from the dead and would join them in heaven. I had studied the Bible for more than forty-five thousand hours, and I never recalled reading any reference to animals in the Rapture or the resurrection.

Are there animals in heaven? The answer is that there are creatures in heaven that have the exact appearance of certain animals that God created on Earth. They appear in spirit form and are living creatures and various types of angels. In the temple of heaven are four living creatures with the faces of a lion, an ox, an eagle, and a man (Rev. 4:7–8). One of the descriptions of the cherubim is that they have faces like a lion and wings like an eagle and feet like calves (Ezek. 1:3–28). When the saints return to Earth, we will join our "commander in chief," Jesus Christ, who will be on a white horse (Rev. 19:11). When Elijah was transported from the plains of Moab into heaven, "a chariot of fire appeared with horses of fire" (2 Kings 2:11).

While there are animals in heaven, and there are mysteries about heaven that even Paul was unable to speak about when he had a vision of paradise, when it comes to earthly pets, there are some points to be made. One of the most important is this: What about the resurrection of a pet that has died?

Everyone I have ever met—especially children—loves animals. I have a pocket parrot, my son and daughter both have cats, and we have fish. If I allowed it, we could become a miniature zoo! Pets are beneficial as fun friends for children and are especially important to those without children. They are also very popular with the elderly. Pets fill a void, which leads to the second observation.

On Earth we marry—as the Lord Himself said, "It is not good that man should be alone" (Gen. 2:18). Companions, friends, and pets are needed on Earth for fun, fellowship, and relationship. Heaven, however, is a different dimension of perfection that we have never experienced on Earth. We are not married or given in marriage in heaven, and yet on Earth God ordained it for companionship and procreation.

Elderly believers whose families live in another state and who are unable to travel as they once did need the warmth of a cat, dog, or other pet on Earth to fill the void. However, in heaven the perfection, the joy, the peace, and the family of God united as one will fill every *emotional* need a person has. We cannot understand this at this time, but that perfection fills all voids.

## The Creature Being Delivered

One of the passages used to teach that pets will be in heaven is the following:

> For the earnest expectation of the creature waiteth for the manifestation of the sons of God. For the creature was made subject to vanity, not willingly, but by reason of him who hath subjected the same in hope, because the creature itself also shall be delivered from the bondage of corruption into the glorious liberty of the children of God.
>
> —ROMANS 8:19–21, KJV

The important word here is *creature*, which is used thirteen times in the King James Version. Three examples of scriptures that use the word *creature* are as follows.

In 1 Timothy 4:4, Paul wrote: "For every creature of God is good, and nothing to be refused, if it be received with thanksgiving" (KJV). The word is used in Galatians 6:15 (KJV) of those who became "a new creature" in Christ Jesus, referring to those who have received salvation through Christ. In 2 Corinthians 5:17, we read: "Therefore if any man be in Christ, he is a new creature" (KJV). It is obvious that the word *creature* can allude to animals and also to humanity that receives Christ. The newer translations say it this way: "If anyone is in Christ, he is a new creation..."

In the context of Romans 8:19–21, Paul mentions the creature delivered from bondage and entering the liberty of the children of God. Redemption of the soul was purchased for humanity to make us "sons and daughters of God."

A second passage often quoted to teach that pets will be in heaven is Luke 3:6: "And all flesh shall see the salvation of God." The word for "flesh" in the Greek can be used of both the fleshly body and the flesh of animals. However, in the Old Testament, the word *flesh* is used of an animal only after the animal is dead. The Old Testament used the word *flesh* when describing the sacrifices that were offered on the altar at the tabernacle, including the lambs, rams, oxen, and other sacrificial animals. When the Bible predicts, "I will pour out of My Spirit on all flesh" (Acts 2:17), this alludes to all nations of people, including sons and daughters and servants and handmaidens—not to the animal kingdom.

A third passage referenced in the theory of the beast kingdom being raised is found in Psalm 36:6: "Thy righteousness is like the great mountains; thy judgments are a great deep: O Lord, thou preservest man and beast" (KJV). The world of humans and most pets have several things in common. Most pets are mammals—blood creatures, just as humans have blood. The "life of the flesh is in the blood" (Lev. 17:11). The word *nephesh* is often translated as "soul" in the Old Testament. It is the "life force" in both humans and mammals. Both humans and mammals came from the dust, and both return to dust at death. Both are given the "breath of life"; however, there are two different words used for "breath of life."

In Genesis 2:7, when God breathed into Adam the breath of life, the word for "breath" is *neshamah*, meaning "breath, inspiration, soul and spirit." God actually imparted into Adam's clay body both a soul and spirit, which gave him earthy life and life beyond death. In Genesis 6:17, at the flood of Noah, all flesh that had the breath of life was destroyed. This Hebrew word for "breath" is *ruach*, which is translated in the King James Bible as "wind," "breath," and "spirit." In the Flood account, this "breath of life" was the physical breath that ceases at death in both men and animals.

## What Happens at Death?

> For what happens to the sons of men also happens to animals; one thing befalls them: as one dies, so dies the other. Surely, they all have one breath; man has no advantage over animals, for all is vanity. All go to one place: all are from the dust, and all return to dust. Who knows the spirit of the sons of men, which goes upward, and the spirit of the animal, which goes down to the earth?
>
> —ECCLESIASTES 3:19–21

This is perhaps the most revealing passage concerning the death of men and beasts in the entire Bible. The writer acknowledged that both man and beasts will eventually die, and both will return to the dust of the earth. They also all have one breath (*ruach*). However, the writer reveals that the spirit (*ruach*) of a man goes upward, and the spirit of the animal goes downward to the earth. This life force in man returns to God as the body returns to dust.

> Then the dust will return to the earth as it was,
> And the spirit will return to God who gave it.
>
> —ECCLESIASTES 12:7

Using just the Scripture and not tradition or personal opinions, it is difficult to find where an earthly animal is raised from the dead to join its former owners. We are told in 1 Corinthians 13:10, "When that which is perfect has come, then that which is in part will be done away."

I am a very rational and systematic person, especially when studying a controversial subject, such as pets in heaven. From just a logical view, if a pet has an eternal soul and spirit and is part of the resurrection, then how would God distinguish which pet is in heaven? I know of people who have pet snakes, yet the serpent was cursed in the garden (Gen. 3). Some have a pet alligator or even a spider or rats, and so forth.

We also have the issue of an animal being killed, either by a hunter or in an accident. This may sound ludicrous and to some sarcastic, but it is not intended as that. Years ago I accidently ran over a dog that ran out in front of my car. I felt sick for days, and it was as though I had run over a person. If the pet has an eternal spirit, was I guilty of a crime? Then we have another issue. God allowed the slaying of lambs, rams, bulls, and birds under the old covenant as a blood sacrifice. Why would the Lord permit the continual slaying of animals that, according to some, would have access to eternity?

This raises another point to consider. Would our pet cats, dogs, and perhaps a few birds be the only creatures permitted into heaven, or does it include all the creatures—such as pigs, bats, rats, and so forth?

There are millions of people who do not, for religious or moral reasons, eat any form of meat. After the Flood, God said to Noah and his sons:

> And the fear of you and the dread of you shall be on every beast of
> the earth, on every bird of the air, on all that move on the earth,
> and on all the fish of the sea. They are given into your hand. Every

moving thing that lives shall be food for you. I have given you all things, even as the green herbs.

—GENESIS 9:2–3

The Lord permitted the sons of Noah to eat meat after the Flood as long as they did not eat the blood, which was the life force. The sacrifices offered and burned on the ancient temple altar were actually eaten by the priests. Jews today have a specific manner in which they slaughter and prepare beef, ensuring there is no blood mixed with the meat. We do not eat dogs or cats in the West. However, there are nations with strong Christian populations where it is permissible to eat dog and cat. I know this is very sad, and I have difficulty writing it, but it is true. Now the logical issue is this: if an uncivilized tribe in a South American jungle were to eat a human (which has happened), it would be cannibalism; if a person were to eat the flesh of any creature considered a pet, would this be cannibalism?

There is the biblical concept of what is a *clean and unclean* animal. God would not allow the Hebrew people to eat certain animals that were classified as unclean or allow certain animals in or near the temple because of their "unclean nature." One of those creatures was the swine. In Judaism, and also among Muslims, a pig is considered an unclean creature. Jews totally avoid pork and pork products, and some Muslims go as far as to believe that contact with pork can defile a person and hinder his or her access to paradise. If a swine is to be considered an unclean animal and a person has a pet pig (which some have) that passes away, would the Lord allow an animal in heaven that He told His own people to avoid?

There are numerous theological and practical questions the idea of pet resurrections brings up that honestly cannot be answered. While it is interesting to quote the historical opinions of popes, scholars, and animal lovers, after more than forty-five thousand hours of studying, I cannot find a clear indication that animals are resurrected at the Rapture, as some are teaching.

According to the prophecies concerning the future, we will only be in heaven for a brief period of time (some suggest seven years), and then we will return to rule with Christ for a thousand years (Rev. 20:1–4). At that time on the earth, there are lions and lambs and even serpents, and the curse on the animal kingdom is removed:

> "The wolf and the lamb shall feed together,
> The lion shall eat straw like the ox,
> And dust shall be the serpent's food.
> They shall not hurt nor destroy in all My holy mountain,"
> Says the LORD.
>
> —ISAIAH 65:25

During the future rule of Christ, we continue to see animals in the millennial kingdom, such as the wolf and lamb feeding together.

## What About My Pet at the Rapture?

There were two examples of judgment that came to the earth that are compared to the time of Christ's return. The first was the days of Noah, followed by the days of Lot. The Flood brought destruction to all living things. Lot saw four out of five cities destroyed, and apparently all life in those cities perished. Noah, however, was commanded to take both clean and unclean animals into the ark to preserve the animal kingdom for future generations:

> And of every living thing of all flesh you shall bring two of every sort into the ark, to keep them alive with you; they shall be male and female.
>
> —GENESIS 6:19

> You shall take with you seven each of every clean animal, a male and his female; two each of animals that are unclean, a male and his female; also seven each of birds of the air, male and female, to keep the species alive on the face of all the earth.
>
> —GENESIS 7:2–3

Since the details of Christ's return are a part of the stories of Noah and Lot, some suggest that as God spared certain creatures in the ark, likewise He would spare certain pets of the righteous; they would be with them during the time of the Tribulation. In the story of Lot, however, we see a complete destruction of four out of five cities, with no record as to what occurred to the creatures in that region—if some escaped, or if all animals perished with the people. In Genesis 19:24–25, we read, "Then the LORD...overthrew those cities, all the plain, all the inhabitants of the cities, and what grew on the ground."

Christ revealed that the eyes of the Lord are upon even two small sparrows when they are sold at the market (Matt. 10:29). The sparrow is very small and would seem insignificant to the average person. This verse reveals the care that God has for even the smallest of creatures in His creation.

Some people are concerned about what will happen to their pets after the ingathering and catching away of the believers. We know the promise of John 14:1–4: "Where I am, there you may be also" (v. 3). We who are caught up will "always be with the Lord" (1 Thess. 4:17). If pets remain after the Rapture, then will they starve to death after their owners are taken? Or, as some suggest, will the pets of believers be somehow removed at the same moment as the believer and actually be taken as a form of protection against what is coming?

## A Woman "Sanctifies" Her Family

In 1 Corinthians 7, Paul gave guidelines concerning marriage between a believer and an unbeliever. He instructed that if a believer married an unbeliever, and the unbeliever wished to remain in the marriage, then the believer should not separate (divorce) from the unbeliever:

> And a woman who has a husband who does not believe, if he is willing to live with her, let her not divorce him. For the unbelieving husband is sanctified by the wife, and the unbelieving wife is sanc-

tified by the husband; otherwise your children would be unclean, but now they are holy.

—1 CORINTHIANS 7:13–14

When a believer lives among unbelievers, there is a special sanctity God places on the home and those dwelling in the home. The word *sanctified* means "to be set apart." It does not mean that the husband is automatically a believer because of his wife; the question is about separating because of the husband's unbelief. The *sanctification* alludes to the fact that God will permit the marriage bond because of the woman and will even bless the children because of her faith and her lifestyle in the home. If the woman separated from her husband, the husband's influence on the children could cause them to be unclean.

To say that everything in the house (including pets) are sanctified by a believer living in the house is not intended in this passage and certainly is not implied in any way.

A believer must have full confidence and trust in God at all times. We must understand that the catching away and the resurrection fall under the classification of *a mystery*. We know how certain things will happen but are uncertain of the many details that are linked to these two events!

## Back to Pets

Here is the summary:

- Both man and beast are formed from the same substance, the dust of the earth.

- Both man and beast return to the dust at their deaths.

- Both man and beast have breath (*ruach*) that departs when they expire.

- The spirit of man goes back to God, and the spirit of a beast returns to the earth.

- Man's spirit is eternal, and the spirit of the beast ceases at death.

- There are animals that appear in spirit forms in heaven.

- There are animals on the earth during the thousand-year reign.

Heaven itself is very much like Earth, with rivers (Rev. 22:1), trees (v. 2), a city (Rev. 21:2), mountains (Heb. 12:22), books (Rev. 20:12), and so many other things. When Moses constructed the tabernacle, he built the structure based upon the patterns he saw of the heavenly temple (Heb. 8:5). The earth is covered with thousands of species of animals, including four-footed beasts, small creatures, and birds. There must be some form of animal life in heaven—albeit most are in some unique *spirit form* (such as the horses we will ride in Revelation 19:14). These are probably creatures that were created from the beginning of time and have been a part of heaven from Genesis 1:1.

It is unclear from the Bible if a person's individual earthly pets would be resurrected and spend eternity with that person. During my lifetime from childhood until before I was married, my family and I had about five dogs, many cats, and a few birds and fish. I enjoyed them all very much *at the time.* However, for me personally, I would have no desire to have all five dogs and all the cats running through my mansion. (Somehow I get a very funny picture of all of them jumping all over the furniture.) However, I have ministry friends and partners who have told me they believe their departed pets, which they loved dearly, will be in heaven. Since Scripture is silent as to whether there will be pets in heaven, it is best to leave the issue up to the Lord, and we can all say, "We'll see in the future." I am 100 percent certain that heaven is such a place of perfection that nothing will be lacking or missing when we enter the land of no time.

Finally, for those who have personal pets (which we too have as a family) and are concerned about the coming of Christ and no one to care for their pets if they remain behind, I am reminded of how God said He watches the sparrows and the lilies of the field (Matt. 10:29–31).

Certainly He will care for anything close to the heart of one of His children. This is where a person must simply trust God in all things.

## What About People in Other Religions?

Often when Protestant ministers are interviewed on secular television, they are asked in blunt, in-your-face tones this question: Do you think Jews and Muslims are going to hell? I have heard well-known ministers stumble, cough, get sidetracked, or try to avoid answering the question. Let me comment on this question. First, the issue is not whether Jews and Muslims are going to hell; the issue is that all men who are lost are sinners and are bound for hell.

In reality, all men are under a death penalty because of Adam's sin, for it is written, "Therefore, just as through one man sin entered the world, and death through sin, and thus death spread to all men, because all sinned" (Rom. 5:12). Thus all men need redemption. Redemption is different from religion. Religion is formed for men to reach up to God (or a god), but redemption is God reaching down to man. Anyone can form a religion, establish a belief, and make certain laws and regulations for their followers, but these activities have nothing to do with redeeming a human soul from hell. People do not spend eternity in hell because they are Hindu, Jewish, or Muslim, but they do so because they have no redemptive salvation covenant that delivers them from the eternal death penalty.

One of the criticisms of Christianity is that Christians believe they are the only ones going to heaven and that anyone who does not believe as they do will be lost. As far as Christians believing they are the only ones going to heaven, I would say that Christ is the only *religious leader* who was predicted to come, called the Messiah, and who had a clear plan for saving mankind, fulfilled that plan, then rose from the dead! I have asked some Muslims if they have an assurance of going to heaven, and they do not. Only if they follow the Quran, pray, give to charity, follow the five pillars of Islam, and make *hajj* in Arabia, *then* they may be found worthy. Even Orthodox Jews follow laws, regulations, rituals, and customs in an attempt to make it into the kingdom of heaven.

Here are reasons a Christian has such confidence: What other religious leader do you know with an empty grave? What other religion has a clear plan of salvation that leads to eternal life? Can you name one religion—outside of the covenant through Christ—that teaches you will never need to pass through hell or experience a purging of fire to enter the kingdom? These are the reasons why a true believer has total confidence in the gospel message.

## What About the Heathens Who Have Never Heard the Gospel?

Two of the most common questions that people have are: Will a person who never heard the gospel be lost? If a person is moral, lives a good life, dies without receiving Christ, and knew little about Jesus, how could God condemn such a person for eternity?

In the Hebrew Scriptures the English translation uses the word *heathen* 143 times. The word for "heathen" is *goyim* and refers to "foreign nations, unbelieving nations and non-Jewish people." In the context of the meanings, the word is used extensively for nations that worship idols or have no knowledge of the God of Abraham. Today, the common meaning of *goyim* is a Gentile, or simply a non-Jew.

God introduced His covenant to Abraham and His commandments to Moses through the Hebrew nation of Israel. Prior to the manifestation of Christ, the nations around the Mediterranean Sea had been influenced by the Egyptians, the Babylonians, and the Greco-Roman culture. All previous cultures and empires were idol worshipers who built temples and managed a priesthood that presented various offerings to their male and female deities.

With the introduction of the new covenant, the gospel of Christ spread rapidly throughout the Roman Empire, due in part to the amazing miracles performed by the followers of Christ. The apostles clearly taught that Christ was the final sacrifice for sin and was the only way to gain access to the kingdom of heaven.

> Neither is there salvation in any other: for there is none other name under heaven given among men, whereby we must be saved.
>
> —ACTS 4:12, KJV

> For I am not ashamed of the gospel of Christ: for it is the power of God unto salvation to every one that believeth; to the Jew first, and also to the Greek.
>
> —ROMANS 1:16, KJV

These men, eleven out of twelve, willingly died as martyrs for their message that Christ is the Savior of mankind. Most of their deaths came at the hands of leaders of other religions who rejected their teachings, which contradicted the ideas of these other religions.

Once an individual has heard the message of the gospel, at that moment that person is responsible for his or her own choice to believe or reject it. "He who believes and is baptized will be saved; but he who does not believe will be condemned" (Mark 16:16). However, for years there has been one major sticking point. Even if a person had never once heard a clear gospel message, would God condemn him or her to a place of separation and eternal confinement if that person were not an idol worshiper and lived a moral type of life?

This is perhaps the most difficult question to answer, because it questions the justice and mercy of God. I know you have heard it said, "How can a loving God send a person to hell?" Some will not accept a teaching on eternal punishment because it does not agree with their logic. I remind such logical thinkers that God never *sends someone to hell*. All men are born under a death penalty, and if a person does not remove this sin penalty passed on through Adam, that person is separated from God. Hell was not intended for man but was prepared for the "devil and his angels" (Matt. 25:41).

In Scripture, many sins are listed that are either sins against man or sins against God. Any sin against God must be confessed to God, but with a sin against another person, the offender must ask forgiveness from the one he offended and also ask God for cleansing (Matt. 6:12–14). There are also *willful sins* and *sins of ignorance*. The writer of Hebrews gives a strong warning (Heb. 10:26–27). Those who sin in ignorance are those who do wrong but are unaware that what they are doing is a sin (Lev. 4).

How does the one true God reveal Himself to humanity? There are basically four types of people on Earth:

1.  People who have no religion and no concept of or access to biblical truth

2.  People who have a belief in a religion and have never heard the gospel

3.  People who have a religion and practice it but have at least once heard a message of the gospel. However, they have never received the truth.

4.  People who have no religion, have heard and believed the gospel, and are saved

The Bible indicates that in ancient times God once winked at men's spiritual ignorance, but He no longer ignores men's ignorance (Acts 17:3, KJV). There are many individuals, perhaps primitive tribes in jungle regions and other remote areas, who have lived on the land and rivers for many generations yet have never heard a clear message of Christ's power to redeem. In light of this, it is written in 2 Peter 2:21: "For it would have been better for them not to have known the way of righteousness, than having known it, to turn from the holy commandment delivered to them." If it is better to have never heard than to have heard and turned, then does this imply that those who never hear the gospel could automatically go to heaven? If those who never hear can have a free pass to the kingdom, then should we quit sending missionaries and printing Bibles and let those who have never heard remain in their ignorance? Certainly not, for Christ told us we were to go into the entire world and preach the gospel to every creature, baptizing them in water and making disciples for Him (Mark 16:15–16).

However, there is another aspect of this that must be considered, written in Romans 1:18–20:

> For the wrath of God is revealed from heaven against all ungod-liness and unrighteousness of men, who suppress the truth in unrighteousness, because what may be known of God is manifest in them, for God has shown it to them. For since the creation of the world His invisible attributes are clearly seen, being understood by the things that are made, even His eternal power and Godhead, so that they are without excuse.

Men, from all parts of the world, can see the magnificent creation of God—the sun, moon, and stars; the rivers, mountains, and trees; the animal kingdom—and come to a conclusion that there is a Creator behind this detailed creation. As these simple men see the creation, they will begin to ask questions in their hearts and search for the Creator. I am not speaking here of those who are following a false religion and worshiping demons and idols but of individuals in remote areas of the world where there is no printed page, no television, radio, shortwave, satellites, or computers. In Luke 12:47–48, Christ gave a parable in which He said:

> And that servant who knew his master's will, and did not prepare himself or do according to his will, shall be beaten with many stripes. But he who did not know, yet committed things deserving of stripes, shall be beaten with few. For everyone to whom much is given, from him much will be required; and to whom much has been committed, of him they will ask the more.

The fact is that people cannot hear the gospel unless they hear a minister preach the gospel.

> For "whoever calls on the name of the LORD shall be saved." How then shall they call on Him in whom they have not believed? And how shall they believe in Him of whom they have not heard? And how shall they hear without a preacher? And how shall they preach

unless they are sent? As it is written: "How beautiful are the feet of those who preach the gospel of peace, who bring glad tidings of good things!"

—ROMANS 10:13–15

There are many people who have yet to hear the gospel because there are not enough people going to where they are to minister to them. However, once a person hears a clear message of the gospel, then that person is responsible for the truth he or she has heard. Those who have never heard the gospel still have within them a special pull that causes them to question where they are from and what their life is about.

## Seven Beliefs About the Unevangelized

We all know that millions of people have died without hearing the gospel message of salvation through Jesus Christ, and there are many more people living in certain parts of the world today—especially within the 10/40 window—who still have not heard. Many Christians, especially those who once adhered to some other religion such as Hinduism or Buddhism, want to know what happened to their relatives who died without hearing the gospel. When my sister was researching material for a book she wrote, she came across a paper that was written by Dr. LaVerne P. Blowers, assistant professor of Christian missions at Bethel College in Mishawaka, Indiana. The paper was titled "Are They Really Lost? What Is the Status of the Unevangelized?"

Throughout church history, many scholars have researched answers to the question, "What happens to people who do not hear the gospel before they die?" Dr. Blowers's paper summarizes the different beliefs that have been held by scholars and theologians throughout church history. You might not be aware that there have been seven different beliefs throughout church history about what happens to the unevangelized.

The seven beliefs are:

## 1. All unevangelized are condemned to hell.

Proponents teach that access to salvation is not universal; therefore, not everybody will have the opportunity to be saved, and most will die condemned to hell. Leading proponents of this position are primarily Augustinian-Reformed theologians such as Augustine, John Calvin, and Jonathan Edwards.

## 2. All unevangelized are saved.

This is referred to as universalism. Ultra-universalists teach that there is no hell, while restorationists teach that there will be a hell from which people will be given the opportunity to escape of their own free will. Proponents of universalism include some Reformed theologians, liberal pietists, and pluralists. Most names you would not recognize, but they include Origen, Charles Chauncy, and William Barclay.

## 3. God will send the gospel message before death.

Proponents teach that nobody is condemned to hell without first being given the opportunity for salvation. They believe that God can send the gospel message through human beings, angels, or dreams. Proponents include Thomas Aquinas, Dante, and some Roman Catholics.

## 4. Universal opportunity at death, also known as the "final option" theory.

This belief states that all people will have an encounter with Jesus Christ at the moment of death and thus have an opportunity to believe on Him. Those who hold this view admit that they have no scripture to back it up. Leading proponents include Roman Catholics, with Cardinal John Henry Newman being one of the most notable.

## 5. God will judge the unevangelized on the basis of how they would have responded if they had heard the gospel.

Proponents believe that God knows what could, would, and will happen; therefore, He knows who would have been saved had they been given the opportunity to hear the gospel. While there are not many proponents of this belief, they include Donald Lake, George Goodman, and William Lane Craig.

### 6. People will receive an opportunity after death to hear about Christ and to accept or reject Him.

Proponents teach that a person must be able to have explicit knowledge of Christ. Therefore, the only reason people are condemned to hell is for explicit rejection of Jesus Christ—not for ignorance of the gospel but for refusal to accept the gospel message and salvation. Also referenced are the scripture passages that speak of Christ's descent into the heart of the earth to preach the gospel there. Proponents include church fathers such as Clement of Alexandria, Gregory of Nazianzus, and John of Damascus. Many nineteenth- and twentieth-century theologians and commentators teach this as well; they include John Lange, Herbert Luckock, Thomas Field, and George Lindbeck, among others.

### 7. The unevangelized are saved or lost on the basis of their commitment to God.

Proponents teach that, even though salvation is through the work of Jesus, salvation can be received through general revelation and recognition of God's providential work throughout history. They teach that while Christ's sacrifice on the cross was necessary for salvation, explicit knowledge of what Christ has done is not necessary for salvation. Thus it is possible for the unevangelized to be saved without having knowledge of Christ or the exact nature of His gift to humanity. There are many well-known proponents of this belief. They include Clement of Alexandria, Clement of Rome, Justin Martyr, Matthew Henry, John Wesley, A. H. Strong, and C. S. Lewis.

Perhaps you were unaware that scholars throughout church history have sought so diligently to answer the question, "What happens to those who die without hearing the gospel?" Dr. Blowers's paper does an excellent job of summarizing the various beliefs, the scriptures used to back up their beliefs, and how each belief impacts evangelization and missions' work. Since his article is available on the Internet, you can go to the link and read it in its entirety. You might be encouraged to do your own research on this topic.[8]

## From Jack Harris

Jack Harris, president of Global Messengers in Fenton, Missouri, is an international missionary. He contributed the following for this section of the book.

> Men of all religions around the world, and those who have no religious background, all search for the *Creator* in some form. There is something within each person that eventually causes that person to make a quest to find out who put him on Earth and how he can communicate with the person responsible for all things. In many civilizations and cultures, god worship takes on many forms, ranging from ritualistic dances to human sacrifices, and even offering infants to a particular god.
>
> It was Solomon who wrote: "He has made everything beautiful in its time. Also He has put eternity in their hearts, except that no one can find out the work that God does from beginning to end" (Eccles. 3:11). When God set eternity in the hearts of men, He put a deep expectation and sense of eternity and of what the future holds. It is like each man has a compulsion to know about God. When Ecclesiastes says, "He made everything beautiful in its time," it tells us that God put in man the ability to see His beautiful creation, and that places within mankind a desire for what may be unknown to him at the present but causes him to search for eternal things. Eventually men realize there must be more to life than what they now see. This *eternal feeling* is especially strong when a person is about to pass from this life.
>
> In my travels around the world, I have visited and lived in several cultures. In India, the Hindus believe there are many gods, even millions of them, and that somehow they all lead to one God. Even though Malaysia is primarily an Islamic nation, my family lived in

a Buddhist community. As we learned about their culture and religious beliefs, we found that when men in their religion die, many go to hell, and it is the responsibility of the living family members to provide for their ancestors in the afterlife. One way they provide for their ancestors is to burn paper money called *hell money*. They also have a set yearly time when they will burn paper credit cards, passports, even paper watches, microwaves, and small paper cars with the belief that once the paper is burned, it transfers into the afterlife, in hell, where the departed spirit of their loved one can use it. Many from this religion are very hesitant to believe in the Christian faith for fear that if they turn to Christ, there would be no one in the family who would provide for their departed loved ones in the afterlife. This is ancestor worship, and it is prominent in the Buddhist religion.

After traveling as a missionary around the world, learning the culture and religions of those living in foreign nations, I have observed that whether educated or uneducated, and with or without an established religion, all men have similar questions that eventually come to mind. The questions are a combination of "Who created the world that I live in?" and "Is there a higher power or Creator God?"

For example, the Aztecs and Incas were highly developed cultures that asked themselves where everything they saw in the world originated. While they had many gods, their philosophers thought the Creator might be the wind, the water, or the waves of the ocean. As their search for their Creator progressed, they realized that the moon was more powerful than water and wind, and for a time they thought the moon might be the Creator. Then they realized that the sun was much more powerful than the moon, and thus they became sun worshipers. What would have happened if a Christian would have reached these philosophers and explained the story of Creation and of the one God who created all things? Instead of worshiping the sun, they would be worshiping the Son!

Because eternity is set in men's hearts, there is always the question of, "Where will I go when I die?" Something in each person, near death, begins to realize there is something beyond this life.

There is an inner feeling that there is more than just a ceasing of existence. The difficulty is that while this desire to know is there, we cannot find God on our own. This is why the apostle Paul wrote in Romans 10:14–15:

> How then shall they call on Him in whom they have not believed? And how shall they believe in Him of whom they have not heard? And how shall they hear without a preacher? And how shall they preach unless they are sent? As it is written: "How beautiful are the feet of those who preach the gospel of peace, who bring glad tidings of good things!"

I once took my family on a tour of one of the largest temple compounds in India. As the priest took us from one place to another throughout this massive structure, I observed many idols made of wood and brass, and some of gold. Some were very large and almost overwhelming to the sight. While I was walking beside the priest, I heard the Lord speak to my Spirit and say, "This priest is sincere in seeking for Me, but he cannot find me." This Hindu priest was using idols and religious rituals to search for God, but the idols were blind, deaf, and could not help this man.

Acts 17:24–30 details this search:

> God, who made the world and everything in it, since He is Lord of heaven and earth, does not dwell in temples made with hands. Nor is He worshiped with men's hands, as though He needed anything, since He gives to all life, breath, and all things. And He has made from one blood every nation of men to dwell on all the face of the earth, and has determined their preappointed times and the boundaries of their dwellings, so that they should seek the Lord, in the hope that they might grope for Him and find Him, though He is not far from each one of us; for in Him we live and move and have our being, as also some of your own poets have said, "For we are also His offspring." Therefore, since we are the offspring of God, we ought not to think that the

> Divine Nature is like gold or silver or stone, something shaped by art and man's devising. Truly, these times of ignorance God overlooked, but now commands all men everywhere to repent.

One interesting missionary story comes out of Southeast Asia in the nation of Burma, among the Karen people. For many generations in their folklore, it was handed down from generation to generation that one day a man would come riding into the area with *leaves* with the answers to eternal life. Generations later, a missionary was impressed to ride over the huge mountains to see if there were people who needed the gospel message on the other side of the mountains. As he arrived, the people from the villages would come out and see him, following him. As the crowds grew larger and larger, he was able to find someone with whom he could communicate. He was told about the folklore and asked the important question by the man who related the old story: "Do you have the leaves with you that give us the answer for living forever?" The missionary pulled out his Bible and began to share the gospel with the people, revealing the Creator, His plan of redemption, and eternal life. In a short period of time, tens of thousands of Karen people became Christians.

The very reason that the gospel message works in all nations of the world and that men, women, and even children respond to a clear message of the gospel is that as the Word is preached, the seed of eternity in the people's hearts begins to grow, and each person, through the Holy Spirit, can actually sense within his or her spirit the life of God as they begin to believe on Him.

The preaching of the gospel is the assignment of all Christians everywhere. Christ revealed that He alone is the door to heaven through His sufferings and resurrection (John 10:7–11). Since the beginning of the church on the Day of Pentecost, apostles, prophets, evangelists, and teachers have, from generation to generation, traveled the globe to bring the good news of Christ to all people. This is why millions of dollars are invested each year as missionaries set up evangelistic meetings, print Bibles, and carry gospel literature to the people of all nations.

It is interesting to note that we now have technology through television, satellite, and the Internet to reach more people than ever before. God allowed the earth's population to grow at a very rapid pace after these tools came into existence. Today, with more than seven billion people on the earth, there is no excuse for Christians not to take the gospel to the nations. Christ taught that the gospel of the kingdom would be preached as a witness unto all nations, and then the "end will come" (Matt. 24:14). The world is waiting for believers to tell them the answer to the feeling of "eternity in their hearts."

## Six Complicated Questions

During my years of ministry, I have been asked many questions about heaven and hell—and about who will be going to each place. Some of the questions asked most often relate to people who have died without ever hearing the gospel story about Christ. This section includes six of these questions, each of which is complicated and must be answered from a scriptural point of view.

### Question 1

"I lost a child whom I love dearly at an early age. She was like an angel to me. I am hoping that in heaven she will be the same age (age five) that she was on Earth. Is this possible, or will she be a grown woman when I see her? Will she know I was her mother? It greatly burdens me that she will not know who I am!"

*Answer:* First, consider that we are all a tripartite creation—a body, soul, and spirit. It is the spirit of a person that, if it stepped out of the body where you could see it, you would recognize as that person. This was the case with the rich man who recognized Lazarus (Luke 16:19–31) and with Moses and Elijah, who were recognized by Christ and by Peter at the Mount of Transfiguration (Matt. 17:3–4). Thus, the spirit and soul have the same appearance as the physical body. This is why we will be known in heaven as we were known on Earth (1 Cor. 13:12).

On one occasion, the disciples rebuked parents for bringing their children to Christ. The Lord rebuked His disciples and reminded them to allow the little children to come to Him, for "such is the kingdom of heaven" (Matt. 19:14). Some have pointed out that in the English translation we read where Christ used the word *children* to describe adults; for example, "children of the kingdom" (Matt. 8:12, KJV), the "children of the bride chamber" (Matt. 9:15, KJV), and the "children of the wicked one" (Matt. 13:38, KJV). However, when speaking of adults being "children," the Bible uses a different Greek word than the word for small children. The word used for "children" when speaking of a person of adult age is *teknon*, which is "the offspring or one that is begotten." This is why we are "children of God," as we are God's spiritual offspring through Christ (Acts 17:29). The "little children" mentioned by Christ is the Greek word *paidion*, which alludes to an infant or a half-grown boy and girl (Matt. 14:21; 18:3; 19:13). The word *paidion* is the word used to describe those little ones who were brought to Christ, and He laid hands upon them and blessed them (Matt. 19:13–15). The word *paidion* is used in the New Testament of an infant just born (John 16:21), of a male child recently born (Matt. 2:8), and of a more advanced child (Matt. 14:21).[9]

The soul and spirit must grow within a person as the physical body grows. A child at ages five to twelve does not have the same physical structure in height or weight as that child will at twenty years of age. When his or her spirit departs from his body at a young age at death, it does appear he will remain in the same form as he was when he was a child. Those who have seen their departed children in a vision or in a near-death experience see them in their young form.

## Question 2

"Prior to her being born, I lost a child who was a little girl. When people were trying to comfort me, they would say, 'Your little girl is with the Lord.' I want to believe this, but I struggle with this, because she would not have been totally developed. However, if *life* begins at conception, then have her soul and spirit departed from her body? Could her soul and spirit enter another infant, and then I would never know her? I am very confused."

*Answer:* As mentioned earlier, the *life force* that begins human life starts at the time of conception. This is when there is fertilization of the male sperm and female ovum, thus beginning an embryo. If this unexplainable life force were absent, then the process would be stopped at that moment and conception would not occur.

From a Christian perspective, the soul and spirit enter the body at the moment of conception in the same manner that God breathed into Adam's nostrils the "breath of life" and Adam "became a living soul" (Gen. 2:7, KJV). Notice it did not say a "human being" but a "living soul." Adam was created from the dust (v. 7), and this *dust body* became his flesh and bone. We know this because when God formed Eve from one of Adam's ribs, Adam said, "She is flesh of my flesh and bone of my bone." (See Genesis 2:23.) However, he would have remained in the dust without the breath of life.

As the fetus begins to grow in the womb, so does the eternal soul and spirit. If the infant passes in the womb, the soul and spirit will depart the body. Job pointed this out when he was very depressed and had lost all that was dear to him. He said, "Why did I not die at birth? Why did I not perish when I came from the womb?" (Job 3:11). He repeats the same thought in Job 10:18. When David's young son had just been born, he said he could not being him back from the dead, but he would go where he was (2 Sam. 12:23).

There is no indication in Scripture that the soul and spirit depart from an infant and enter into another infant who has been conceived. According to the Bible, there is a foreknowledge of all living people, long before they are ever born upon the earth. Jeremiah said that God knew him before he was formed in the womb (Jer. 1:5). If an infant passes, then the soul and spirit will return to God: "Then the dust will return to the earth as it was, and the spirit will return to God who gave it" (Eccles. 12:7).

It is true that the infant spirit would be very small, and if the body was underdeveloped, then the mystery is, how could such a tiny spirit know the mother? This is one of the biblical mysteries that cannot be answered. I recall reading many years ago a story that was reported by Gordon Lindsay, the founder of the Voice of Healing out of Dallas, Texas. He related the account of a Miss Marietta Davis, who experienced nine days of being in a trance-like condition. She lived in Berlin, New York, and in 1848, at twenty-five years of age, experienced visions while being in this trance-like condition for nine days.[10]

According to Miss Davis's experience, there is a special infant paradise; infants who die from around the globe are carried by a guardian angel to this special place. She described this place as a type of a heavenly nursery, where the spirits of the infants are taught and remain, until they receive a higher degree of understanding and eventually enter a more youthful paradise. Seven angelic guardians supervise each large edifice. As the angel guardian breathes on the little spirit, it causes the life to expand. As the infant spirit expands and knowledge is taught to each spirit, it will move to a higher level in paradise.

There is no doubt that the spirit comes from God, and He cares for each living spirit that returns to Him. There is much mystery that surrounds the death of an infant. This may be why Paul wrote that he saw things in paradise that it is not "lawful to utter" (2 Cor. 12:4). Perhaps there is more than one meaning to the psalm, and to the words of Jesus, which state, "Out of the mouth of babes and nursing infants You have ordained strength" (Ps. 8:2).

## Question 3

"I have read a lot of stories of individuals who have claimed a life-after-death experience or a near-death experience. In almost all cases, if the people saw heaven (or paradise), when they saw their grandparents or parents they described them as being very young, perhaps in their twenties or no older in appearance than when they were in their thirties. Is there any Bible reference to indicate how old a person will appear when he or she is in heaven?"

*Answer:* There is not a specific scripture on how old we will look in heaven. Some point out that when King Saul had the visitation from what appeared to be Samuel, Samuel was covered in a mantle and looked like an old man, suggesting that since Samuel died old he appeared old before Saul (1 Sam. 28:14). However, as is pointed out in this book, Saul never visibly saw the apparition that appeared, but the witch claimed she did. This was a familiar spirit and not actually Samuel, according to many scholars.

In heaven, there are twenty-four elders sitting upon thrones. These are believed to be the twelve sons of Jacob from the Old Testament and the twelve apostles of Christ (Luke 22:30). Scripture calls them elders, which is a Greek word (*presbuteros*) translated sixty times throughout the New Testament to mean "an older, senior person." In the New Testament, the word was used when describing the elder of two persons (Luke 15:25), a person who is advanced in life (Acts 2:17), and the elders who are the forefathers of Israel (Matt. 15:2). It does not allude to respect of position but seniority in age, rank, and position of responsibility. When Paul was giving advice concerning elders in the church, he mentioned elders being married and mentioned the elders' children (1 Tim. 3:2; Titus 1:6–7). Young men could only enter the common priesthood at the tabernacle and temple at age thirty up to the age of fifty (Num. 4:3, 23, 30, 35). It can be *suggested* that between the ages of thirty to fifty is the time frame in which a person could mature into the position of an elder. If the twenty-four elders around the throne are the sons of Jacob, they all passed away at a very old age. The same is true with the majority of the apostles. It is believed that the apostle John passed shortly after penning the Book of Revelation, in his nineties!

Now back to the original question, which is how old a person is in heaven. While the spirit and soul may grow as the physical body grows, the spirit reaches a certain maturity or dimension as the person reaches full statute, and the soul and spirit cease to grow because the body has reached physical maturity. From that moment, the spirit-soul ceases to age as the body ages. We read, "Therefore we do not lose heart. Even though our outward man is perishing, yet the inward man is being renewed day by day" (2 Cor. 4:16). The inward man is the spiritual man or the spirit of a redeemed person. It is "renewed" each day—a word in Greek (*anakainoo*) alluding to "make new back again and again."[11] Thus, as we become feeble with age and our skin wrinkles with time, the inner spirit is continually made new. It will be this eternal spirit that will join a new body at the resurrection.

I have also noticed individuals who have allegedly experienced a near-death encounter describe how youthful their departed loved ones appear. When asked what age they appeared, the common answer is, "They looked about the same as when they were thirty years old." When Christ began His public ministry, He was about thirty years of age (Luke 3:23). The four Gospels record several Passovers that Christ attended before His death. Scholars believe Christ was between thirty-two and thirty-three years of age at His death. Since the age of thirty was the age of entering the spiritual ministry as a priest, the age of thirty could be the age a person *appears* once they enter the heavenly paradise. Others point out that Adam was created a full-grown man at the time of his creation. When he opened his eyes, he was one day old on the first day, but his body was that of an adult man.

It is unclear how old loved ones will appear when we arrive in heaven. Will they maintain their same appearance if they pass at age ninety? I suggest not. Women especially would never be happy in eternity with any form of wrinkles on their faces—much less the men! However, we will know them as we knew them on Earth. That is the most important fact.

## Question 4

"I once heard you teach about 'Four Seconds From Eternity,' in which you related a story of a man in a plane accident who had four seconds before the plane crashed. He survived and later told you what went through his mind before the accident. I have numerous unsaved brothers and sisters who were raised in church. This story gave me hope that the seed of God's Word planted in their spirits would not return void at the end of their lives. Even in the event of an accident they could have time to repent. Please relate this story again."

*Answer:* Many years ago I preached each year in Deland, Florida, for a dear friend, Pastor Mike Coleman. One afternoon he was invited to fly with a friend who owned a two-seater show plane. As they took off from the runway and were several hundred feet in the air, the rudder became stuck, and the plane began to turn to one side. Mike had a headset on, and the pilot yelled, "We're going down." Mike said he had about four seconds before the plane hit the ground and everything went black.

I asked him, "What went through your mind during those four seconds?"

He said, "It was the most amazing thing I have ever experienced. It was like a computer hard drive filled with information was turned on. My mind went back to the time I was a child and called my dad a name. My thoughts recalled sermons I heard as a child. I instantly began to think about missing my daughter's graduation, the insurance I left my family, and a check on my desk in my office that I should have signed."

I was amazed to hear this.

Mike said, "I literally remembered things that I had long forgotten, including my many mistakes, words I had spoken, church services I had sat in—and it all hit in my mind and spirit within those four seconds!"

I asked Mike a very important question that I knew many family members would have asked him had they had the opportunity. I said, "Mike, in those four seconds would you have had time to repent and ask for God's forgiveness?"

He immediately replied, "There is no doubt. In fact, with all of that information flooding my mind and spirit, I was actually asking God to forgive me of anything in my life that may have been wrong!"

This brought me great comfort in knowing that if a person has the seed of the Word of God planted in them and is about to pass into eternity and has only a few seconds of breath or life remaining in his or her body, that person is able to recall the loving warnings and messages and to call on the name of the Lord for forgiveness or mercy.

Some would say that a person needs to say a long sinner's prayer in order to have true redemption. Well, this *long prayer* was not what the thief on the cross prayed. The fellow was bleeding to death and said to Christ, "Remember me when You come into Your kingdom" (Luke 23:42).

Christ replied, "Today you will be with Me in Paradise" (Luke 23:43).

The poor dying thief did not say, "Lord, I am a thief, and I have stolen from many people, and that's why I'm here. Let me confess all my sins." By the time he was finished *confessing*, Jesus could have passed, and he could have missed his opportunity for forgiveness. Perhaps this is why it is written, "Whoever calls on the name of the LORD shall be saved" (Joel 2:32). Receiving salvation and forgiveness is not a complicated event that takes hours of travail. Christ has already provided the suffering, the travail, and the pain of purchasing our redemption. He is looking for *faith* in the heart of that person.

I have taught my children and my closest friends the importance of keeping a repentant spirit, and I know that in the event of a sudden tragedy, they will have made their peace with God before they leave this life. Men and women should never take the risk of living their lives without Christ and hoping that in the end they will have time to repent. There are many who pass in their sleep or depart with a sudden and unexpected heart attack. There may be a split second of time between the death and the departure of the soul and spirit in which a person could call on the name of Christ. However, it is far better to know each day that you have a covenant, redemptive relationship with the Savior.

## Question 5

"I have a family member who was a strong Christian throughout his life. He went through a terrible time of losing almost everything he had and committed suicide. This was a shock to the entire family and the church. It caused a great cloud of darkness and depression to come over the entire family. The biggest concern was if a person killed another person without cause (such as in self-defense or war), the killer would be classified a murderer. Would the suicide be *self-murder*, and did this person make it to heaven?"

*Answer:* Without a doubt you have just asked me the most difficult question that anyone could attempt to answer. First of all, let me discuss *why* a person who is a devout believer would do such a thing. The Bible says, "Hope deferred makes the heart sick" (Prov. 13:12). Hope is the positive expectation that something good will occur. When a person begins to feel his faith waver and become weak, then it is *hope* that undergirds him, along with the belief that the bad things will not always be as they are but are subject to a positive change. For example, Job lost his ten children, their homes, and all of his livestock. His health also began to deteriorate before his eyes (Job 1–3). Job became so despondent that he said he cursed the day he was born and wished he had never been born (Job 3:1–11). However, Job also looked forward knowing that the Lord was still with him and that he would one day stand before his Redeemer (Job 19:25). Job held on to his trust in God, and eventually the Lord reversed the captivity and blessed Job with twice as much in the end as in the beginning (Job 42:10).

The power of hope is seen when a cancer patient is told, "You have cancer, but it can be treated," or in the life of a prisoner when he or she is told, "You have been given thirty years, but I believe you will only serve a few." It is hope that keeps a person wanting to live longer. Once a patient believes a disease is hopeless, that person will pass much faster than a person who fights, believing there is hope.

A person can experience weak faith, as did the disciples on occasions (Matt. 8:26). However, when hope is delayed, then the heart begins to feel sick. There is an uncomfortable sense of doom and despair that will take root. It is sad, but some see taking their life as a form of escape from the pressure they are feeling. As believers, we must never lose hope and must surround ourselves with praying individuals during our weak moments, knowing that our trials will bring patience and bring us forth as gold (1 Pet. 1:7).

In the Bible there are three examples of people who took their own life. The Spirit of the Lord had departed from Saul because of his jealousy against David. Saul was wounded in battle and requested that a young man pierce him through with a sword. When his armor bearer refused, Saul took his own life by falling on his sword (1 Sam. 31:4).

The second incident was Ahithopel, a counselor to David. This leader went behind David's back to attempt a coup against the king. Ahithopel made plans to set up David's son as the next king and to assassinate David. The plan backfired. We read, "Now when Ahithophel saw that his advice was not followed, he…went home to his house…put his household in order, and hanged himself" (2 Sam. 17:23).

The third person was Judas, the man who betrayed Christ. After he sold Christ for money, he realized his sin and was regretful. Judas went out and hung himself (Matt. 27:5).

In all three instances the men were not believers but were in complete rebellion. Saul had slain eighty-six priests (1 Sam. 22), made twenty-one attempts to kill David, and sought a witch for advice (1 Sam. 28). We are not told where Saul's spirit went after his death, although the familiar spirit prior to the battle said to Saul, "Tomorrow you and your sons will be with me" (v. 19). This would have been the Sheol compartment under the earth at that time. With Ahithopel, it simply tells us he took his life. Judas is an entirely different subject. He was an apostle, but Christ also said he was a "devil" (John 6:70). He was also called a "thief" while he was the treasurer of Christ's ministry (John 12:6). Prior to Judas's betraying Christ, we read where Satan entered his heart (Luke 22:3). Christ said it would have been better for the man who would betray Him to never have been born (Matt. 26:24). After Judas took his life, we read that he went "to his own place" (Acts 1:25). This phrase "own place" indicated that his spirit did not go to the same place where the spirits of just and righteous men are, but to a special compartment in the underworld of his own. These are the three examples of men who in some form of another took their own life. However, in all three cases these men were in complete rebellion against God and spiritual leadership.

These examples are not the same as a person who loves the Lord yet has fought a hopeless spirit. In some instances there have been Christian people who were on a very high level of medication that actually caused severe confusion and depression in their minds. I believe that when God judges a person, He will judge him or her by the knowledge he had and by the condition of his mind and spirit when the events occurred. If a person had no clue what he or she was doing because of legal medication that somehow clashed with their thinking, then God will judge according to each particular circumstance.

In Christ's time there was a man from Gadera who was being tormented by many spirits. We are informed that he was "cutting himself with stones" and was crying night and day (Mark 5:5). After Christ's prayer, these spirits departed from the man and entered a herd of wild pigs. The pigs ran off a cliff into the Sea of Galilee, where they perished (v. 13). It is clear that this strong spirit was pressing the man to take his own life, but the limestone rocks that he used in an attempt to "cut himself" were not sufficient to take his own life. After he was cured, the Bible says, "He was in his right mind" (v. 15). The phrase "right mind" is from a Greek word (*sophroneo*) meaning "a sober and sound mind." Obviously the man did not have a *sound mind* when these spirits were tormenting him. In fact, he had little control over his own actions because of the tormented condition he was experiencing. The adversary may not be able to possess a believer, but he does attempt to oppress believers and make them think God has forsaken them.

I have known of older believers who lived a spotless and holy life. However, in their latter years they suffered certain illnesses and would begin to use profanity, become angry, and even curse their own family members. They are not accountable for a physical disease or illness that has affected their blood vessels or their neurological systems, which they cannot control or alter.

When a believer takes his life and does not fulfill his earthly assignment, he can hinder himself from receiving a reward for his works in life. This may seem insignificant, but it should be an important part of a believer's expected future.

It is very important for all who are living never to take the risk of discovering what lies beyond this life if we take our own life. It is the unknown that often forms a restraint in the hearts of those who battle depression and anxiety. The thought of the judgment, losing rewards, or perhaps not being a part of the eternal kingdom restrains a believer from giving up or saying, "I am finished with life." Hold on to your hope. Bad things today are changeable tomorrow, and the Lord said He would go with you even to the end of the world!

## Question 6

"I have served in the military, and it was necessary to take the lives of those we were fighting against. Years have passed, and I am often bothered about standing before God and answering Him for taking those lives. I wonder whether I will have to meet these people in heaven one day, and what if they died lost?"

*Answer:* It would be a wonderful world if we could prevent all future wars and live together in harmony. However, wars and rumors of war will continue until the time of the end and are indicators of the *birth pains* that precede the return of Christ (Matt. 24:6–8). As Americans, our nation has never gone to war just for the purpose of going to war. In every war America and her allies were assigned to prevent an evil dictator or an evil regime from taking control of an entire nation or region that would cost the lives of thousands or millions of innocent people. Whether it was Hitler or Saddam Hussein, America is not an aggressive nation but a nation that seeks freedom for peace-seeking people.

Some people will quote the commandment "Thou shall not kill" and condemn a soldier who took the life of an enemy. First of all, there are two distinct Hebrew words translated in the English Bible as "kill." The word used in the commandment "Thou shall not kill" is the Hebrew word *ratsach,* meaning, "to dash in pieces or *commit murder*." It is dealing with the premeditated slaying of an innocent person. A man who would rob a home and kill the owner, kill a woman by raping her or a child by abusing him then taking his life is a manslayer and a murderer.

There is a difference between this immoral action and the action required to protect innocent people from a demonically controlled dictator. Saddam Hussein used chemical and biological weapons against the Kurds in northern Iraq, killing thousands and maiming thousands of others.

He also prepared mass graves as he and his henchmen slew thousands of Shiite Muslims in the south of Iraq. To remove this wicked man was a moral obligation to the people of Iraq and the world. Had the Allies not entered Europe and fought against the Nazis during World War II, can you imagine the destructive power that Adolf Hitler would have in his hands? Few Jews would have existed in the world if this criminal mind had fulfilled his total vision of Jewish annihilation. War is not the best choice, but at times war becomes necessary for the greater cause of humanity and for preserving the moral and social societies that have emerged.

In times of war, there is an enemy. The enemy is instructed to take out the opposition by whatever method is possible—either with bombs, hand-to-hand combat, guerrilla warfare, or torture. In war a soldier understands that when he is confronted with an armed enemy, it will be either his life or the life of the armed enemy. It is a matter of survival.

Because many United States troops have family and friends who continually pray for their safe return, and since America was founded on high spiritual and moral principles, men enter war with certain convictions, mixed with their determination to defeat the enemy. At times these convictions, especially spiritual convictions, can clash with the necessity of taking the life of an enemy geared toward the destruction of our troops and the very people of his own nation.

Also there is nothing wrong with a man defending himself. During Christ's ministry, He told His disciples not to take money on their journey. This was because Christ was the director of this evangelistic team, and He would provide what was needed for them (Luke 22:35). Near His death, Christ told them that if possible, the one who had no sword should sell his garment and purchase a sword (v. 36). The apostle Paul mentioned that during his missionary journeys he was in danger of "robbers" (2 Cor. 11:26). The only need for a sword would be for personal protection.

In the case of a soldier who took the life of an enemy, it would have been in the realm of self-defense and for the reason of freedom for the innocent people who were suffering in that nation. Let me use this example. What if you were to come across a small armed gang and they stopped your car, putting your entire family in danger, approaching with clubs, knifes, and other dangerous instruments? If you had a method to protect your family, would you allow the gang to destroy your car, beat your family with clubs, and leave you in the road while they drove off in your car? There are times when a person must protect himself, which is both a natural instinct and permitted in Scripture.

When another life is taken in war, in many instances the enemy comes from either a pagan background or is a follower of a false religion or an idol worshiper. If this person died in a natural condition, he would enter eternity lost. If his life is taken in a battle, he will enter the next life in the same condition and to the same place as he would have if he had lived and eventually passed. This is why there is such a need for the gospel message, even following a time of war. America often rebuilds the nation, assists the poor and needy, and, in some instances, helps the people to find religious freedom, including allowing the Christian faith to be practiced without oppression.

# Chapter 12

# The BEMA and the GREAT WHITE THRONE JUDGMENTS

Τhere are so many comforting promises for an exciting future for the believer who has received Christ and the redemptive covenant of eternal life. However, there is one aspect of eternity that to this day is rather frightening, and even Paul himself recognized the time as very significant and fearful. Just as it is appointed for every man to die, it is appointed for every man to be judged before God in heaven.

> I beheld till the thrones were cast down, and the Ancient of days did sit, whose garment was white as snow, and the hair of his head like the pure wool: his throne was like the fiery flame, and his wheels as burning fire. A fiery stream issued and came forth from before him: thousand thousands ministered unto him, and ten thousand times ten thousand stood before him: the judgment was set, and the books were opened.
>
> —DANIEL 7:9–10, KJV

Throughout the Bible the throne room in heaven serves as the center of all heavenly activity. We know that the entire area is patterned as a heavenly temple, with sacred furniture—the menorah (Rev. 1:12), the golden altar (Rev. 8:3–4), and the ark of the covenant (Rev. 11:19). At times the heavenly temple becomes a war counsel room, as seen in 2 Chronicles 18:18 when God and His warring angels secretly counseled together to determine the outcome of a war and discussed the way that a wicked king would be deceived to go into battle where he would perish. In the Book of Revelation we are made aware that the heavenly temple also serves as a heavenly courtroom where judicial decisions regarding men's eternal futures are set.

## Solomon's Divine Pattern

King David desired to build a temple for God but was refused by the Almighty because David was a man of war and blood. The Lord allowed David's son Solomon to take the plans from his father at death and prepare the most magnificent temple in world history.

- Solomon made a throne of ivory and overlaid it with pure gold (1 Kings 10:18).
- He made six steps leading up to his throne in Jerusalem (1 Kings 10:19).
- Solomon placed twelve carved lions—six on each side—on the steps going up to his throne (1 Kings 10:20).
- The top of Solomon's throne was round—just as there is a rainbow in heaven (1 Kings 10:19; Rev. 4:3)

> Then he made a hall for the throne, the Hall of Judgment, where he might judge; and it was paneled with cedar from floor to ceiling.
> —1 KINGS 7:7

The colors of the heavenly throne change colors as the atmosphere of heaven begins to change. In Ezekiel 1:26 the throne appears as a sapphire. In Daniel 7:9 the throne appears with fiery wheels of fire. Out of the throne proceed lightning, thunder, and voices (Rev. 4:5). Later in Revelation 20:11, at a major judgment, the throne is described as a "great white throne."

## The Throne Room Is the Courtroom

The courts that exist on Earth are set up in a manner similar to the heavenly court. Every court must have a judge, and the heavenly judge is God Himself (Gen. 18:25). Every court must have a prosecutor and an attorney. Satan is identified as the "accuser of the brethren" who appears in the heavenly court attempting bring accusations against the believer (Rev. 12:10). Christ counters the assaults of the prosecutor against the saints, and Christ is called the *advocate,* or the lawyer, who defends and protects His *clients* (1 John 2:1). Every court must have a jury, and in most courts there are twelve selected jurors who hear the information in the case and assist in the verdict. In heaven we read of twenty-four elders who are sitting on smaller thrones around the throne of God. These appear to be the twelve sons of Jacob from the Old Testament and the twelve apostles of the Lamb from the New Testament. The apostles were told:

> So Jesus said to them, "Assuredly I say to you, that in the regeneration, when the Son of Man sits on the throne of His glory, you who have followed Me will also sit on twelve thrones, judging the twelve tribes of Israel."
>
> —MATTHEW 19:28

In every court there are also witnesses who sit in on the case and observe the events. They do not participate in the verdict but are often relatives or close friends of the individuals linked to the case. I believe these witnesses are identified in Hebrews 11 as the many saints who have gone before us, called "so great a cloud of witnesses" (Heb. 12:1). This concept may be somewhat of a stretch, but each court has police officers assigned to protect the judge, along with a bailiff who announces for the court to rise when the judge enters the room. Surrounding the throne are four living creatures that are continually drawing attention to the heavenly judge and His righteousness (Rev. 4:6). It will be this area of heaven where the judgments will unfold.

## Two Different Judgments Are Set in Heaven

The Book of Revelation identifies two different judgments that will occur in heaven. The first is a judgment for believers, and the second is a judgment for unbelievers and for those who die during the millennial reign of Christ. The purpose of the first judgment is to reward those who have labored faithfully for the gospel cause, and the second is to show men (and women) why they are condemned to the second death and to judge the angels.

> "The nations were angry, and Your wrath has come,
> And the time of the dead, that they should be judged,
> And that You should reward Your servants the prophets and the
>     saints,
> And those who fear Your name, small and great,
> And should destroy those who destroy the earth."
>
> Then the temple of God was opened in heaven, and the ark of His covenant was seen in His temple. And there were lightnings, noises, thunderings, an earthquake, and great hail.
>
> —REVELATION 11:18–19

The timing for this judgment is during what scholars identify as *mid-Tribulation*, somewhere in the middle of the seven years of tribulation that will unfold on Earth. The saints and righteous will have been "caught up" to meet the Lord, and the dead in Christ will have been raised (1 Cor. 15:52–54; 1 Thess. 4:16–17). Jesus said, "For the Son of Man will come in the glory of His Father with His angels, and then He will reward each according to his works" (Matt. 16:27). Paul calls this time of judgment and reward the judgment seat of Christ:

> But why do you judge your brother? Or why do you show contempt for your brother? For we shall all stand before the judgment seat of Christ. For it is written: "As I live, says the LORD, every knee shall bow to Me, and every tongue shall confess to God." So then each of us shall give account of himself to God. Therefore let us not judge

one another anymore, but rather resolve this, not to put a stumbling block or a cause to fall in our brother's way.

—ROMANS 14:10–13

Paul also wrote:

Therefore we make it our aim, whether present or absent, to be well pleasing to Him. For we must all appear before the judgment seat of Christ, that each one may receive the things done in the body, according to what he has done, whether good or bad.

—2 CORINTHIANS 5:9–10

The phrase *judgment seat* is found ten times in the King James translation of the New Testament. It is used when Pilate sat down to judge whether Christ should or should not be crucified (Matt. 27:19). It is found in Acts 18:12–17, where Paul was brought before the judgment seat and had to defend the gospel and the accusation from the Jews that he was preaching contrary to the Law of Moses. He was beaten at that judgment seat for the message he was declaring in the area (v. 17). Another use of the term is when Paul wrote that we would appear before the judgment seat in heaven (Rom. 14:10; 2 Cor. 5:10).

The Greek for judgment seat is the single word *bema*. The word *bema* means "to set foot on" or "foot room" and was used of the raised platform a person stood on, reached by steps. The original *bema* seats were in Athens, Greece, and were raised platforms that existed on Pnyx Hill. From these raised platforms speeches were made to those who gathered together. Later the word was used to mark a tribunal in the Greek courts in which the accused would defend himself from one platform and the accusers would speak from the other.[1]

The bema was also used in the time of the Olympics. It was the raised platform near the finish line where the judge would sit and determine who had crossed the line first, second, and so forth during foot races. The writer to the Hebrews listed numerous saints, from righteous Abel to Noah, Abraham, Isaac, Jacob, and others who "died in faith" (Heb. 11:13). He then informs his readers:

> Wherefore seeing we also are compassed about with so great a cloud
> of witnesses, let us lay aside every weight, and the sin which doth
> so easily beset us, and let us run with patience the race that is set
> before us, looking unto Jesus the author and finisher of our faith.
>
> —HEBREWS 12:1–2, KJV

Running the race and looking unto Jesus would indicate that He is the rewarder and the judge at the finish line and that we must lay aside anything that would hinder our effectiveness and prevent us from receiving the prize at the end of our race.

John wrote that it was time to judge the dead. The dead in Christ will all be judged at one time at the great resurrection. Paul gives a powerful revelation on how a believer will be judged and the methods God will use to reveal the deeds done while a person lived on Earth.

> For no other foundation can anyone lay than that which is laid,
> which is Jesus Christ. Now if anyone builds on this foundation with
> gold, silver, precious stones, wood, hay, straw, each one's work will
> become clear; for the Day will declare it, because it will be revealed
> by fire; and the fire will test each one's work, of what sort it is. If
> anyone's work which he has built on it endures, he will receive a
> reward. If anyone's work is burned, he will suffer loss; but he himself
> will be saved, yet so as through fire.
>
> —1 CORINTHIANS 3:11–15

Many people would consider this passage as some form of metaphor. However, there is a golden altar in heaven where prayers are offered before God (Rev. 8:3–4). There is also an angel over fire:

> And another angel came out from the altar, who had power over
> fire, and he cried with a loud cry to him who had the sharp sickle,
> saying, "Thrust in your sharp sickle and gather the clusters of the
> vine of the earth, for her grapes are fully ripe."
>
> —REVELATION 14:18

How would our works "be revealed by fire"? First, we are not saved by works but only by grace (Eph. 2:8–9). Our works are the deeds that were done while living in our bodies on Earth. For example, Christ taught: "Whoever gives one of these little ones only a cup of cold water in the name of a disciple, assuredly, I say to you, he shall by no means lose his reward" (Matt. 10:42). Christ revealed that when you are persecuted, it increases your heavenly reward:

> Blessed are you when they revile and persecute you, and say all kinds of evil against you falsely for My sake. Rejoice and be exceedingly glad, for great is your reward in heaven, for so they persecuted the prophets who were before you.
>
> —MATTHEW 5:11–12

Helping to care for true men of God will also bring you a special reward:

> He who receives a prophet in the name of a prophet shall receive a prophet's reward. And he who receives a righteous man in the name of a righteous man shall receive a righteous man's reward.
>
> —MATTHEW 10:41

There is a special reward for those who serve others willingly, not for self-gain, but doing it as a service to the Lord:

> Servants, obey in all things your masters according to the flesh; not with eyeservice, as menpleasers; but in singleness of heart, fearing God; and whatsoever ye do, do it heartily, as to the Lord, and not unto men; knowing that of the Lord ye shall receive the reward of the inheritance: for ye serve the Lord Christ.
>
> —COLOSSIANS 3:22–24, KJV

This Scripture passage reminds me of the numerous volunteers who assist our ministry each year during our main conferences. Without these dedicated and trusty volunteers, it would be very difficult to conduct the regional conferences and to assist the crowds of fifteen hundred to thirty-five hundred who attend. Our volunteers are often asked why they spend their vacations and pay their own expenses to assist the ministry. They always answer that they are doing this "for the Lord," not just for the ministry.

They understand the spiritual principle that my grandmother Lucy Bava understood. After Granddad's passing, "Granny Bava" moved to Cleveland and would volunteer a few hours a day to my ministry doing odds and ends. I would say, "Granny, I need to pay you something for this work you are doing!"

She would look up with a slight grin and point to a plate that had a small cross on a purple pillow with a small gold-plated crown above on it, which read "Give for the Crown." "I don't need money," she said. "I am working for that in heaven!" These volunteers have the "reward of inheritance" and will inherit all of the blessings of the future kingdom since their hearts and motives were pure in a desire to be a blessing to others.

Many ask, "What will our rewards be if we are found faithful to Christ?" The Bible lists a series of crowns that will be awarded to individuals for particular aspects of ministry and obedient labor in their life.

## Five Crowns in the Bible

There are two common Greek words for the word *crown* in the Bible. One word used in the New Testament is the word *diadema*, found in the Apocalypse (Rev. 12:3; 13:1; 19:12). This word is used of the crowns on the dragon's heads, the crowns on the ten kings in the Antichrist's kingdom, and the "many crowns" on the head of Christ when He returns to Earth to set up His kingdom. The English word is *diadem* and always refers to the crown of a king or imperial dignitary.

The second word is the Greek word *stephanos*, which is the main word used to describe the crowns believers will receive if they are found faithful (1 Thess. 2:19; 2 Tim. 4:8; James 1:12; Rev. 2:10). The word comes from *stepho*, meaning "to encircle," and alludes to a victor's crown. In the Greco-Roman period, this crown was given to the victor of the games. It was woven as a garland of oak, ivy, myrtle, or even olive leaves, or, in some cases, an imitation of these in gold.[2] Nowhere is a believer promised a diadem, as there is only one King of kings worthy to wear this crown of kingship, and that is Christ. Believers will, however, receive the *stephanos*, which is the reward to a person who won the games, ran the race, and crossed the finish line.

There are five distinct and different types of crowns that believers are promised as a part of their *heavenly retirement package*!

## The incorruptible crown

> Know ye not that they which run in a race run all, but one receiveth the prize? So run, that ye may obtain. And every man that striveth for the mastery is temperate in all things. Now they do it to obtain a corruptible crown; but we an incorruptible.
>
> —1 CORINTHIANS 9:24–25, KJV

The idea of an incorruptible crown indicates a crown that will endure throughout eternity. This crown indicates a reward that a believer will receive that will always be a reminder through ages without end that the wearer was faithful in his or her earthly life to follow the Lord and be obedient to Him.

## The crown of rejoicing

> For what is our hope, or joy, or crown of rejoicing? Is it not even you in the presence of our Lord Jesus Christ at His coming? For you are our glory and joy.
>
> —1 THESSALONIANS 2:19–20

This crown is often called the soulwinner's crown, as there will be a special reward for all soulwinners. Paul was addressing the church at Thessalonica, Greece, in what was the first of thirteen letters he penned in the New Testament. The letter is divided into five chapters, and in each chapter Paul alluded to the return of Christ. He told this church that at the coming of Christ, they would be given a "crown of rejoicing." We will be rewarded for the souls we have won to Christ, and a special soul-winner's crown will be given to each believer who was a soulwinner!

## The crown of life

> Blessed is the man who endures temptation; for when he has been approved, he will receive the crown of life which the Lord has promised to those who love Him.
>
> —JAMES 1:12

Scholars identify this crown with the crown promised in Revelation 2:10, which is the reward of believers who endure and overcome temptation and testing. When Christ warned, "Hold fast what you have, that no one may take your crown" (Rev. 3:11), He was warning the church of Philadelphia to be faithful and endure the attacks of the enemy. There is a special crown for those who have disciplined their bodies, minds, and spirits to follow the Lord until the end. It is a crown of life.

## The crown of glory

> And when the Chief Shepherd appears, you will receive the crown of glory that does not fade away.
>
> —1 PETER 5:4

In 1 Peter 5, the apostle Peter was addressing the elders and instructing them to remain faithful to feed the flock of believers, not to be greedy of money, and to be an example to other believers. If they are found faithful, then at the appearing of Christ they will receive a "crown of glory." This particular crown is for those who have served as elders, pastors, and spiritual bishops over the believers as a shepherd would care for his sheep.

## The crown of righteousness

> Finally, there is laid up for me the crown of righteousness, which
> the Lord, the righteous Judge, will give to me on that Day, and not
> to me only but also to all who have loved His appearing.
>
> —2 TIMOTHY 4:8

It is interesting that Paul mentions that this crown is given for those
who "love His appearing." Once would think that all believers would
love the appearing of the Lord. However, there are some who claim to be
believers who actually scoff and mock the idea that Christ is returning (2
Pet. 3:3–4). Others will be "ashamed before Him at His coming" (1 John
2:28). For those who look for His appearing, there is a crown of righteousness. Only those in an active covenant with Christ, who are made the
righteousness of God through Christ, will receive this particular crown.

There are seven blessings promised for those who overcome, mentioned
by John in Revelation chapters 2 and 3. The blessings are:

1. The overcomer will eat from the tree of life in the heavenly paradise of God (Rev. 2:7).

2. The overcomer will not be hurt by the second death
   (Rev. 2:11).

3. The overcomer will eat the hidden manna and will be
   given a new name, written on a white stone (Rev. 2:17).

4. The overcomer will be given authority over the nations
   (Rev. 2:26).

5. The overcomer will not have his or her name erased from
   the Book of Life (Rev. 3:5).

6. The overcomer will be a pillar in the temple and will
   receive a new name (Rev. 3:12).

7. The overcomer will sit upon the throne of Christ
   (Rev. 3:21).

All of the above are a part of the rewards believers will receive for serving God faithfully.

Other rewards will include ruling on the earth with Christ during the millennial (one-thousand-year) reign. In Luke 19, Christ gives a parable concerning servants who were receiving rewards for their faithfulness. Based upon how these dedicated and loyal servants invested their time and income into the Lord's work, they were given rule over numerous cities. In the Apocalypse, all believers are called "kings and priests" and are promised to "reign on the earth" (Rev. 5:10). During the Millennium, there will be thousands of cities in which leaders will be set to rule over entire regions. These rulers and kings will be the saints who are living on Earth during this time.

## Losing Your Reward

There are some very soul-stirring things that are linked to the bema judgment. While a person must have a redemptive covenant to stand at this judgment, there will be people who will lose their eternal reward. This warning is found throughout the Scriptures.

> Let no one cheat you of your reward, taking delight in false humility and worship of angels, intruding into those things which he has not seen, vainly puffed up by his fleshly mind, and not holding fast to the Head, from whom all the body, nourished and knit together by joints and ligaments, grows with the increase that is from God.
> —Colossians 2:18–19

> Behold, I am coming quickly! Hold fast what you have, that no one may take your crown.
> —Revelation 3:11

Christ said that by helping others, you will "by no means lose [your] reward" (Matt. 10:42). I have often wondered how believers who make it to heaven—or people who were dead and then raised with the "dead in Christ"—could have made it into the kingdom of heaven and yet lost their rewards or their crowns?

In light of the warnings not to lose your reward and not to allow another man to take your crown, warnings were given to five of the seven churches in Revelation, instructing them to repent of their spiritual and moral failures or face severe spiritual and judgmental consequences.

1. "Repent and do the first works, or else I will come to you quickly and remove your lampstand from its place" (Rev. 2:5).

2. "Repent, or else I will come to you quickly and will fight against them with the sword of My mouth" (Rev. 2:16).

3. "I will cast her [Jezebel] into a sickbed, and those who commit adultery with her into great tribulation, unless they repent of their deeds" (Rev. 2:22).

4. "Hold fast and repent. Therefore if you will not watch, I will come upon you as a thief, and you will not know what hour I will come upon you" (Rev. 3:3).

5. "[Repent, or] because you are lukewarm, and neither cold nor hot, I will vomit you out of My mouth" (Rev. 3:16).

All believers at the bema will have their works tried through some form of fire.

## The Books in Heaven

How does God know what we have done? God is omnipotent, thus all knowing. Heaven also has numerous books (perhaps scrolls) with information recorded in the heavenly records. There are at least five different types of books in heaven that record information about those living on Earth.

## 1. The Book of the Living

There is a Book of the Living in heaven, which some suggest is the same as the Book of Life, which contains the names of the righteous. However, this Book of the Living appears to be a book revealing the destinies of all humans born on Earth. God spoke to Jeremiah and said, "Before I formed you in the womb I knew you; before you were born I sanctified you; I ordained you a prophet to the nations" (Jer. 1:5). This is an example of the foreknowledge of God. David knew about this foreknowledge when he wrote:

> Your eyes saw my substance, being yet unformed.
> And in Your book they all were written,
> The days fashioned for me,
> When as yet there were none of them.
>
> —PSALM 139:16

Prior to the physical birth of every human, there is information in heaven concerning the details of each living person. This is the Book of the Living, and the details for each infant were written before the infant was formed in the womb (Ps. 139:16). God not only knew you before you were born, but He also knows the number of days you will live! God Himself has a specific name that He has given to each person, and when we enter the heavenly kingdom, He will reveal to us our new name (Rev. 3:12).

At times in the Bible God changed a person's earthly name and gave that person a new name with a new meaning. Jacob was changed to Israel (Gen. 35:10), Simon to Peter (Matt. 16:17–18), and Saul to Paul (Acts 13:9).

Let me add that God created you to be different from any other human being who will ever live! You have a distinct set of fingerprints and footprints that identify you personally. The retina in your eyes has a specific, one-of-a-kind design. Even the form of your teeth is distinct from all other living humans, and your signature is all your own. You have a voice pattern that a computer program can identify as the real you, not someone imitating you!

## 2. The Book of Life

> He who overcomes shall be clothed in white garments, and I will not blot out his name from the Book of Life; but I will confess his name before My Father and before His angels.
>
> —REVELATION 3:5

This book, the Book of Life, is mentioned twelve times in the Bible, in both Testaments. In the Old Testament it is mentioned by Moses (Exod. 32:32–33), by David (Ps. 69:28), and Daniel (Dan. 12:1); in the New Testament it is mentioned by Paul (Phil. 4:3) and John in the Apocalypse (Rev. 22:18–19).

This book is a unique book that contains the names of those who repent of their sins and trust God for their salvation. The great prophet Moses knew that names could be added to or blotted out of this heavenly ledger. When Christ became the High Priest in the heavenly temple and was positioned as the mediator between God and man, this heavenly book was named the Lamb's Book of Life after Christ, who was called the Lamb of God (John 1:29, 36). We are told that names are inscribed or recorded in the Book of Life in heaven (Luke 10:20). To enter the eternal kingdom of heaven, a person's name must be in this book:

> And anyone not found written in the Book of Life was cast into the lake of fire.
>
> —REVELATION 20:15

## 3. The Book of Tears

There is also a record of the tears of the saints, as revealed in Psalm 56:8: "Thou tellest my wanderings: put thou my tears into thy bottle: are they not in thy book?" (KJV). In the time of Christ there were small *tear bottles* that were used to collect the tears of men and women at a funeral. Tears were collected and placed in these small bottles and sealed. The imagery in this verse is that God watches over every tear that we shed. God said, "I have seen your tears" (2 Kings 20:5). We know that God is moved by a "broken heart" and a "contrite spirit" (Ps. 34:18).

## 4. The Book of Remembrance

> Then those who feared the LORD spoke to one another,
> And the LORD listened and heard them;
> So a book of remembrance was written before Him
> For those who fear the LORD
> And who meditate on His name.
>
> —MALACHI 3:16

In Malachi chapter 3 the prophet was dealing with Israel's lack of obedience in giving their tithes and offerings at the temple in Jerusalem. He informed them of a special book in heaven that held the names of those who feared the Lord, gave their tithes and offerings, and witnessed to others about the Lord and His name. The Hebrew word for "remembrance" here is *zikrown* and alludes to something done as a memorial. An example of this book is found in Acts 10:1–4:

> There was a certain man in Caesarea called Cornelius, a centurion of what was called the Italian Regiment, a devout man and one who feared God with all his household, who gave alms generously to the people, and prayed to God always. About the ninth hour of the day he saw clearly in a vision an angel of God coming in and saying to him, "Cornelius!" And when he observed him, he was afraid, and said, "What is it, lord?" So he said to him, "Your prayers and your alms have come up for a memorial before God."

For a person's name to be recorded in the Book of Remembrance, that person must be a giver (Mal. 3:10), must fear God, and must witness of His name. Cornelius was giving alms, which is an English expression for offering charity for the needy. He feared God and was in prayer at the time of the visitation. His prayers and giving record came up before God, and the Lord honored this man with a special family blessing as a result of his faithfulness! If you have ever wondered how God keeps up with your tithes, offerings, and charity to the poor, they are recorded in this Book of Remembrance in heaven.

## 5. The Book of Rewards

The fifth book is the most important, because it relates to the rewards of a believer. There are records in heaven of our deeds and works that are done while we live on Earth.

> A fiery stream issued
> And came forth from before Him.
> A thousand thousands ministered to Him;
> Ten thousand times ten thousand stood before Him.
> The court was seated,
> And *the books* were opened.
> —Daniel 7:10, emphasis added

> And I saw the dead, small and great, standing before God, and books were opened. And another book was opened, which is the Book of Life. And the dead were judged according to their works, by the things which were written in the books.
> —Revelation 20:12

Our deeds include the words we speak. Christ said, "But I say to you that for every idle word men may speak, they will give account of it in the day of judgment. For by your words you will be justified, and by your words you will be condemned" (Matt. 12:36–37). An idle word can allude to something useless, lazy, and barren. These are words that harm people and statements that are useless and produce no spiritual fruit. Words are very important, because "death and life are in the power of the tongue" (Prov. 18:21). James gave a series of instructions regarding the power of the tongue and the importance of a believer controlling what he says. He said, "Let your 'Yes,' be 'Yes,' and your 'No,' 'No,' lest you fall into judgment" (James 5:12). Remember, if you don't say it, then you'll never have to face it! Christ also gave a strong warning to anyone who would use words to offend a little child (Matt. 18:6) and to those who would lead an offense of some kind, thereby creating a stumbling block for others (v. 7).

Our judgment at the bema will include judgment for the deeds we have done while living on Earth in our bodies, whether good or bad. The King James Version mentions deeds and how our deeds are judged (Rom. 2:6). The Greek word for "deeds" is *ergon* and comes from the word *ergo* or "to work." It alludes to the ethical sense of human action, whether good or bad. It is not just what you did in the form of labor, but also the ethical or spiritual reason behind what you did. We would say it was the true motive for why you worked. If your motives were selfish, self-serving, and all about you and how you could get to the top, then you received your reward here and will have no reward in heaven. Christ revealed, "Take heed that you do not do your charitable deeds before men, to be seen by them. Otherwise you have no reward from your Father in heaven" (Matt. 6:1).

For example, consider two different ministers. One uses his or her income for personal gain, personal needs, and to live a rather expensive lifestyle—all in the name of prosperity. Another person—for example, Mother Teresa—lives in absolute poverty in India and gives all her donations to the poor, helping to feed, clothe, and care for the poorest and most despised on Earth. Both die and stand before the judgment. I suggest that the rich minister has already enjoyed much of his reward on Earth, but Mother Teresa will have huge rewards because she accepted little on Earth but truly cared for the poor. Christ spoke about some on Earth who "have their reward" because their deeds are seen of men, and they desire the honor and praise of men (Matt. 6:1–2). Others do their praying, giving, and helping in secret, and the heavenly Father will reward them openly (v. 4).

## Who Is Watching You?

If our words and deeds are reserved in heavenly books, then who is recording the information? In the days of Lot, the Lord appeared with two angels. After meeting with Abraham, both angels, in the form of men, went to Sodom because, as the Lord said, "The outcry against Sodom and Gomorrah is great, and because their sin is very grave, I will go down now and see whether they have done altogether according to the outcry against it that has come to Me; and if not, I will know" (Gen. 18:20–21). Certainly God knew the wickedness and did not need a search team to determine how bad the moral situation had become. However, He checked with Abraham for two reasons. First, Abraham had family (Lot) in Sodom, and God was not going to destroy the city without giving Lot and his family a way of escape. Second, as Amos 3:7 says, "Surely the Lord GOD does nothing, unless He reveals His secret to His servants the prophets." Angels were assigned to confirm the information already known in heaven that the cry of wickedness was great from Sodom.

Another example can be seen from the vision of Jacob in which he saw a golden ladder reaching from Earth to the top of heaven, with angels ascending the steps and other angels descending from heaven to Earth. Because Jacob mentioned tithing ("a tenth," Gen. 28:22) after seeing this vision, some suspect the ladder was sitting at the site of the future temple (Mount Moriah in Jerusalem), where tithes would one day be received by Jacob's descendants. Thus, the angels were carrying the tithe up to heaven and releasing the blessing back to those on Earth. Jacob called the area "the house of God, and this is the gate of heaven" (v. 17).

Angels are ministering spirits sent to minister for those who are the heirs of salvation (Heb. 1:14). They are fully aware of who we are and are especially protective of children (Matt. 18:10). In heaven, angels worship God (Rev. 5:11), have access to the seven trumpets and seven vials used to pour out the future Tribulation judgments (Rev. 8:6; 15:6), and guard the twelve gates of the city (Rev. 21:12). There are so many angels that they are called an "innumerable company of angels" (Heb. 12:22). I believe each believer has an assigned angel that stays with him or her throughout that person's lifetime:

The angel of the LORD encamps all around those who fear Him, and delivers them.

—PSALM 34:7

It appears that each person's angel may be responsible for compiling any information related to that individual while living on Earth and for keeping a detailed record in the heavenly files that will be used at the bema. When John was caught up into the heavenly temple in Revelation, he saw the throne, the twenty-four elders, the four beasts, and the multitude of angels. These angels may be the angels that are going to present the information about each person to the Lord at the bema.

## How the Books Will Work

These books in heaven will each serve a distinct purpose at the bema judgment.

1. *The Book of the Living*—your entire destiny was recorded in the Book of the Living.

2. *The Book of Life*—by receiving Christ, your name was inscribed in the Lamb's Book of Life.

3. *The Book of Tears*—details of your words and tears and other actions are recorded in a Book of Tears.

4. *The Book of Remembrance*—as you give finances to the kingdom's work and pray, your actions are marked in the Book of Remembrance.

5. *The Book of Rewards*—as you work on Earth for God and help others, your deeds are recorded in heaven.

At the judgment seat of Christ all these books will be placed in a fire. If your works are burned, then you will receive no reward. If your works endure the test and come forth, you will be rewarded and hear the Lord say, "Well done, good and faithful servant..." (Matt. 25:21). If you hear these words, then the next statement from Christ at the judgment will thrill you for eternity: "You were faithful over a few things, I will make you ruler over many things. Enter into the joy of your lord."

I once heard a person say that he did not care if he received a crown or a reward, just as long as he made it to heaven. One day while reading the Apocalypse, I noticed that the twenty-four elders will cast their crowns on the crystal floor of the throne room and begin singing a song of praise to the Lamb (Rev. 4–5). I realized that a crown on the head of an overcoming believer is an eternal sign to the Lord that the person wearing the crown loved Christ so much while on Earth that he or she willingly sacrificed time, finances, prayers, and works to help others enter the kingdom. Without a crown, you will have nothing to present to Christ, nothing to lay at His feet, and nothing that throughout the eternal ages demonstrates your faithfulness to the Lord. You will be ashamed at His coming.

## The Terror of the Great White Throne

> Then I saw a great white throne and Him who sat on it, from whose face the earth and the heaven fled away. And there was found no place for them. And I saw the dead, small and great, standing before God, and books were opened. And another book was opened, which is the Book of Life. And the dead were judged according to their works, by the things which were written in the books.
>
> —REVELATION 20:11–12

This second judgment will take place at the conclusion of the one-thousand-year reign of Christ on the earth. There has never been, nor ever will be, such a major judgment on humanity as will occur at this particular time. The heavenly court will be called to session, and those standing in the courtroom will be individuals who lived on Earth since Creation until the end of the Millennium. The individuals present at this judgment will include:

- All unrighteous men and women who died, from the time of Cain to the time of the crucifixion of Christ
- All unrighteous men and women who died since the Crucifixion to the time of the Rapture of the saints
- All who died in the seven-year Tribulation period, including those with and without the mark of the beast
- All who lived during a part of the one-thousand-year reign of Christ on Earth and died before it was over
- All people who lived at the end of the one thousand years and must be judged
- All fallen angels, including Satan and his spirit rebels

There is a rather peculiar passage in Revelation 20:12, which says, "The dead were judged according to their works, by the things which were written in the books." We know that those from the Old Testament era who died without faith in the one true God and those who died without a covenant of redemption from the time of the Crucifixion to the end of the millennial age are lost, so who are those judged by what is "written in the books"?

> The sea gave up the dead who were in it, and Death and Hades delivered up the dead who were in them. And they were judged, each one according to his works. Then Death and Hades were cast into the lake of fire. This is the second death. And anyone not found written in the Book of Life was cast into the lake of fire.
> —REVELATION 20:13–15

First, notice that "the sea" gave up its dead, followed by death and hell (Hades). Hades is the fiery part of Sheol where the unrighteous dead have been confined since as far back as the people who died before the Flood during Noah's day. These souls come up from the underground chambers through the sea and are taken to the heavenly temple for this one judgment. Why must these lost souls be judged? God is a righteous judge and would never condemn anyone into a final, eternal separation without allowing that person to see the evidence written about him or her in the books of heaven. This is why the books are opened. There are many books, but only one Book of Life. Those who did not receive the mark of the beast but were slain for their testimony during the Tribulation are raised and permitted to live with Christ for the thousand-year reign (Rev. 20:4). Those who received the mark of the beast are not permitted to rule with Christ and are cast into outer darkness, where there is weeping and gnashing of teeth (Matt. 8:12). Those with the mark of the beast are among those being judged at this judgment.

Those who are judged according to their works would be the men and women who served the Lord during the one-thousand-year reign of Christ but die before the Millennium was over. Their deeds were recorded in the books of heaven, their names are found in the Book of Life, and their rewards will be given at the bema.

## The Mystery of the Second Death

In the sixty-six books of the Bible, the phrase "second death" is only used in the Book of Revelation.

> He who has an ear, let him hear what the Spirit says to the churches. He who overcomes shall not be hurt by the second death.
> —REVELATION 2:11

> Blessed and holy is he who has part in the first resurrection. Over such the second death has no power, but they shall be priests of God and of Christ, and shall reign with Him a thousand years.
> —REVELATION 20:6

> Then Death and Hades were cast into the lake of fire. This is the second death. And anyone not found written in the Book of Life was cast into the lake of fire.
> —REVELATION 20:14–15

But the cowardly, unbelieving, abominable, murderers, sexually immoral, sorcerers, idolaters, and all liars shall have their part in the lake which burns with fire and brimstone, which is the second death.

—REVELATION 21:8

Just what is the "second death"? When original sin entered the world through Adam, he was told, "But of the tree of the knowledge of good and evil you shall not eat, for in the day that you eat of it you shall surely die" (Gen. 2:17). Adam did not instantly die physically, but he died spiritually when he was separated from God and sent out from the garden, losing access to the tree of life. He lived 930 years, and then he died physically. Thus, there was a spiritual death first and a second death (physical) last. All men must die, both righteous and unrighteous. The righteous will only die once, which is physically, and then there is no more death, for we will be part of the first resurrection, after which the second death has no power over us!

The unrepentant sinner, however, will experience death twice. The first death is separation from God in the Hades compartment of Sheol. Some have been confined in the depths of the earth for centuries. Their "death" is not a destruction of their soul or spirit but is eternal existence without the presence of God, loving righteous people, and the beauty found in God's creation, the earth. The Bible indicates that the second death follows the Great White Throne Judgment, when all humanity, including Satan and his cohorts—the beast and false prophet—are cast into the lake of fire, "which is the second death" (Rev. 21:8).

## Is There a Final Annihilation in the Lake of Fire?

There are many who believe that God will not permit these souls to continue in this form of punishment eternally, but will, at some point, allow them to be consumed in the final fire, the "second death." There are many scriptures used to underpin this theory. Here are several:

For evildoers shall be cut off…

—Psalm 37:9

For yet a little while and the wicked shall be no more;
Indeed, you will look carefully for his place,
But it shall be no more.

—Psalm 37:10

But the wicked shall perish;
And the enemies of the Lord…
Into smoke they shall vanish away.

—Psalm 37:20

May sinners be consumed from the earth,
And the wicked be no more.

—Psalm 104:35

The Lord preserves all who love Him,
But all the wicked He will destroy.

—Psalm 145:20

The destruction of transgressors and of sinners shall be together,
And those who forsake the Lord shall be consumed.

—Isaiah 1:28

"For behold, the day is coming,
Burning like an oven,
And all the proud, yes, all who do wickedly will be stubble.
And the day which is coming shall burn them up,"
Says the Lord of hosts,
"That will leave them neither root nor branch."

—Malachi 4:1

The many references stating that the wicked will be destroyed, consumed, and perish usually allude to the destruction of the wicked while they are living on Earth—not to their annihilation when they enter the lake of fire.

Following the Great White Throne Judgment, sinners are cast into the lake of fire. Following this event, God creates a new heaven and a new earth, and the holy city, New Jerusalem, descends from God out of heaven onto the new earth. After this gemstone-jeweled city rests on the earth, we read the following statement:

> But the cowardly, unbelieving, abominable, murderers, sexually immoral, sorcerers, idolaters, and all liars shall have their part in the lake which burns with fire and brimstone, which is the second death.
>
> —REVELATION 21:8

Later, John describes the fact that in the New Jerusalem there is a river of life and a tree of life on each side of the river. There is no more curse on the earth and no need of the sun, because the Lamb lights the city (Rev. 22:1–5). Notice that the river of life with the two trees is located *outside* the gates of the fifteen-hundred-square-mile city:

> Blessed are those who do His commandments, that they may have the right to the tree of life, and may enter through the gates into the city. But outside are dogs and sorcerers and sexually immoral and murderers and idolaters, and whoever loves and practices a lie.
>
> —REVELATION 22:14–15

Why are these individuals—"dogs" (a phrase in Judaism for an unclean person, not a literal animal), sorcerers (the Greek is *pharmakos*, drugs and potions), whoremongers (sexual perverts and perversion), along with liars, murderers, and idol worshipers—still being identified as outside the city after the earth has been purified (2 Pet. 3:7)?

It appears that the lake of fire will also be located under the new earth. God does not destroy the earth into oblivion and set the heavens on fire, re-creating a new one from scratch. He actually renews the planet and the heavens through a purging fire that Peter spoke of. This occurs following the Great White Throne Judgment when everyone, including the saints, will be in heaven. Peter wrote:

But the heavens and the earth which are now preserved by the same word, are reserved for fire until the day of judgment and perdition of ungodly men.

—2 Peter 3:7

But the day of the Lord will come as a thief in the night, in which the heavens will pass away with a great noise, and the elements will melt with fervent heat; both the earth and the works that are in it will be burned up. Therefore, since all these things will be dissolved, what manner of persons ought you to be in holy conduct and godliness, looking for and hastening the coming of the day of God, because of which the heavens will be dissolved, being on fire, and the elements will melt with fervent heat? Nevertheless we, according to His promise, look for new heavens and a new earth in which righteousness dwells.

—2 Peter 3:10–13

In the Apocalypse John does not mention the burning of the earth and heaven with a purging fire (Isa. 65:17; 66:22; 2 Pet. 3:1–13), but he does allude to the new heavens and new earth (Rev. 21:1). John said there was no more sea on the new earth. This observation was important for John. When he wrote the Apocalypse, he was a political prisoner on the rocky island of Patmos and was surrounded with the waters of the Aegean Sea. To John, this massive body of water separated him from his churches and those he loved. On the new earth there are no more boundaries and limitations! The only way the seas of the world could become nonexistent is if they evaporated in a global fire of some type, similar to what Peter said: "The elements shall melt with fervent heat" (2 Pet. 3:10).

## The Men in Hell

Isaiah alludes to the new heaven and new earth. We mentioned this passage earlier, but now look at this prediction in light of the words in the Apocalypse:

For as the new heavens and the new earth, which I will make, shall remain before me, saith the LORD, so shall your seed and your name remain. And it shall come to pass, that from one new moon to another, and from one sabbath to another, shall all flesh come to worship before me, saith the LORD. And they shall go forth, and look upon the carcases of the men that have transgressed against me: for their worm shall not die, neither shall their fire be quenched; and they shall be an abhorring unto all flesh.

—ISAIAH 66:22–24, KJV

Earlier I mentioned the possible link of the Dead Sea during the time of the millennial reign of Christ. However, after the re-formation of the earth and heaven, lost souls are located outside the gates of the city. Thus it does not appear that the spirits of the angels or fallen men will be annihilated or destroyed in the lake of fire.

The Great White Throne Judgment will separate these sinners from those faithful who died in the millennial reign with Christ. There will be no unbelievers on that day. Atheists will become believers, and agnostics will be stunned to see the Creator on His throne. The mockers will be silent, and the wicked will regret their ways…but it will be too late.

For the righteous, the future looks great. The best is yet to come.

Chapter 13

# HOW WILL YOU
# BE REMEMBERED?

As a teenager, I was ministering in Carmi, Illinois, and studying in the pastor's office when I came across a small booklet with pictures called *The Infidel's Grave*. The book recounted a true story and showed pictures from a cemetery with a bronze statue of a man. On his bronze statue were two scrolls. The first, which represented the Bible and was inscribed "Superstition," was under his feet. A second scroll was engraved with the words "Universal Mental Liberty" and was in his uplifted hand. The marker was the grave of Chester Bedell, who died at age eighty-two and was buried in North Benton, Ohio, in 1908. The man was outspoken against God and the Bible. (He wrote a book against the Bible called *Universal Mental Liberty*.) It was reported that Mr. Bedell had stated, "If there is a God or any truth in the Bible, let Him infest my grave with snakes."

According to an interview in the 1930s with Bedell's daughters, when the sexton dug the grave, two snakes were killed. When the casket was laid in the ground, a third snake was removed from the grave. From 1908 to the 1930s, the grave became a popular tourist site, as the story of the infidel's grave spread to surrounding areas. There were photos in the old book showing as many as seven snakes coming from the grave in one day's time.

In the 1930s, people from all over the United States came to the cemetery to visit the grave and see the bronze statue. According to the old sexton who was interviewed by B. E. Perigo in the 1930s, there were as many as two hundred visitors on one Sunday. During a major storm, the statue was blown down and removed and was replaced by a tombstone.[1]

Years ago I read a story that was published by Gordon Lindsay, founder of Christ for the Nations, about a Mr. Stanley Carter, who observed a strange marker in a cemetery near Lafayette, Indiana. The marker was inscribed with these words:

> Martin P. Jenners
> Was born August 21, 1832 in a log cabin on the Northwest
> Corner of Ferry and Fourth Streets
> Died December 22, 1919
> My only objection to religion is that is not true
> 1 Corinthians 15:52; Isaiah 26:14
> No preaching, no praying, no psalm reading permitted on this lot

This man believed he had found a major contradiction in the Bible that led him into total disbelief in the inspiration of the Scriptures. The two scriptures in question read:

> …in a moment, in the twinkling of an eye, at the last trumpet. For the trumpet will sound, and the dead will be raised incorruptible, and we shall be changed.
> —1 CORINTHIANS 15:52

> They are dead, they will not live;
> They are deceased, they will not rise.
> Therefore You have punished and destroyed them,
> And made all their memory to perish.
> —ISAIAH 26:14

To the casual reader, these passages seem to contain opposite teachings. However, a closer examination of the context in which they were written reveals that there is no contradiction. The 1 Corinthians passage deals directly with the resurrection of the dead in Christ at the return of Christ. In context of the chapters before and after it, Isaiah 26:14 was dealing with nations that God was going to judge, making their memories perish, but the nation of Israel would endure. Poor Mr. Jenner fell for the oldest trick in the adversary's playbook—believing that the Bible is full of contradictions and lies.

Both of these cemetery markers are a statement to the men who once lived. The statement is: *We did not believe what was written in the Scriptures.* This defines how these departed souls were remembered by their friends and those in their communities.

Go with me now to the mountains of West Virginia. We have traveled by car through winding roads paved over rolling hills. We are about three miles from Davis, the highest town east of the Rockies. Just before reaching the old bridge at the quaint town of Thomas, we make a left turn and head toward a wooded area on a gravel road that appears to lead to nowhere. In a brief moment we see a sign that reads Rose Cemetery. This old-time graveyard has served as the final resting place for people from the surrounding community since the 1800s. Many of the markers on the backside of the road are so weather-worn they have become unreadable. Some have been broken and are leaning to one side, ignored centuries ago by surviving relatives. Some more recent monuments have plastic flowers lying lifelessly in front of the memorials, while others are well kept and manicured.

We stop about fifteen yards from the entrance, turn off the ignition, and exit the car. What we want to see are two simple marble markers on the right side of the gravel road. The grass has been trimmed, and new plastic flowers are sitting in a small vase at the base of the tombstones. We pause and remember the two wonderful people who died years ago, both in their eighties. They were married for more than sixty-five years before the husband's departure. The wife missed her loving friend so much and followed him several years later. They were buried side by side.

Today they still live, but at this moment only in our memories. He was always laughing and telling jokes. He was never sad, and the children and grandchildren never saw the couple argue and never heard them talk negatively about anyone. She was a great cook, and the aroma of her homemade vegetable soup would bring the family to the table before being invited to come.

They are two of hundreds buried in this cemetery. Their grave markers are passed every week without notice, except by relatives and friends who visit occasionally to remember two special people whose physical remains are laid to rest in that small mountain cemetery.

However, over the years, it is the simple words on the man's marker that people have commented about. Along with his name, date of birth, and date of death, are carved into the hard granite four simple words:

A MAN OF GOD

Shortly after his death, the family met and asked: "What should we place on the marker?"

The grandson said, "Put *Man of God*, because that's what he was to everyone who knew him." He never, I mean never, missed church, even on a snowy day and during holidays. He always paid his tithe up to the day he died, and he was a minister in the same church he had organized and built physically in 1959. It was that little church where I preached my first revival. That man was my granddad, John Franklin Bava.

He died in 1996, shortly after having surgery in the Elkins Hospital in Elkins, West Virginia, but we still remember him.

*What will they remember about you?*

Will people pass by your earthly remains, say farewell, and in a few days forget you ever existed? Will they whisper in the funeral home and comment, "He sure caused a lot of trouble for his wife and never had much to do with his biological kids." Will the business community have stories to tell of how you were always in debt, would never pay your bills, and left your family holding the burden? What will they say about you?

Or will your closest friends be hanging your picture on the mantel for years to come as a reminder of their dear friend who is no longer with them? Will people in the community say, "He was a great example of a good husband and father; I hope I can be like him"? Will business colleagues say, "He had a sharp business mind and always tried to do what was right; he knew how to plan for the future"? Will your children miss you and tell stories of their relationship with you and the fun they had with Dad to their children?

How men and women will view your departure is all up to you. You choose your own destiny. You decide the paths you take and where they will ultimately lead you. The same is true concerning your eternal destination. Where will you end up?

God has given each person the power to choose between life and death (Josh. 24:15). The plan of redemption, often called the plan of salvation, was set in motion long before Adam ever sinned (1 Pet. 1:19–20). Christ took our sins to the cross, and if we repent and turn to God and receive by faith the finished work of Christ, then we can be delivered from this body of death and spend eternity with the Lord (Rom. 7:24; 8:1–11).

The process begins by believing with your heart that Jesus Christ is the only way to heaven.

> Nor is there salvation in any other, for there is no other name under heaven given among men by which we must be saved.
> —Acts 4:12

Then we must confess that we are sinners and ask for Christ to forgive us of our sins. As Paul said:

> For with the heart one believes unto righteousness, and with the mouth confession is made unto salvation.
> —Romans 10:10

This process of believing and confessing leads to an inner transformation, which cannot be explained but has been experienced by hundreds of millions of people over time. From this point, as you study the Scriptures and join with other believers, you will discover what you have been missing—righteousness, peace, and joy (Rom. 14:17). You will be amazed at the wonder of God's written Word, the Bible, and as you learn to communicate one on one with the Lord, you will grow in grace and knowledge in Him.

You should also seek out a church or a fellowship of believers who love Christ and are teaching the pure Word of God. As you remain faithful to your commitment to Christ and walk in this new covenant, you are preparing yourself for the greatest journey of all time. You will either depart this life through death or be translated and changed in a moment at the return of Christ. Either way, you leave a winner!

If you hear the truth and willfully choose to reject it, your final eternal destination will be a land of barrenness and darkness, fire, and loneliness in subterranean chambers under the earth. You don't have to go there, and you never have to see the place if you will only believe the gospel.

As I conclude, please never forget that *forever never ends*, and you are headed into forever!

## Conclusion

# A PRAYER for REDEMPTION

*Dear Lord Jesus,*

*I come before You knowing that I am a sinner. I realize my weakness and my sin, but I believe You came to redeem me and forgive me of my sins and bring me into Your family. I am asking You to forgive me of all my sins, cleanse me through Your precious blood and sacrifice, and remember me as Your child when the time comes to enter the kingdom.*

*Through Your Word and Your power, change me. Deliver me out of my bondages, and bring me joy and peace. Help me to make new friends and to follow You and learn of You. I receive You as my Savior, and I believe You have received me as Your child into the family of God. I ask this all in Christ's name, amen.*

# NOTES

## Chapter 1
## Journey Beyond the Grave

1. Finis Jennings Dake, *Dake's Annotated Reference Bible* (Lawrenceville, GA: Dake Publishing, 1996), s.v. "Genesis 1:1."

2. *Biblesoft's New Exhaustive Strong's Numbers and Concordance with Expanded Greek-Hebrew Dictionary,* Copyright © 1994, Biblesoft and International Bible Translators, Inc., s.v. "*tehom.*"

3. W. E. Vine, *Vine's Expository Dictionary of the Old and New Testament Words* (Nashville, TN: Thomas Nelson, 2003), s.v. "Hades."

4. *The Ante-Nicene Fathers*, vol. 5 (Grand Rapids, MI: Wm. B. Eerdman's Publishing House, 1957), 221.

5. As quoted in Francis A. Schaeffer, *The Church Before the Watching World* (Downers Grove, IL: InterVarsity Press, 1971), 54–55.

6. John Lightfoot, "Chapter 39: The Valley of Hinnom," in *A Commentary on the New Testament From the Talmud and Hebraica*, http://philologos.org/__eb-jl/cent04.htm (accessed April 9, 2010).

7. Flavius Josephus, *War* 2:155, as referenced in Steve Mason, *Flavius Josephus on the Pharisees: A Composition-Critical Study* (Leiden, The Netherlands: E. J. Brill, 1991), 159.

8. WorldAtlas.com, "The Bermuda Triangle," http://www.worldatlas.com/aatlas/infopage/bermudat.htm (accessed January 7, 2010).

9. Library.Thinkquest.org, "Ocean Facts," http://library.thinkquest.org/6234/newpage1.htm (accessed January 7, 2010).

10. Bibliotecapleyades.net, "Ten Vile Vortices Around the World," http://www.bibliotecapleyades.net/mapas_ocultotierra/esp_mapa_ocultotierra_11.htm (accessed January 7, 2010).

11. Ibid.

## Chapter 2
## The Dead Sea—the Area of the Future Lake of Fire

1. "Science Update," *Nature*, July 22, 2002, as quoted in Terry Watkins, "The Truth About Hell," http://www.av1611.org/hell.html (accessed April 12, 2010).

2. TravelEgypt.com, "Dead Sea," http://www.travelegypt.com/siteinfo/DeadSea.htm (accessed January 8, 2010).

3. Zayne Bilkadi, "Bulls From the Sea," *Saudi Aramco World*, July/August 1994, http://www.saudiaramcoworld.com/issue/199404/bulls.from.the.sea.htm (accessed January 8, 2010).

4. "LV.3–LVI.4: Final Judgment of Azazel, the Watchers, and Their Children," *The Book of Enoch*, http://www.heaven.net.nz/writings/thebookofenoch.htm (accessed January 8, 2010).

5. Strabo, *Geographika* XVI, 764, as quoted in Stephen John Spencer, *The Genesis Pursuit* (Longwood, FL: Xulon Press, 2006), 199.

6. Wisdom of Solomon 10:6–7, The Apocrypha, Revised Standard Version, copyright © National Council of Churches of Christ in America, http://quod.lib.umich.edu/cgi/r/rsv/rsv-idx?type=DIV1&byte=3905445 (accessed January 8, 2010).

7. Diodorus, *Book II*, as quoted in Sir William Smith ed., *Dictionary of Greek and Roman Geography*, vol. 2 (London: Spottiswoods and Company, 1873), 522.

8. Philo, *On Abraham*, XXVII: 140–141, http://www.earlychristianwritings.com/yonge/book22.html (accessed January 8, 2010).

9. Volney, *Travels*, vol. 1, 281–282, as quoted in Newswatchmagazine.org, "Jude's Example," http://www.newswatchmagazine.org/restknowledge/rk2/lakeoffire2.htm (accessed January 8, 2010).

10. William Francis Lynch, *The Official Report of the United States Expedition to Explore the Dead Sea and River Jordan* (Baltimore: John Murphy & Company, 1852), 34, 38.

11. Jamal Halaby, "Mideast Conflict Slows Dead Sea Work," *USA Today*, May 5, 2007, http://www.usatoday.com/news/world/2007-05-05-deadsea_N.htm (accessed January 8, 2010).

12. Joe Anuta, "Probing Question: What Heats the Earth's Core?" Physorg.com, March 30, 2006, http://www.physorg.com/news62952904.html (accessed January 11, 2010).

13. National Academy of Sciences, "Project Mohole, 1958–1966," http://www.nationalacademies.org/history/mohole/ (accessed January 11, 2010).

14. RitchieWiki.com, "Kola Superdeep Borehole," http://www.ritchiewiki.com/wiki/index.php/Kola_Superdeep_Borehole" (accessed January 11, 2010).

15. Anuta, "Probing Question: What Heats the Earth's Core?"

16. Isaiah 66:24 from the Chaldee, taken from *Barnes' Notes*, Electronic Database, Copyright © 1997 by Biblesoft.

17. Isaiah 66:24, the Vulgate.

18. Isaiah 66:24, the Septuagint.

19. Isaiah 66:24, the Syriac.

# Chapter 6
## More Secrets of the Third Heaven

1. *International Standard Bible Encyclopedia*, Bibleencyclopedia.com, s.v. "candlestick," http://bibleencyclopedia.com/candlestick.htm (accessed April 19, 2010).

2. Ali Sina, "7 Layers of Heaven," *Islam Watch*, November 20, 2005, http://www.islam-watch.org/AliSina/7Layers.htm (accessed January 12, 2010).

3. *Bereishis Rabbah* 19:7, as quoted in "Hide and Go Seek," Rabbi Winston's Weekly Parsha Page, http://www.neveh.org/winston/parsha63/nitzvylc.html (accessed January 12, 2010).

## Chapter 7
## Man Is a Three-Part Being—One Part Dies, and Two Parts Live

1. WhatHappensNow.com, "Average Funeral Costs," http://www.whathappensnow
.com/articles_show.cfm?id=37&cat=6&sub=4 (accessed January 14, 2010).

2. KehillitIsrael.net, "A Summary of Jewish Practices in Death and Mourning,"
http://kehillatisrael.net/docs/chevra_summary.htm (accessed January 22, 2010).

3. Earl A. Grollman, "Rituals: Ceremonies Following Death and Their Meanings
for Jewish Children," in *Bereaved Children and Teens: A Support Guide for Parents
and Professionals* (Boston, MA: Beacon Press, 1995), 142.

4. Alfred J. Kolatch, *The Jewish Book of Why* (Middle Village, NY: Jonathan
David Publishers, 1981), 49–83.

5. Eusebius, *Church History*, book VI, chapter 37, "The Dissension of the
Arabians," NewAdvent.org, http://www.newadvent.org/fathers/250106.htm (accessed
April 21, 2010).

6. C. F. Hogg and W. E. Vine, *The Epistles to the Thessalonians With Notes
Exegetical and Expository* (London: Pickering & Inglis, 1929), 172.

7. Robert A. Morey, *Death and the Afterlife* (Minneapolis, MN: Bethany House,
1984), 50.

8. Flavius Josephus, *The Wars of the Jews*, Book II, chapter 8.11, Christian Classics
Ethereal Library, http://www.ccel.org/j/josephus/works/war-2.htm (accessed April 21,
2010).

9. Justin Martyr, "Chapter XX: Heathen Analogies to Christian Doctrine," in *The
First Apology of Justin*, http://www.tertullian.org/fathers2/ANF-01/anf01-46.htm
(accessed April 21, 2010).

10. John Deedy, *The Catholic Fact Book* (n.p.: Thomas More Press, 1990), 374.

11. *The Council of Trent: The Sixth Session*, trans. J. Waterworth (London: Dolman,
1848), Hanover Historical Texts Project, "Decree on Justification," Canon XXX, http://
history.hanover.edu/texts/trent/ct06.html (accessed April 21, 2010).

12. *The Council of Trent: The Twenty-Fifth Session*, ed. and trans. J. Waterworth
(London: Dolman, 1848), Hanover Historical Texts Project, "Decree Concerning
Purgatory," http://history.hanover.edu/texts/trent/ct25.html (accessed April 21, 2010).

13. F. L. Cross and E. A. Livingstone, eds., *Dictionary of the Christian Church*,
3rd edition (n.p.: Hendrickson Publishers, 2007).

14. Plato, as quoted in Homer William Smith, *Man and His Gods* (n.p.: Grosset's
Universal Library, 1956), 127.

## Chapter 8
## The Mystery of Near-Death Experiences

1. Maurice Rawlings, *Beyond Death's Door* (Nashville, Thomas Nelson, 1978), 3.

## Chapter 9
## The Greatest Homecoming Ever Known

1. This story happened during the Vietnam War, and I heard it related by Jimmy Swaggart when he preached a message in the late 1970s from a local church.

2. For more information about the discovery of DNA, see Lotta Fredholm, "The Discovery of the Molecular Structure of DNA—The Double Helix," NobelPrize.org, September 30, 2003, at http://nobelprize.org/educational_games/medicine/dna_double_helix/readmore.html.

3. Kitta MacPherson, "'Junk' DNA Has Important Role, Researchers Find," cited in Mariusz Nowacki, Brian P. Higgins, Genevieve M. Maquilan, Estienne C. Swart, Thomas G. Doak, and Laura F. Landweber, "A Functional Role for Transposases in a Large Eukaryotic Genome," *Science* 324, no. 5929 (2009): http://www.sciencemag.org/cgi/content/abstract/324/5929/935 (accessed January 14, 2010).

4. Walt Brown, *In the Beginning*, 8th ed. (Phoenix, AZ: Center for Scientific Creation, 2008).

5. Ibid.

6. One Web site giving additional information about the DNA testing of the Dead Sea Scrolls may be accessed at http://www.smithsonianmag.com/history-archaeology/Who-Wrote-the-Dead-Sea-Scrolls.html.

7. Vine, *Vine's Expository Dictionary of the Old and New Testament Words*, 1168.

## Chapter 10
## The Time-Light Mysteries and Eternity

1. To learn more about how melatonin works, go to "Questions and Answers About Melatonin," Society for Light Treatment and Biological Rhythms, http://www.sltbr.org/melfaq.htm (accessed June 30, 2010).

2. Isaac M. McPhee, "Traveling at the Speed of Light," Suite101.com, http://physics.suite101.com/article.cfm/traveling_at_the_speed_of_light (accessed January 15, 2010).

3. "Laser Smashes Light-Speed Record," PhysicsWorld.com, July 19, 2000, http://physicsworld.com/cws/article/news/2810 (accessed January 15, 2010).

4. "Engineers Discover Procedure That Can Make Tissue Temporarily Transparent, Potentially Improving Medical Procedures," Cockrill School of Engineering, August 23, 2000, http://www.engr.utexas.edu/news/releases/4468 (accessed January 15, 2010).

5. Paul Rincon, "Wormhole 'No Use' for Time Travel," BBCNews, May 23, 2005, http://news.bbc.co.uk/2/hi/sci/tech/4564477.stm (accessed January 15, 2010).

## Chapter 11
## Who Will Be in Heaven, and Who Will Be Missing?

1. For more information about the forty-eight temples at Fengdu, China, see Nancy Muenker, "To Hell and Back," *The Well Seasoned Traveler*, http://www

.wellseasonedtraveler.com/Muenker/MuenkerArticles/China/ToHellAndBack.htm, or "Fengdu Ming Mountain Scenic Area," ChinaHotel.com, http://www.chinahotel.com .cn/ch_scenic_info.php?sl41_No=1090 (accessed January 18, 2010).

2. MyHealingHands.com, "The Buddhist Perspective on Paper Offerings," *The Dharma*, January 2004, http://www.myhealinghands.com.sg/thedharma/ buddhistburningpaperoffering.htm (accessed April 22, 2010).

3. R. K. Jones et al., "Abortion in the United States: Incidence and Access to Services, 2005," *Perspectives on Sexual and Reproductive Health* 40, no. 1 (2008): 6–16, referenced in Guttmacher Institute, "Facts on Induced Abortions in the United States," July 2008, http://www.guttmacher.org/pubs/fb_induced_abortion.html (accessed January 18, 2010).

4. L. B. Finer et al., "Reasons U.S. Women Have Abortions: Quantitative and Qualitative," *Perspectives on Sexual and Reproductive Health* 37, no. 3 (2005): 110–118, referenced in Guttmacher Institute, "Facts on Induced Abortions in the United States."

5. Lawrence Jones, "Planned Parenthood Director Resigns After Witnessing Abortion," ChristianPost.com, November 6, 2009, http://www.christianpost.com/ article/20091106/planned-parenthood-director-resigns-after-witnessing-abortion-on -ultrasound/ (accessed January 18, 2010).

6. Bishop Earthquake Kelley, *Bound to Lose, Destined to Win* (Cleveland, TN: CopperScroll Publishers, LLC, 2007).

7. Ibid., 105–118.

8. Dr. Laverne P. Blowers, "Are They Really Lost? What Is the Status of the Unevangelized?" Christian Higher Education, Bethel College, http://www.bethelcollege .edu/academics/library/Archives/reflections/v7n1p127.pdf (accessed March 5, 2010).

9. Vine, *Vine's Expository Dictionary of the Old and New Testament Words*, 179–180.

10. Gordon Lindsay, *Scenes Beyond the Grave: Visions of Marietta Davis* (n.p.: Christ for the Nations, 1975).

11. Vine, *Vine's Expository Dictionary of the Old and New Testament Words*, 950.

## Chapter 12
## The Bema and the Great White Throne Judgments

1. Vine, *Vine's Expository Dictionary of the Old and New Testament Words*, 612.
2. Ibid., 250.

## Chapter 13
## How Will You Be Remembered?

1. "Snakes in an Atheist's Grave," FaithPublishing.com, http://www.theshop.net/ faithpub/snakesin.html (accessed January 21, 2010).

# GOD'S PROMISE OF PROTECTION FOR YOU AND YOUR FAMILY

A ngels on Assignment shows you how to enter into a covenant relationship with God that engages the help of His angels. You will learn…

- How angels protect us
- What kinds of assignments God gives to angels
- Biblical and current examples of angelic protection
- Five things that hinder their protection of us

Discover the amazing Mizpah covenant and its power to protect your family

*Angels* ON ASSIGNMENT

GOD'S RELENTLESS PROTECTION OF YOUR LOVED ONES AND YOU

PERRY STONE

ISBN: 978-1-59979-752-6 / $15.99

Charisma
HOUSE
A STRANG COMPANY
9389

ENGAGE THE POWER OF GOD'S ANGELS TO KEEP YOUR FAMILY SAFE.

# FREE NEWSLETTERS
## TO HELP EMPOWER YOUR LIFE

## Why subscribe today?

☐ **DELIVERED DIRECTLY TO YOU.** All you have to do is open your inbox and read.

☐ **EXCLUSIVE CONTENT.** We cover the news overlooked by the mainstream press.

☐ **STAY CURRENT.** Find the latest court rulings, revivals, and cultural trends.

☐ **UPDATE OTHERS.** Easy to forward to friends and family with the click of your mouse.

**CHOOSE THE E-NEWSLETTER THAT INTERESTS YOU MOST:**

- Christian news
- Daily devotionals
- Spiritual empowerment
- And much, much more

SIGN UP AT: **http://freenewsletters.charismamag.com**

8178